Britain's Prime Ministers

Britain's Prime Ministers

Roger Ellis
and
Geoffrey Treasure

SHEPHEARD-WALWYN (PUBLISHERS) LTD

First published in 2005 by
Shepheard-Walwyn (Publishers) Ltd
Suite 604, The Chandlery
50 Westminster Bridge Road
London SE1 7QY

British Library Cataloguing in Publication Data
A catalogue record of this book
is available from the British Library

ISBN-13: 978-0-85683-234-5
ISBN-10: 0-85683-234-0

Typeset by Alacrity,
Banwell Castle, Weston-super-Mare
Printed through Print Solutions, Wallington, Surrey

Contents

List of Illustrations

THE PUBLISHERS and authors gratefully acknowledge permission to reproduce the illustrations from the following:

Nos 1-15, 17, 19, 21, 23 the National Portrait Gallery, London
No 16 copyright reserved: collection National Portrait Gallery, London
No 18 courtesy of Felix Rosentiel's Widow and Son Ltd
No 20 Yousuf Karsh/Camera Press, London
No 22 the estate of Pamela Chandler/National Portrait Gallery, London
No 24 Gemma Levine/Camera Press, London

Preface

LUDWIG WITTGENSTEIN'S approach to philosophy was based on the precept that philosophers should not look for the meaning of terms but should observe the way in which the terms are used. I have often felt that the same approach should be used for analysing the role of the Prime Minister in the United Kingdom. This is what Roger Ellis and Geoffrey Treasure have done in this book.

The powers of the Prime Minister are not defined in any statute or constitutional settlement. They have emerged over the last three hundred years from the need for the Sovereign to have someone, firstly, to advise him or her on those matters which are not the statutory responsibility of individual ministers; and, secondly – since the Sovereign ceased to take the chair at meetings of the Cabinet in the eighteenth century – to convene ministers when they need to act collectively.

Since the matters which are not the statutory responsibility of individual ministers are principally those which fall within the Royal Prerogative – and include the appointment and dismissal of ministers and other Crown appointments, the summoning and dissolution of Parliament, the conferral of royal honours, and much in the field of international relations, including declarations of war and the making of treaties – this role has put major powers in the hands of Prime Ministers. But the use of these powers, and to some extent the powers themselves, change with time and with the way individual Prime Ministers behave (or, it might be said, what Parliament and fellow ministers let Prime Ministers get away with).

One example of this is the issue of whether advice to the Sovereign on dissolution of Parliament and the calling of a general election is a matter for the Prime Minister alone or for the Cabinet collectively. There is no doubt that the decision of a Prime Minister to resign is a personal one; but it has always seemed to me that the decision to advise the Sovereign to dissolve Parliament should be for the Cabinet since all ministers thereby put their appointments to the hazard of an election. Yet it has come to be accepted that this is the personal prerogative of the Prime Minister. One reason may be that the Cabinet has accepted that this is a price worth paying for maintaining security and retaining the initiative against the opposition parties.

In some other respects circumstances have increased the power of the Prime Minister in recent years. In an increasingly media-dominated age, the Prime Minister – and the Prime Minister's Press Secretary – have come to be regarded as the leading spokesmen for the government. The televised weekly jousting at Prime Minister's questions gives the Prime Minister an ideal public platform on the controversies of the day. I remember Margaret Thatcher saying to various Cabinet colleagues, 'This is what I am going to say at Prime Minister's questions this afternoon unless you can change my mind in the next thirty seconds; and then it will be Government policy.' In foreign affairs, important issues are now settled in direct discussions over the telephone with other Heads of State rather than through the rigmarole of Foreign Secretary visits or instructions to ambassadors.

Yet the Prime Minister's office is not equipped to support a presidency. 10 Downing Street is not big enough to accommodate much more than a secretariat and, even after the annexation of neighbouring buildings in recent years, the space is more suitable for a colony of gadflies than a fully-fledged Prime Minister's department. The statutory powers and the main expertise lie in the Whitehall departments with the Prime Minister's colleagues.

So I have always seen the role of the Prime Minister as being more akin to a team captain than a chief executive. The system, if it works well, demands that each minister and each department contributes its skill and expertise to a collective endeavour which comes together at the Cabinet table. There is no law which requires this to be so: it just works better that way.

Even so, the five Prime Ministers I have seen at close hand have each done the job in different ways, ranging from Harold Wilson in his second term, playing as centre half and distributing the ball to his talented team mates, to Margaret Thatcher and Tony Blair, who have definitely been centre forwards.

So I think that Roger Ellis and Geoffrey Treasure take the right approach to the role of Prime Minister by describing how each has used the position in practice. If the book is not to run into several volumes each treatment has to be short, and it is well known that it is harder to write a leader for *The Daily Mirror* than for *The Times*. Nevertheless the descriptions of the Prime Ministers I have served seem to me to capture admirably the essence of their times in power and I hope that more expert readers will conclude the same of the other vignettes in this book.

LORD BUTLER OF BROCKWELL

Introduction

LORD BLAKE ended his lectures on the Office of Prime Minister, delivered in 1974, with 'a plea that the study of an office such as this depends very largely on the study of individuals.' This book offers brief portraits of each occupant of the highest political office in Britain. Those who have managed to climb successfully to the top of the 'greasy pole' were sometimes lesser men than contemporaries who slipped from it tantalisingly near their goal. Among the Prime Ministers are several who, by any criterion, must be judged remarkable individuals; several, too, whom the more severe historian might be tempted to dismiss as nonentities. That power and its pursuit can be corrupting should come as no surprise. There is a gambling element that has always had appeal. It can be seen notably in the careers of Disraeli and Lloyd George: eloquent, imaginative, high in self esteem, ready to leap the stream where others would look for stepping stones; each in his way an adventurer, though capable of rising to statesmanship; each an outsider, willing to challenge convention; regarded at different times as outrageous. But it was often the steadier men who proved more successful, those considered in the eighteenth-century phrase as having 'bottom'. Those who lacked it, in the eyes of their contemporaries, had to wait long in the wings, a Canning or a Churchill. Reliability, assiduity, management skills, as demonstrated by Pelham, Liverpool, Attlee and Major, were as likely to be rewarded as flamboyant genius. But successful politicians of all types have shared a sustained appetite for power, the *sine qua non* of ultimate success. A Grafton or a Rosebery rose to the top in favourable circumstances, but they did not stay there long, for there was something in them of Trollope's Duke of St Bungay, who 'enjoys the game and the rest from the game'.

A Prime Minister can only be as effective as the tradition and expectations of his times will allow: tradition as cherished by his party, expectations defined by his own statements or by manifesto. When Prime Ministers have chosen to change course radically, to 'break faith' as supporters might put it, through perceived necessity

or personal conviction, they have paid a price, as Peel and Mac-
Donald found. Politics being 'the art of the possible', compromises
are inevitable. So wheeling and dealing (at least through underlings,
Disraeli's Tapers and Tadpoles), the enforcing of party discipline
within Parliament and testing of public opinion outdoors, may come
to seem defining characteristics of successful government. Read as a
whole, however, the story of Britain's Prime Ministers challenges the
pessimist and confronts the cynic with its examples of courage and
magnanimity. Seen at its finest in the careers of a younger Pitt or a
Gladstone, a persistent note is that of a responsible use of authority
and a sense of obligation to the country. Societies change, and fash-
ions and values with them, but one value has been pervasive until
recent times – and may still not be obsolete – that of a sense of
public service in those equipped and willing to enter the fray. It has
been a fine thing to strive for political office, a very fine thing indeed
to be Prime Minister. This view has been reflected in public
expectations, in aristocratic and democratic society alike. Honest
and honourable conduct has been looked for: to mislead Parliament
and the country is regarded as a most serious offence.

Until near the end of the nineteenth century – some would say
until the end of the First World War – the prevailing tone in British
politics was aristocratic, and its organisation oligarchic. Where birth
did not confer the opening to a career there, education would. Of
the twenty nineteenth-century Prime Ministers, nine were at Eton,
five at Harrow; nine Oxford men were at Christ Church, while
towards the end of the century Jowett was consciously nurturing
leaders at Balliol. We may be taken aback by the confident attitudes
of young men from these political nurseries for whom borough
seats were found: the young Grey, for example, not feeling obliged to
meet the voters or even attend the poll. They came to politics from
intensive study of the classics, a system aimed 'at the training of
statesmen at a time when statesmanship consisted largely of winning
and retaining the confidence of some six hundred gentlemen'
(J.R.M. Butler). It was a narrow education, insufficient in some
respects for the challenges of industrial Britain, but it gave them 'a
common fund of experience and a common hinterland of thought';
a training in classical oratory, 'large, dignified, lofty, appealing to
the sense of honour and responsibility of a particular class'; and
the moral lessons to be learnt from Thucydides and Cicero, with
noble examples to inspire and tyrants and charlatans to condemn.

To this shared background should be added family tradition as exemplified by the Russells, Cavendishes and Cecils, infused often with the earnestness of Christian purpose to be seen in the evangelical Perceval or the Tractarian Gladstone: all contributing to the strong sense of calling that characterised many politicians, Prime Ministers among them. With the arrival of Lloyd George, followed by the emergence of the Labour Party, the assumptions of a shared education disappeared. Twentieth-century Prime Ministers were born in places as different as Blenheim Palace and a Lossiemouth but-and-ben, and though all but four of them went to a university (nearly half of those to Oxford), they brought with them into government a wider and less cohesive upbringing. Yet the House of Commons has retained a strong corporate sense. While it appeared after the Great War that political success might be achieved by those with industrial experience – Law, Baldwin, Chamberlain – the Westminster village has become closed to out-siders again. Whatever their background, subsequent Prime Ministers, wartime service apart, have been professional politicians for nearly all their working lives. Moreover, with Parliament in session for more than twice as long as it was in Victorian times, the activities of government spreading inexorably, and the pressures of travel and the media insistent throughout the year, few have found time once in office to refresh themselves, like Macmillan with his Trollope or Heath on his 'Morning Cloud', with experience out-side the 'village' or the international political circuit. This obsessive life proved damaging in different ways to Wilson and, eventually, Thatcher.

There being no written constitution in Britain, the role and the powers of the Prime Minister have never been prescribed. The title first appeared officially on paper as recently as 1878, when Disraeli, looking to pull rank amongst European dignitaries, signed the treaty at the end of the Congress of Berlin as 'First Lord of Her Majesty's Treasury, Prime Minister of England'. In 1905, Edward VII, punctilious in such matters, introduced the Prime Minister into the order of precedence on state occasions (just behind the Archbishop of York), but it was only in 1917 that the title appeared on the Statute Book. Walpole, with whom we start, was called 'Prime Minister' only by his opponents, as a term of mild abuse. Historians, however, have generally agreed that he was the first to be properly so described; as holding the King's favour, substantial control of patronage as First Lord of the Treasury and consequent influence over elections, undisputed leadership of his party, authority in the House of Commons and, for most purposes, a majority in the Lords. This was the reality of power then. There have been changes since. William IV was the last King to dismiss a ministry which had a majority in the Commons because he did not like it, in 1834. Although Victoria stopped Peel from forming a Tory government by refusing to accept any Tory ladies into her bedchamber, she never dared to go beyond fulminating against Palmerston or Gladstone. The present monarch still formally appoints her Prime Minister, but the last occasion when the choice was sufficiently open for the King to exercise his own judgment was when, with no advice from the dying Bonar Law, George V chose Baldwin rather than Curzon in 1923. George VI would probably have preferred Halifax to Churchill in 1940 had he been willing to serve, but by then other forces were in play, as we shall see. By the 1870s, Bagehot believed that the role of the monarch was 'to be consulted, to encourage and to warn', little more. A majority in the House of Lords is convenient for a Prime Minister, but since the Parliament Act (1911) the Lords have only been able to delay rather than defeat legislation. Patronage, the gradual passing of which from the King to the Prime Minister explains how the balance of power shifted decisively between them, cannot, after the end of 'pocket' and 'Treasury' boroughs, influence elections. But Prime Ministers still use it, within and outside government and especially within the House of Commons, to encourage the loyalty of the members of their parties in order to bolster their majorities there, as well as to keep support against internal rivals.

For King's government has become party government. A King's government first lost a general election in 1835: patronage could not keep Peel in office after William IV summoned him to form a minority administration. Since the Second Reform Act (1867), party machinery has developed in the constituencies and party discipline in the House of Commons. With a 'first past the post' electoral system, voters have become so conditioned to the two-party system that independent candidates hardly ever get returned, and the only third party eventually to gain a majority so far has been the Labour Party – and then only after two minority administrations. The leader of the largest party after an election is therefore the person whom the monarch has to select as Prime Minister, and once selected he is normally able to carry through his legislative programme.

The Prime Minister thus getting to Downing Street on the back of his party has responsibilities and wields power covering far wider areas than those of his eighteenth- and nineteenth-century predecessors. Between 1700 and 1815 military expenditure and debt servicing accounted for over 80% of government expenditure. The mid-Victorian state was cheaply run, with free trade and a peace-promoting foreign policy, a suspicion of government activity ('Not English' said Dickens's Mr Podsnap of the Public Health Act), and an amateurish and threadbare civil service. Gladstone was not interested in social reform, and Disraeli knew nothing of its details. The Welfare State was a twentieth-century creation, and it and two world wars transformed the role of government. At the same time, the popular press, radio and television were bringing government closer to the people. Prime Ministers were expected to run it efficiently, and present it excitingly. Many managed one or the other, not all achieved both, one or two could do neither. Nor is this surprising. Peter Hennessy concludes that, 'the model of a modern Prime Minister would be a grotesque composite freak – someone with the dedication to duty of a Peel, the physical energy of a Gladstone, the detachment of a Salisbury, the balls of a Lloyd George, the word power of a Churchill, the brains of an Asquith, the administrative gifts of an Attlee, the style of a Macmillan, the managerialism of a Heath and the sleep requirements of a Thatcher' (*The Hidden Wiring*, 1995). Lord Blake, an academic looking out wryly at the democratic world, thought that essential requirements were tact and an unoriginal mind.

From Walpole's time onwards, ministers, of whom the Prime Minister is chief, have been spoken of as a Cabinet. Until the end of the eighteenth century, the King regarded them separately as his own ministers. Yet in 1746 Henry Pelham and his fellow ministers forced George II to accept as one of them the elder Pitt, whom he wanted to keep out of government, by resigning one after another when he proved obstinate. In 1782 all Cabinet Ministers changed on the appointment of a new Prime Minister, and in 1792 the younger Pitt established the principle of the collective responsibility of the Cabinet by persuading George III to dismiss Lord Chancellor Thurlow when he was openly disloyal to it. Thereafter the Cabinet operated as an executive body. The Prime Minister chose its members and dismissed them, chaired its meetings, and from 1856 held them in 10 Downing Street (though Lloyd George once called a meeting in the Station Hotel at Inverness, to fit in with his holiday arrangements). The Cabinet became as much a part of constitutional convention as the Prime Minister. It formulated policy and its members were kept informed of each other's activities. It became more effective, and capable of managing more complex government, through Cabinet committees, which prepared legislation and reported back to the main body. So important was it considered that Asquith even tried to run the Great War through it at first, even though, astonishingly, there was no Cabinet Secretary, nor were minutes of its meetings taken, until 1916.

Inevitably management of the war soon had to be undertaken by a smaller War Council, a precedent to be followed by Churchill and Thatcher. The peacetime bypassing of the Cabinet was started by Lloyd George, with his Garden Suburb, so called because its members lived in temporary accommodation in his Downing Street garden. This disappeared with him, denounced by Baldwin as unconstitutional, but Prime Ministers from Heath onwards have had formal advisory bodies outside Cabinet. In the second half of the twentieth century the Cabinet gradually ceased to govern as a body. Under Attlee it met on average 87 times a year, and 340 Cabinet papers were circulated. By the early 1990s the average was 40 meetings, and in only one year were there more than 20 papers. Ministers have had less and less knowledge of each other's work. They have to run large departments with junior ministers under them, staffed by a professional and committed civil service: a demanding and all-absorbing task. The amount of ministerial work, the need for quick decisions, modern methods of communication and the prevalence of leaks from its discussions have removed the Cabinet from the centre of the decision-making process, and significantly increased the power and the exposure of the Prime Minister. Yet the Cabinet is still with us, surviving as a consultative body, and used by the Prime Minister to bond a government together, as in the eighteenth century. Until towards the end of her premiership, Margaret Thatcher scrupulously held discussions with her Cabinets over policy, even though she led them forcefully. Significantly, it was her Cabinet Ministers that she consulted, one by one, when she was deciding whether to fight on or resign. Cabinet meetings under Blair have become brief. But they are still regular.

Recently it has become clear that it is not enough for a Prime Minister to command the confidence of the House of Commons, and that he has to be a national figure if he is to keep a firm hold on his position. Canning and Palmerston were the first to cultivate the press. Gladstone took politics to the people, with speeches to large crowds, so successfully that even Salisbury felt it necessary to learn the art and do likewise. Baldwin quickly mastered the technique of talking to people in their homes through the wireless, and Macmillan brought the television cameras into Downing Street. Readers of the tabloids look for heroes and heroines, villains and guilty men, and it is in this context that political leaders are recognised today. Victory in the jousting over Prime Minister's questions in the Commons counts for little at the polls, as William Hague discovered as Conservative leader. In May 1940, George VI asked Churchill to succeed Chamberlain, against his own wishes and those of many in the Conservative Party, because it was clear that this was the will of the nation.

Yet without a majority in the Commons, a government cannot long survive. Churchill recognised this, giving the Conservative leader Chamberlain a central position in his Cabinet and delivering many of his most famous speeches to the House. The Prime Minister is not a President. His powers are in one way greater than those of the President of the USA, since he leads the legislature as well as the executive; and there have been occasions when Thatcher, and Blair too, have seemed to the public to behave presidentially. But the reality is different, for in this era of party government Prime Ministers are dependent on the support of their back-benchers. With elections to be faced every five years, this support may depend on their standing in the country, for no MP wants to face his constituents under the banner of a loser. In this way, the public continues to exert its influence on politics even between elections, and a Prime Minister today looks for support in the opinion polls; but it is from his control of the House of Commons that his power ultimately derives. In the time of Walpole, Britain was an oligarchy, governed by a King and his ministers. Today it is a parliamentary democracy, with the Queen as Head of State, governed by a Prime Minister and his party. In his lectures, Lord Blake cited, as pairs operating in the same constitutional framework but to very different effect, Portland and Pitt, and Peel and Aberdeen: talking today, he might well have added Thatcher and Major. Even though they are

more closely hedged around by economic and diplomatic circumstances difficult to control, the personalities of British Prime
Ministers count for as much as they have ever done in the story of
their country.

Sir Robert Walpole

SIR ROBERT WALPOLE, IST EARL OF ORFORD (1676-1745), was
First Lord of the Treasury from 1721 to 1742. The manner in which
he used his high office to maintain his grip over fellow ministers
and over policy meant that the informal, often derogatory, title of
'prime minister' would be likely to last and to acquire official status.
No single politician in modern times has had a more significant
influence on the development of the constitution.

He was born at the old manor house at Houghton in North
Norfolk, the third son of nineteen children. He was evidently clever
enough to thrive at Eton and at King's College, Cambridge.
Intellectual challenge and family tradition drew him to politics. His
father had broken away from the Cavalier tradition of this old
county family and sat as a Whig in William III's parliaments. His
early death in 1700 left Robert, because of the death of his elder
brothers, to manage the family estates. In the same year he married
Catherine Shorter, heiress to a timber merchant; her extravagance
would match his own taste for good living, add to his debts, and
sharpen his appetite for office. Altruism would not have been looked
for in the new member for the pocket borough of Castle Rising
(1701). But the borough of King's Lynn, to which he transferred in
the following year, was another matter. It was a thriving port and
offered its energetic member training in matters of trade – the workings, for example, of the customs system – which would later prove
invaluable.

Queen Anne's reign saw intensified party conflict around several
related issues: religion, foreign policy and war, finance and, above all
and lending a dangerous edge to contention, Jacobitism. Though
some preferred to be independent, most would by now call themselves Whig or Tory. Within the parties groups tended to form and
work together through relationships. Herefordshire members
looked to the influential Robert Harley. In the Norfolk interest
Robert Walpole was soon acknowledged leader. He took pains to
cultivate the interest of friends and relations, notably his cousin

and brother-in-law, Lord Townshend, and Charles Turner, a leading citizen of Lynn. From his earliest years he showed the capacity for taking pains over people as well as material concerns: invaluable practice for the management of Parliament. In the chamber he soon showed that he could be formidable in debate. His friendship with Townshend drew him into Whig society where he was valued for his direct manner, quick grasp of issues, and jovial manners. In the Commons it certainly helped that most of the Whig leaders sat in the Upper House. In town, with experienced mentors such as Somers, Halifax and Wharton, he got the feel of politics in the smoke and gossip of the Kit Kat Club.

In June 1705 Walpole was made a member of the naval council of Prince George, Lord High Admiral. In February 1708 he succeeded his Tory rival, St John (later Bolingbroke), as Secretary at War; this gave him control, at the height of the War of the Spanish Succession, of all aspects of military life in England and Scotland. In January 1710 he became Treasurer of the Navy. So he was associated intimately with the conduct of the war, now exclusively a Whig war, since the Whigs had eased the Tories out of office and stood firm for Marlborough as commander-in-chief, and for the cause of the Arch- duke Charles. So after the Tory victory of 1710 Walpole was marked for destruction. In 1711 he was committed to the Tower after accus- ations of corruption in the negotiation of contracts. They were political charges, although there was evidence to support them, and Walpole's 'martyrdom', coming at the same time as Marlborough's disgrace, enhanced his stature with the Whigs.

The failure of Bolingbroke's plans for the accession of James Edward in 1714 found Walpole strongly placed amongst the Whigs who looked for places under George I. He was made first Paymaster, then in 1715 First Lord of the Treasury and Chancellor of the Exchequer. He could now indulge his love of building and display. A Paymaster was entitled to take a percentage of sums which passed through his hands. But even by contemporary standards he was careless of the distinction between public and private money; war veteran pensioners may have put it less delicately as they saw Orford House rise majestically in the grounds of Chelsea Hospital. But the country benefited too from Walpole's financial sense. His measures for the redemption of debt, consolidation of rates of interest and the establishment of a sinking fund were models for subsequent work in this field.

The precarious harmony of the Whig ministers was, however, wrecked when Secretary of State Townshend crossed George I over foreign affairs. Tensions had already been created by the King's prolonged absences in Hanover. A soldier-king with a mind of his own and inclination to favour his native duchy – and therefore ministers like Stanhope sympathetic to his ideas – provided a sobering lesson to the ambitious politician: he must find ways of securing the support of the King without jeopardising his position in Parliament. Walpole's career would depend on the way in which he responded to this challenge.

Meanwhile he showed that he had the self-confidence to accept immediate loss for future gain. After Townshend's dismissal he followed his friend into opposition. He was accompanied by a significant group, present allies, potential future rivals: Pulteney, Methuen, Orford, and his devoted friend, Devonshire. From April 1717 until June 1720, when he became Paymaster again, he enjoyed the calculations and pleasures of faction. On one issue his opposition was far-sighted. He helped to destroy the Peerage Bill which, if it had been passed in 1719, would have turned the House of Lords into an oligarchy. Long before the emergence of a formal, recognised, coherent opposition to government it could be that a man was better fitted to govern if he had first tested his ideas, weighed interests and studied tactics unrestrained by office. To the hungry politician, however, to be 'out' could only be endured if it was seen as prelude to being 'in'. Talent and persistence could do so much. Luck was needed to provide the crucial chance.

Walpole speculated heavily on the rise and fall of South Sea Company stock in 1720. The inside knowledge which enabled him to escape without heavy loss also made him vulnerable to the furious reaction after the Bubble's collapse. But he was not so closely involved as the principal ministers, Sunderland, Stanhope, Aislabie and Craggs, father and son. So there was a potential advantage. The suicide of the elder Craggs, the disgrace of Aislabie and the younger Craggs, the fortuitous deaths of Stanhope in 1721 and of Sunderland in the following year, cleared the course of potential rivals. But there were obstacles to overcome and his horse could still fall. It was the way in which he rode, skilful and fearless, that ensured not just survival but the basis on which to build a lasting authority: the re-establishment of public credit.

What Walpole actually did may have been less important than

what he appeared to be doing. His scheme (proposed by his banker Jacombe) for incorporating South Sea stock in that of the bank was not eventually adopted. But it bought time and helped to counter panic and persuade men to invest again. To contemporaries Walpole was not a financial wizard but the 'skreen-master general'. Defending directors and surviving ministers against bitter attacks, he showed political courage. It might not endear him to the House of Commons but it made him influential friends, not least at court.

From 1721 to 1742 Walpole was First Lord of the Treasury. During this time, without precedent in length or stability, he obtained a mastery over Parliament and an initiative in the conduct of affairs which transformed his office. He was not the first to be called 'prime minister'. Godolphin and Harley had enjoyed sufficient influence at Queen Anne's court, command of patronage and standing in Parliament to earn the title, and the odium that went with it. Harley in particular might be seen as a model for Walpole: 'indefatigable man of business, of a lively and aspiring spirit, and manages the caballing parties with that dexterity that he keeps in with both' (Prince Eugene reporting contemporary views). But Harley was soon 'Robin the Trickster' to his opponents. In any case, like Godolphin, he was the Queen's minister, dependent wholly on court favour. Walpole too was the Kings' minister. It was his achievement, taking advantage of changing circumstances, to establish himself as the minister that the King found he must have. It was what George II found on his accession in 1727, after promoting his man, Wilmington. Without support in Parliament the royal choice could not govern and the King, a constitutional lesson hard learned, had to turn back to the man who could.

After Walpole there were to be other First Lords who were not 'prime' ministers; the elder Pitt, who plainly was, was a Secretary of State. In the government of the Pelhams there was no distinct head. But Henry Pelham, controlling the purse, had the crucial role in most aspects of policy. Before that be assumed, as eventually it would, to be the criterion for primacy, the career of Carteret must be taken into account. He was certainly seen as 'sole minister' during his time as Secretary of State (1742-4) because of his dominant role in the formation of foreign policy – and that in a manner entirely pleasing to the King. The that was the undoing of Walpole was the exceptional opportunity for Carteret. Yet exceptions only serve to highlight the trend, even if it is plainer to us than it could have been to contemporaries. The office of 'prime minister' would continue to evolve logically from the Crown's retreat from the active centre of government. It was Walpole's long tenure of office that proved decisive. That would not have been surprising in the emergencies of war; it was Walpole's special achievement that it happened during the 'pudding times' of a long peace. He was relentless in the pursuit of power, tenacious in holding on to it. He was committed to no programme or timetable. He had to study the interests, every seven years, of an electorate of some 200,000 whose uneven, sometimes freakish, distribution in counties and boroughs had owed more, over five hundred years, to the needs of sovereigns and influential subjects, than to reason or theory. Privileged electors expected no manifesto – but due regard to material concerns.

It may be that principle was prominent only when wedded to political advantage. That does not mean that there are no steady notions to be deduced from Walpole's acts and speeches. He held by the House of Hanover. His opposition to Toryism was as vindictive as it was shrewd. The 'Atterbury Plot' of 1722, when he undoubtedly doctored evidence to ensure the bishop's banishment, was well-timed to rally men behind so staunch a Whig and leave Toryism indelibly tainted with Jacobitism: he made much capital out of it, and particularly Bolingbroke's past errors. It was not until 1726 that he was convinced that his old enemy was harmless and allowed his return from exile.

Blooded in faction, Walpole valued stability above all. What suited him suited the country: lower taxes, cheaper commodities, rising rents. He became the unrivalled master of a system which was 'flexible enough to contain the competing demands of different interests and rival pressure groups' (Dickinson). At its heart was the parliamentary forum where the powerful and wealthy were sufficiently well represented to assume that they could make the system work to their advantage. Even when, at some point, it did not, they could always hope to effect a change. Parliament was open to external pressures through lobby, petition and the voices, strident or seductive, of a free press – and, until Walpole brought it under the Lord Chamberlain's control, a free theatre. Parliament also provided a well-publicised arena for debate. Walpole there maintained his dominance by unremitting vigilance by noting what would impress the crowded benches of St Stephen's House, not least the lucid presentation of facts and figures; above all by his handling of the

Crown patronage. This gave rise to the complaint that he reduced corruption to a system. Unless they have prior loyalties as partisans or hirelings, political journalists rarely support government for long: readers look for intrigue and blunder, and circulation thrives on scandal. He had to contend with a press consistently hostile, often scurrilous, and did little to propitiate it. His own hacks were mediocre. Critics had the better story, and massive evidence in the wealth that enabled him to play Maecaenas, build palatial Houghton on the family acres and fill it with fine paintings. Yet the judgement of a later political pundit – and no friend to political corruption – should count in his favour: Burke wrote that 'he governed by party attachments. The charge of systematic corruption is less applicable to him, perhaps, than to any minister who ever served the crown for so great a length of time.' Certainly the means of such 'corruption' did not increase during his ministry. Nor did Walpole monopolise patronage. His 'Pope', Edmund Gibson, bishop of London, was a helpful advisor but he had ideas of his own, and ecclesiastical preferment remained only partly in Walpole's hands. Both kings retained control over military and naval appointments.

Walpole had 'bottom', as men then described those qualities of sound judgement and staying power that even rivals had to recognise. One after another they were elbowed into eccentric corners, society's 'insiders' left to brood on the frustration of being permanently 'out': Pulteney and Carteret, Wilmington, Chesterfield, and, after 1730, his old ally Townshend. Memory of the Schism, the menace of Jacobitism (which the rising in 1745 would prove was not just a convenient Whig myth), the remembered cost of an ambitious foreign policy, and the savagery of domestic mobs were all arguments of weight with King and Parliament. In a country virtually unpoliced, where soldiers had to be sent in when riot threatened, there were examples to scare the most fervent admirers of English liberty: the destruction of toll-gates in Herefordshire in 1734, attacks on Irish labourers in the Rag Fair riots of 1736, and most alarming, in that year, the lynching of Captain Porteous in Edinburgh for acting against the ever popular trade of smuggling. Pleas for tough action were all the stronger when presented in the bluff language of the country squire, sceptical of fine talk that 'buttered no parsnips'. The lolling figure of the Commons chamber, stout and ruddy, munching his Norfolk russets, the ardent horseman who would hunt in Richmond Park if he could not get down to Houghton – cultivated image or natural style – provided cover for the shrewdest political mind of his generation. London laughed when it heard that Walpole had landed face down in the Richmond mud; in the political saddle he had a surer seat.

In assessing his political skills style has its place. In the end, however, it was policies that counted. In Parliament the squire predominated and many (though not all who professed disgust) spurned the places and jobs that might bind them to 'Robinocracy'. Alienated, given a big issue, these men of 'the country party' could endanger the dynasty. So Walpole wooed them, supporting the stern Game Laws, notably the comprehensive 'Black Act' of 1723, and furthering the private bills for enclosures and turnpikes which strengthened the rural economy and the position of the landowner within it. Simple or sophisticated, honest or venal, electors have short memories and limited reserves of gratitude. The Land Tax, when levied at 4s, had placed a large share of the state's expenditure on the backs of the squirearchy; when Walpole reduced it he could count on warm appreciation from the men who, in boroughs of limited franchise, or in the counties, had most electoral influence. An essential part of the strategy behind Walpole's ill-fated Excise Bill of 1733, extending the duties already imposed on tea and coffee (1723) to wine and tobacco, was that it would enable him to perpetuate the low rate of 1s. But there were other political interests beside that of land, notably those of commerce and finance, beneficiaries of peace and of the expanding trade with Europe and the colonies. Inertia raised to the level of principle, or 'let sleeping dogs lie' in the phrase most often used – such reductionist judgements of Walpole do less than justice to the balancing act that so long frustrated his rivals and which, he could reasonably claim, brought benefits to the country as a whole.

Walpole cannot be called a free trader; nor was he a rigid protectionist. Always pragmatic, he studied the needs and sentiment of city merchants and bankers. The lowest interest rates in Europe, down to 3% by the late 'thirties, reflected their confidence in his management and encouraged them to invest. His Sinking Fund was responsible for a significant reduction in the capital of the National Debt. So far was he from being a purist in financial matters that he periodically raided it to keep expenditure down. He removed all customs duties on the export of agricultural produce and of over a hundred articles manufactured in England. He abolished import duties on raw silk, flax and dyes. He laid down regulations of quality to maintain the standard of English products. To keep costs down justices were empowered to fix wages. To protect home industry Walpole retained high duties on the import of foreign goods that competed with English manufactures. Colonies he looked on as a source of valuable raw materials and a market for English products, and they were forbidden, generally, to trade directly with other countries. When the West Indian planters complained that colonies were buying sugar more cheaply from the French he produced the Molasses Act (1733), placing duties on foreign sugar. He placated the planters but upset the colonists and encouraged smuggling. He would not have expected legislation to be without drawbacks, if not counter-productive. So such acts stand out like monoliths on an empty plain. Government action was for emergencies, or when there was a clear consensus.

British statesmen have tended in the main to veer between two foreign policies, drawn to one or the other by personal inclination, domestic pressures, or external events outside their control: involvement in the rivalries of the Continental powers, with the commitment that this required, or isolation, with some insurance in the shape of a close understanding with another major power. Walpole knew from ministerial experience the hazards of the former course; the latter was the Tory idea as expressed by the ruthlessly realistic Treaty of Utrecht; in essentials it would be Walpole's too. In 1730 he parted company with Townshend, who seemed to him to be precipitate in his engagements and to be endangering peace. After 1730 he was in control, with Newcastle and Harrington Secretaries of State. In 1731 was signed the Treaty of Vienna: England guaranteed the Pragmatic Sanction while the Emperor admitted Don Carlos to the Italian duchies that had long been a cause of strife. This treaty marked the end of the Stanhope-Townshend idea of co-operation with France and the return of the earlier system of alliance with the Emperor. Unfortunately Walpole, an isolationist at heart, did not foster the alliance. England's influence was seen to dwindle when France and Spain made the first of the Family Compacts. When Fleury led France into the Polish Succession War Walpole refused to commit England to the support of the Emperor. He rejoiced that he thus saved English lives and shillings but he found, as other Prime Ministers have found since, that diplomatic influence has to be paid for. Fleury edged him out of the peace negotiations. The Austrians were sore at what they regarded as desertion. A year after a second Treaty of Vienna (1738), by which France gained Lorraine and the Emperor nothing but the French guarantee of the Pragmatic Sanction, Walpole was forced into a war against Spain without an ally in Europe.

Between the outbreak of war in 1739 and his fall in January 1742, Walpole fought to hold his ground. His conduct of the war was unsure, but he remained master of Parliament to the end. His survival in these years testifies to the strength of the position he had built for himself. The death of Queen Caroline, his clever friend and confidante, in 1737, was a severe blow, but the King remained loyal. An opposition had evolved over the years composed of the hard core of Tories, the deprived Whigs led by men like Pulteney and Chesterfield, whom Walpole had ousted, and those aspiring politicians who saw the old minister as an obstacle to their advancement. The Leicester House faction clustered round Frederick Prince of Wales, counting on his patronage when he became King. The 'Cobham Cousinhood' were marshalled by the ambitious young William Pitt. With their distinctive views and plans the opposing groups could only be effective when there was an issue big enough to override conflicting interests. They had forced Walpole to withdraw his Excise Bill after a countrywide campaign of vilification and distortion. They triumphed when they drove him reluctantly into war with Spain, ostensibly for the rights of Jenkins, the Welsh captain who lost an ear, so he claimed, at the hands of *gardacostas*, but really for freedom of the lucratic trade in Spanish colonial waters. Walpole secured the Convention of Pardo and a small monetary compensation, sufficient, he urged for an honourable settlement. But moderation and peace lost the day to Pitt and 'the despairing merchants' of his perfervid imagination.

The ensuing war was popular but fruitless, after Admiral Vernon's seizure of Porto Bello. The old minister could not rise to the scale of the European war that developed when Frederick of Prussia seized Silesia from Austria in 1740. In the election of 1741 Walpole's majority was reduced but he clung on until February 1742; then he was defeated on an election petition – but he had already decided to resign. He had lost the support of the House of Commons without which no minister could survive long. He knew it. 'I have lived long enough in the world, Sir,' he said in one debate, 'to know that the safety of a minister lies in his having the approbation of this House

... I have always made it my first study to obtain it ...'. When he met Pulteney in the House of Lords, soon after both men had accepted peerages, the new Lord Orford is supposed to have remarked: 'You and I, My Lord, are now two as insignificant men as any in England.'

This could not have been said in the reign of Queen Anne when the Whig junta ruled the country from the Lords. Walpole had raised the Commons to a unique sense of authority. Even if, in his management, he relied chiefly upon the 'old gang', the body of about 150 placemen who could be counted on to support the government in all weathers, he never became insensitive to the needs of the more independent members. He explained and defended his policies with clarity and the plain words that earned respect. He approached debate with an open mind and he could always be converted by good arguments. During the *Pax Walpoleana* there were few great issues but there was plenty of good debate.

Walpole did not live long enough to enjoy his earldom or the treasures of Houghton. The King still consulted him 'in the closet'. The danger of impeachment for peculation receded after committees found insufficient evidence. Gout and the stone tormented his last years, but he was game to the end. One cannot admire Walpole without reservation. Relatives and dependents enjoyed office at every level of the 'Robinocracy'. He professed no idealism: 'I am no saint, no Spartan, no reformer.' He was a man of coarse fibre. 'I have the right sow by the ear,' he said of his relationship with Queen Caroline, one of the most enlightened of royal consorts. Less true connoisseur than avid collector, he filled Houghton with the pictures which now adorn the Hermitage in Saint Petersburg. Caricaturists dwelt upon his homely features and vast bulk (he weighed twenty stone). Election lists, petitions, and a voluminous correspondence reveal a complex character. But certain qualities are beyond dispute. He was endowed with a prodigious capacity for work. He devoted himself to the interests of his class and country and saw there no conflict of interests. He was a man of great physical and moral courage. He is not out of place among the leading statesmen of the Enlightenment. Within the limits dictated by common sense and a keen instinct for self-preservation he worked, not in vain, for toleration at home and peace abroad.

J.H. Plumb, *Walpole: The King's Minister* (1960).
H.T. Dickinson, *Walpole and the Whig Supremacy* (1973).

Spencer Compton

SPENCER COMPTON, 1ST EARL OF WILMINGTON (1673?-1743) was First Lord of the Treasury from February 1742 to his death in July 1743. Sandwiched between Walpole and Walpole's preferred successor, Henry Pelham, it is unsurprising that he has been generally regarded as unimportant – 'an amiable nonentity' (B. Williams) – and that the chief interest in his career has been found in what it reveals about the political process of his day. Indeed it is likely, had he lived longer, that he would have managed affairs less adroitly than Pelham. 'Old dull important lord / Who at the long'd for money board / sits first, but does not lead' (Hanbury Williams) was probably how many saw him. But 'important' nonetheless? He had staying power. Like his friend Bubb Dodington he impresses by his persistence in the political game. Unlike Dodington he had a long experience of office. For nearly forty years he operated near the centre of government.

The sixth, second surviving son of the Tory, James Compton, 3rd Earl of Northampton, and of Mary, daughter of Viscount Campden, he came young into Parliament as member successively for Eye (1698-1710), East Grinstead (1713-15) and Sussex (1715-28). The gap of three years followed his sensible decision to bow before the Tory storm over Dr Sacheverell. The county seat indicates his standing with the Whig grandees, enhanced undoubtedly by his role as manager of the High Tory cleric's trial, partisan and untypically violent in denunciation. As chairman of the Commons Committee of Privileges (1705-10) he acquired a knowledge of the ways of the House that he put to good use as Speaker (still then part of the ministerial team) through two Parliaments, 1715-27. His successor, Speaker Onslow, thought him 'very able in the chair' but lacking 'the powers of speech out of it'. 'Rare of his speech, but then positive' was Egmont's view. Meanwhile he amassed a large fortune in key financial offices, first as Paymaster of the Queen's Pensions (1707-13), then Treasurer to the Prince of Wales (1715-27), finally Paymaster-General of the Forces (1722-30). During the Whig schism of 1717-20 he worked with Walpole from the vantage point of the Prince's household. It was a position that he expected to pay a political dividend. Indeed on George I's death in 1727, the new King wanted Compton to take the Treasury. But it appears that he lost his nerve, 'being frighted with the greatness of the undertaking and more particularly as to what related to money matters'. Yet he was not short of practice in the financial sphere. More likely, against Walpole's solid front, support among other ministers and sheer expertise, he realised that he could not form an administration. Better therefore to bide his time and accept a peerage: in 1730 his barony became an earldom and he was made Lord President of the Council.

In 1740 Egmont noted that there were three parties at court: Walpole's, Newcastle's and Wilmington's with the Duke of Dorset (an early patron) and friends. Up till then his interest and influence had lain mainly in supporting Walpole. But he was not the man to go down with a sinking ship, nor to yield advantage to the Pelhams. Men deduced plotting from his frequent conferring with Bubb Dodington. In February 1742, after Cock Robin's fall, Wilmington joined Argyll, who could answer for a number of Scottish members, in promoting the idea of a Broad Bottom ministry – as distinct from the Whig 'Old Corps' who would have nothing to do with Tories or Whig fellow-travellers. In this approach they had the support of George II who resented the way in which the Whigs closed ranks. He chose Wilmington for the Treasury but his wholehearted backing of Carteret, Secretary of State for the North, and his ambitious Continental strategy – and his own spirited performance at the Battle of Dettingen – meant that Wilmington gained little advantage from the royal favour. Even if not 'the sole minister' of Pitt's invective, Carteret called the tune. Indeed Wilmington found 'His Majesty so resolved to narrow the bottom and withstand the voice of the people that he saw his very crown in danger' (Egmont). When he threatened to resign, however, George reproached him with tears: 'What My Lord, would you desert me?' Like Wilmington he saw his ministers as owing a primary and personal loyalty to him and resented anything that suggested combination. Meanwhile Henry Pelham consolidated his position in the Commons and found himself strongly positioned to take the Treasury on Wilmington's sudden death. It was as Walpole wished and it came to seem a natural extension of the Whig ascendancy.

1   Sir Robert Walpole, 1st Earl of Orford
     (Artist: John Michael Rysbrack)

2   Henry Pelham
(Artist: John Shackleton)

3   William Pitt, 1st Earl of Chatham
        (Artist: William Hoare)

4   Frederick North, 8th Lord North and 2nd Earl of Guilford
(Artist: Nathaniel Dance)

5   William Pitt
    (Artist: John Hoppner)

6   Spencer Perceval
(Artist: George Francis Joseph)

7   Robert Banks Jenkinson, 2nd Earl of Liverpool
(Artist: Sir Thomas Lawrence)

8   Charles Grey, 2nd Earl Grey
     (Artist: att. Thomas Phillips)

Unmarried, Wilmington left only illegitimate children, and his large fortune therefore to his nephew, the Earl of Northampton. Without any notable legislative achievement, he has left an indistinct mark on the political history of his time. Perhaps he was unlucky in his rivals, but he plainly lacked the toughness and single-mindedness required for success at the highest level. Though tenable at the time, his constitutional position would soon look anachronistic. It was his avowed belief that 'the true interest of England was to have no chief minister but that every great office should be immediately dependent on the king and answer for itself' (Egmont). George II might approve but the future lay with the Pelhams and a political balance tilting gradually from royal prerogative to Cabinet responsibility.

Henry Pelham

HENRY PELHAM (1695-1754), was Prime Minister from 1746 until his death in 1754. He had indeed been in a leading position from 1743, when he was promoted from Paymaster to First Lord of the Treasury, but the dominance of Carteret, and the instability following his fall (November 1744), when George II continued to consult Carteret and took every opportunity to undermine his ministers, meant that it was not until 1746 that he was in effect Prime Minister. His elder brother, Thomas, Duke of Newcastle, though with difficulty, was then ready to acknowledge it. In the words of his biographer, Coxe, 'his understanding was more solid than brilliant'. He himself disclaimed 'Court ambition' and had 'very little interested views'. Yet he established, over eight years, such an ascendancy in the House that concerted opposition virtually ceased. In 1753 there were no amendments to the royal address.

Serving a King, George II, whose 'Pow'r, coerced by Laws, still leaves them [people] free' (Desaguliers), in his conception of duty and of what was proper he exemplifies the best features as well as the limitations of the 'politics of politeness' and 'that pursuit of harmony within a propertied society' (Langton) which might suit the governing class, but also, they easily believed, the governed. So long as the governed, at least the more articulate among them, were generally content, occasional eruptions of the populace only reinforced the patrician view of priorities. Neither in Parliament, nor indeed in the country at large, was there much evidence of a desire for change, let alone radical criticism of the use of Crown patronage or the anomalies of parliamentary franchise. The Industrial Revolution, which would engender new forces in society, was in its infancy. There was throughout the assumption that the prime duty of the statesman was to maintain order. In dynastic terms, against the Jacobite threat that meant Hanover and the status quo; at home, the rights of property, whether against country poachers or urban mobs; in the Treasury, the balancing of the nation's books.

The second son of Thomas Pelham MP and of his second wife Lady Grace Holles, he was schooled at Westminster, Oxford and Padua. Family lands and influence ensured early entry to Parliament, as member for Seaford (1717-22), and, for the rest of his career, for Sussex. Marriage in 1725 to Lady Katherine Manners brought the Rutland interest and money to bear. Newcastle was well placed to assist his rise and would continue to be his partner in an ever-growing empire of patronage and influence. But Henry had a mind of his own and the ability to earn promotion by merit. A Lord of the Treasury, 1721-4, Secretary at War, 1724-30, it was as Paymaster-General that he came to have a vital role in financial management. He was in sympathy with Walpole's methods and priorities – 'my oracle' he called him. Walpole was impressed and came to see him as a likely successor. Pelham's comment on the furore over the Excise Bill shows him absorbing a lesson in crisis management. 'We have all been put to our stumps but by the steadiness of the party ... and the firmness of our master [Walpole] in the main point, we are now gott pretty firm in our seats again.' He did not take advantage of the Paymaster's traditional cut to enrich himself. With £5,000 a year he could afford to be honest – but it was in his nature to be so, as it was to work hard. It is unclear what part he played in Walpole's downfall beyond intimating that he had lost the confidence of the Commons, that the game was up. When Walpole's lifelong and eloquent rival Pulteney went with him to the Lords, Pelham became the undoubted leader in the Commons. Many would then have subscribed to Hervey's view that he was 'a gentleman-like sort of man, of very good character, of moderate parts ... not a bright speaker but a useful one.' He earned respect for his competence and was liked for his affable manners. As would others in a chamber where, as in a club, men were closely observed, he rose to the top above cleverer, less steady men. He had the gift for conciliation needed to create a semblance of unity during the early post-Walpole years, as Whig cliques conducted their 'stately minuet' (Hill) in and out of office. But he needed a friend at court and it was undoubtedly through Walpole's continuing influence there that he was appointed First Lord of the Treasury in August 1743. Like Walpole he also took the office of Chancellor of the Exchequer and, to ensure complete financial control, he removed Pulteney's nominees from the Treasury Board.

Would-be rivals sometimes played into his hands. Pulteney, now

Lord Bath, was by this time more suited to opposition than to office. Carteret had a self-destructive streak. As Secretary of State, following Walpole's fall (February 1742) he sought through subsidy and alliance against France to revive the glories of Marlborough. He seemed to think that he could act like a statesman without needing to be a politician. He affected to despise the small change of patronage by which the Pelhams accumulated their balance of power. But it was their success in controlling small constituencies that counterbalanced the shire freeholder vote and secured their position. When his policies failed, the King, on whose support he assumed he could rely, had to dismiss him with a consoling earldom (November 1744), for the Pelhams by then had the whip hand. In 1746, now Granville, Carteret tried to form an administration when the Pelhams threw up their offices, but found no support. 'What is it to me', he had asked, 'who is a judge or who is a bishop? It is my business to make kings and emperors.' It was precisely because the Pelhams made patronage their business that they were able to join forces to foil him, form the 'Broad Bottom' ministry and defy the King. Rosebery (was he thinking of his own career?) wrote that Granville was 'incapable of that self-contained patience, amounting to long-suffering, which is a necessary and costly condition of the highest success in official life.' That was a characteristic of Henry Pelham, as of his brother, steadily focused on essential business, tenacious of power.

During Carteret's ministry taxation to support his Continental alliances was the business of 'the chief clerk', as Carteret loftily called Henry Pelham: it made the First Lord vulnerable to the vehement opposition of Pitt and his Grenvillite group. He knew the temperament of the country gentleman: 'We Englishmen are very stout upon our own dunghill ... but when this nation is engaged in a war ... the country must pay for it and then who is to bear the blame?' After 1744 the chances of war lent weight to the Pelhams' policy of reducing Continental commitments. The British fought bravely at Fontenoy (1745) but it could not be presented as a victory. After that year's alarm when Charles Edward reached Derby came the crushing verdict of Culloden (April 1746) on the future of Jacobitism, and Pelham could claim credit for the suppression of the clans by the subsequent Disarming Acts, with the prohibition of native dress, abolition of hereditary jurisdictions and confiscation of estates. Though the brutal hounding of clansmen by 'Butcher' Cumberland left a sour taste, ministers were unruffled. The plight of rebels in distant mountains beyond the law was of little concern to polite society.

The Broad Bottom could be so called because Pelham had recruited such notable opponents as Bedford and Chesterfield. Its weakness, with the war continuing as a contest of attrition between Continental armies, was that it was not noticeably different from what had gone before. Magnanimous, also aware of his talent, Pelham wanted to bring Pitt into government. George II, whom Pitt had insulted in his tirades against Hanover, could not stomach it and looked to have Granville back. In an exchange with the King, Hardwicke stated the Whig case starkly while George expressed his frustration. 'The disposition of places is not enough if Your Majesty takes pains to show the world that you disapprove of your own work.' 'My work! I was forced. I was threatened.' 'Your ministers are only your instruments of government.' 'Ministers are the kings in this country.' In February 1746 ministers put it to the test: Newcastle and Harrington resigned, followed by Pelham, Bedford and others. Neither Granville nor Bath could form a government. They were up against a majority in Parliament and influential voices in the City: 'No Pelham, no money.' George dared not call an election and was forced to recall the brothers. They were now in a stronger position, able to draw on talent from diverse Whig groups. Pitt became Paymaster-General. The old gang could now be seen as 'the natural party of government'. There had been a momentous shift in the balance of power between King and Parliament, the legacy and unresolved issue of the Glorious Revolution. The Commons could not yet dictate whom the King could employ; but it could render a Prime Minister's place untenable if he lacked support in Parliament. Pelham's place was now unassailable. It rested on the approval of the House but eventually too the respect of the King, who came to rate his financial management superior even to Walpole's. So Pelham would never know the discomfort of Walpole's last years, with opponents closing in for the kill.

Once established, 'his eloquence cleared up, and he shone with much greater force' (Horace Walpole). In Pelham's view, the House was 'a great unwieldy body which requires great art and some cordials to keep it together'. The cordials came in the form of place and preferment sufficient, with soft words and promises, to leave opponents isolated and without a cause worth fighting for. Besides Pitt, Pelham also had some able spokesmen for the government, notably Henry Fox, George Grenville and George Lyttelton. Leading ministers were in the Lords and so shielded from attack. A tactical coup, calling an election in 1747, a year before due, caught opponents off-guard. As the King aged the reversionary interest became a factor. But the Leicester House group, centring on Frederick Prince of Wales, was never a serious threat and it was left shattered in 1751 by his premature death. In November of that year Henry Fox wrote that 'a bird might build her nest in the Speaker's chair or in his peruke. There won't be a debate that can disturb it.'

Gains at the peace of Aix-la-Chapelle (October 1748) were modest and opponents jeered. But the timely assertion of naval power in 1747 by the victories of Anson and Hawke at Finisterre and Belle-Isle, had reinforced the prejudice against Continental war campaigns and Pelham was able to prevent Newcastle's authorising a further campaigning season. Now he could offer a peace dividend in the shape of drastic reductions in the size of the Army and Navy: the Navy from 51,000 to 10,000 in two years, the Army from 50,000 to 18,850. Within four years he had balanced the budget and was able by stages to reduce the Land Tax, from 4s to 2s. The price of these economies would be unpreparedness for the next war, but they found general favour. Only in emergencies would the British regard themselves as a military nation.

Typically Pelham shrank from the administrative reform that might bring further savings but alienate voters in 'Treasury boroughs'. His priority was the National Debt. It had swollen to £77 million and interest payments accounted for 44% of government expenditure. Taking advantage of the buoyancy of stock he got Parliament's approval for a conversion scheme to cut interest to 3½% by 1750, then 3% by 1757. To brave the hostility of the Bank of England and the financial rings which had floated loans on the basis of a closed subscription took political nerve and sound judgement. But he had allies, notably Sir John Barnard and the Jewish financier Sampson Gideon. He could soon point to benefits: a reduction by 1750 of 12% in the servicing of the debt. In time the consolidated debts, or 'consols' could be a source of strength to government. A low rate of interest would encourage investment and trade. Prosperity would reach a wider range of citizens and provide a healthy base for taxation. Like other aspects of his political achievement Pelham's financial management can appear unspectacular. In the wider context of industrial advance, in the application of capital to invention and provision of better transport, it was of the greatest importance.

His ability to take a long view and act upon it reflects the advantage of continuity in administration. 'Harry the Ninth' had no need to look over his shoulders to electors and other critics outside Parliament. More vexing, though never likely to threaten the cohesion of government, was the sniping and carping of his brother, his pride offended when he was crossed in Cabinet, personal sensitivities giving point to the perennial friction of Treasury and Foreign Office: between the concern for economies and that for security and prestige abroad, seen by Newcastle, not without reason, as needing to be reinforced by Continental alliances. Lord Chancellor Hardwicke's role was vital; tactful and emollient, he had the ear of each brother and he was at home at court. Every government needs its Hardwicke. But personal differences would evaporate when unity was threatened, as by Bedford, Newcastle's fellow Secretary of State. In 1751 Bedford was forced to resign, Holderness was promoted in his place and Granville was recalled to be Lord President of the Council. Judged by its own criteria the Pelham system was undeniably successful.

Finance apart, Pelham's was not a notable reforming government. Most helpful measures were promoted by independent members. He supported Oglethorpe's bill of 1750 creating the Free British Fishery Company to develop the herring industry and he allowed the export of wool from Ireland, hitherto forbidden. That island was relatively quiet, grievances muted. Despite Newcastle's misgivings Pelham supported Chesterfield's measure for reform of the Calendar. He also spoke warmly in favour of the Jewish Naturalisation Bill in 1753, mindful perhaps of his obligation to Jewish financiers for support of his debt conversion. But he allowed his brother, and the clamour of the mob to cause its repeal. It was ignoble but Whig oligarchs could not afford to be insensitive to public opinion in the year before an election. The satirical prints of Hogarth revealed the squalor and misery of 'Gin Lane' and were another uncomfortable reminder of the potential in crowded cities for riot, looting and arson. The trade and its illicit vendors were brought under control by Nugent's bill, the Tippling Act of 1751. In 1753 Hardwicke steered through his Marriage Act, to control clandestine and irregular marriages, but Pelham was embarrassed by the opposition of Henry Fox, his main ministerial supporter in the Commons, himself a beneficiary of a 'Fleet marriage'. There was room, however, for public as well as personal disagreements in this administration, appearing to be loosely bound but held together, under careful direction, by common interests.

Much of the legislation of the Pelham years was indeed humdrum, directed towards private interests, enclosures or turnpike roads. Some was aimed at the perennial problem of smuggling. There was a medley of measures to deal with specific problems: like deep rutted roads and the width of carriage wheels. The record reveals a steady advance in the economic strength of the country and a stirring of concern about public morals. Pelham may remain one of the least known of the great Prime Ministers but his sudden death was a loss to his friends and to the country. An inclination to gluttony, a sometimes hasty temper, were the worst men could say about him. Faithful in a childless marriage, single-minded and altruistic, he earned a tribute from a usually caustic critic. Was Horace Walpole mindful of his father's rather different record when he wrote that Pelham 'lived without abusing his power and died poor'. George II too had come to recognise his worth and his comment is no bad memorial: 'Now I shall have no more peace.'

J. Wilkes, *A Whig in Power: The Political Career of Henry Pelham* (1964).

Duke of Newcastle

THOMAS PELHAM-HOLLES, 1ST DUKE OF NEWCASTLE (1693-1768) may have been fortunate to live in the first half of the eighteenth century when the political system was such as to afford the widest scope for his extraordinary, single-minded devotion to the political game. Most assiduous and prominent of Old Corps Whigs, he was sustained through a career of fifty years, and high office of nearly forty, by a strong sense of duty and of his own importance. He was indeed more important than might appear from the relatively short period, March 1754 to November 1756, in which he can be called Prime Minister, between periods acting as an indispensable but subordinate partner, first of his brother, Henry Pelham, and then of William Pitt.

He was the eldest son of Thomas, 1st Lord Pelham and of his second wife, Lady Grace Holles, sister of John, Duke of Newcastle. He added the name Holles on succeeding, in 1715, as adopted heir, to the ducal estate and title. He married, in 1717, Lady Henrietta, elder daughter of Earl Godolphin. With large estates and rentals of £30,000 a year came the traditions and expectations of two notable political families.

He was Lord Chamberlain from 1717 but it was the disgrace or premature death of several leading Whigs following the South Sea Bubble's collapse, together with Walpole's favour, that opened up the chance of higher office. In 1724 he became Secretary of State for the Southern department, in place of Carteret who, by his rash connection with a French diplomatic intrigue, had provided Walpole with a pretext for removing him. Newcastle could benefit from the faults or mistakes of abler men. He was ever immersed in the details of patronage, specialising in the promotion of bishops who could be relied on to support ministers in the Lords. He had staying power – and he knew when to bend the knee. Junior to his colleague Lord Townshend, he would usually fall in with his arrangements – until Walpole decided, in 1730, that he must go: the old ally grown too independent for comfort. Newcastle found his successor Harrington less threatening. He was steadily gaining knowledge of the diplomatic scene, though always from his desk, for he was a nervous traveller.

Vox populi would always resonate with Newcastle. In 1739 it sounded loud and clear over Captain Jenkins' Ear. Supporting war against Spain, he was, in effect, undermining Walpole. As he said to Newcastle: 'It is your war and I wish you joy of it.' Seeing the steady erosion of support for the old minister, Newcastle worked closely with his brother to make dispositions for survival and for power. To Old Corps Whigs, who could easily have dissolved into fragmentary groups, the Pelhams, with the invaluable, emollient Lord Chancellor Hardwicke, promised a welcome continuity: office for some; for the rank and file place, pension or support in some private cause and act. It was thus that, by the narrowest of margins, Newcastle was able to see off a move to mount an enquiry into Walpole's ministry. 'The politics of stockjobbers', in Dr Johnson's scornful phrase, could also be seen as working in 'the publick interest' – Newcastle's constant plea. To the King Newcastle was 'an impertinent fool'. But for two years the partners maintained sufficient cohesion among the Old Corps Whigs to withstand his hostility and Carteret's scorn. Newcastle was necessary – but no less resented. In August 1743 he complained: 'No man can bear long what I go through every day in our joint audience in the closet.' He was repaid for the suffering and alarms which were a recurring theme of his voluminous correspondence when, in November 1744, the Pelhams secured Carteret's dismissal. Henry Pelham was now effectively Prime Minister. Favour in the closet was not enough. The lesson was reinforced in February 1746. By resigning together ministers challenged the King to find another who could form a ministry. Granville and Bath failed and the King had to turn back to the Old Corps.

George could have done worse. The Pelhams were prepared to compromise, to reconcile opposites, a Hanoverian King, an anti-Hanoverian Parliament, to broaden the ministry by appointing former opponents, like Pitt and Bedford. They alone, through an ever-tightening grip on patronage, could ensure the control of Parliament that was essential if the mounting cost of war and diplomacy was to be met. Because they were interested as much in power as in measures, they made government possible. His more self-confident brother was sorely tried by Newcastle's fussiness and jealousies, verging at times on the obsessive. But shared Whig principles and grasp of political realities enabled them to rub along. As First Lord, holding the purse-strings, Henry was clearly in prime position. But Newcastle managed to convince himself that his diplomatic role was equally important. He overcame his fear of the Channel to attend the King and to supervise negotiations at Aix-la-Chapelle. Louisburg and Cape Breton were handed back to the French but England retained Gibraltar and Minorca. Pitt considered that ministers 'had done well to secure so good a peace as they did'. The outraged reaction in France supports the view. The war had been as unpopular as it was expensive and Newcastle returned content with having secured peace and laid the base for economies and lower taxes.

It was not his fault that the loose ends left by Aix were to lead to another war, since Maria Theresa was not reconciled to the loss of Silesia, nor France to the poor reward for her military exertions. He can be blamed, however, with his brother, for failing to prepare the country for another war; in particular to maintain the Navy. Should he have seen, with France thirsting for revenge and colonies, that neutrality was not an option? With his brother bent on economies, did he have any option but to trust to diplomacy? Unfortunately, his initiatives betrayed a superficial understanding of foreign institutions and attitudes. So he busied himself with his 'Great System, the great object of my life, in foreign affairs': to secure, by lavish bribes, the election of Maria Theresa's son as King of the Romans. To Henry Pelham it was 'expensive moonshine'. The Austrians dismissed the scheme as an impertinence and came to terms – the 'Diplomatic Revolution' – with France. Frederick King of Prussia was self-righteous about interference in German affairs, though soon to be thankful for the British alliance. Having replaced Bedford in 1751 with the less robust Holderness – Newcastle's ideal colleague – there was no restraining influence or independent view. Newcastle was gullible in thinking that his treaties with Russia and Prussia were compatible. Ever anxious that no enemy should gain the King's ear, Newcastle twice braved the perils of Continental travel to stay close at his side. So there was point to Pitt's objection that Hanover appeared to be the centre of England's diplomatic interest.

Newcastle was hard hit by his brother's death in 1754. He moved as if by right to Henry's place as First Lord of the Treasury. He still had much to learn, for instance, from Henry's Secretary John Roberts, about the detailed management of elections. He believed that he could maintain his grip over the Commons from the Lords without an effective leader in the House. For that role he needed Henry Fox, but Fox would not do it without a share in, or information about, the distribution of patronage – a point on which Newcastle would not yield. From March 1754 to November 1756 he was Prime Minister, with Holderness, and first Robinson, then Fox, as Secretaries of State, but without the essential coherence that his brother had secured. He began with the reassuring returns from an election in which only 42 seats were actually contested. He soon lost Pitt (November 1754), who was therefore free to attack. The impression of drift and incompetence was confirmed by the way in which the country was drawn into war, and by early setbacks: Braddock's defeat in America, ambushed on the Monoongahala, the surrender of Calcutta to Siraj-ud-Daula, the abortive naval action of Byng and subsequent loss of Minorca. Byng paid the price for the poor state of his ships and confused instructions. 'Indeed he shall be hanged,' said Newcastle when pressed. After a travesty of a trial he was shot on his own quarterdeck (April 1757). It did not deflect criticism of responsible ministers. But by then Newcastle was out.

Newcastle was never comfortable sharing power and preferred to have docile colleagues. It had been clear by September 1755 that the ministry must be strengthened and that the necessary men were Fox, to be Secretary, in place of Robinson, and Leader of the House, and Pitt, who had been dismissed the previous November and since found ready listeners in the Commons for his inflammatory speeches. Pitt refused, when told that Newcastle was not empowered by the King, to offer him the other Secretaryship. He demanded a free hand to direct the war effort. It would need the novel experience of being out of office to persuade Newcastle, reluctant delegator, jittery colleague, that this had to be. Newcastle's report of the conversation reveals the man: 'I never sat down to write to your lordship [Hardwicke] with more melancholy apprehensions for the Publick than at present. I see nothing but confusion and it is beyond me to point out a remedy.' Two months later, following Fox, he resigned, whereupon George had to send for Pitt. It had been a debacle, but one that could have been foreseen. No partner acceptable to Newcastle could command the fractious Commons; no strong man in the Commons would bear with Newcastle. Pitt was such a man. It was now his turn to experience the difficulty of managing without the patronage, without

Newcastle's support. Denied the boon of an early victory, he was ineffective.

From 6 April, when he was dismissed, till 29 June when he joined Newcastle, the country was without a government. The country wanted Pitt, but without Newcastle he could not count on support in Parliament, nor enjoy the confidence of the King. Newcastle was again First Lord of the Treasury but in no meaningful sense Prime Minister. From June until October 1761 the unlikely duumvirate lasted: it endured because of the necessities of war; it succeeded because of Pitt's leadership and nerve, and the heroic efforts of British soldiers and sailors. Newcastle could bask in their glory and take credit for ensuring a regular flow of money. At his 'labouring oar' (his phrase) the old duke played a useful part.

The accession of George III in 1760, Pitt's determination to carry the war to a further phase by attacking Spain, and his haughty, unco-operative ways, were among the causes of his fall in October 1761 and replacement by Lord Bute. For all their differences in policy Newcastle did not want it. But he was now trying to operate in a new political world. George might have done well to heed the earlier advice of the Duke of Devonshire to Lord Bute. It is the insider's view and aptly summarises the significance of the old Whig. 'The Duke of Newcastle had united with him the principal nobility, the moneyed men and the interest which had brought about the revolution [1688] ... and were not only the most considerable party but the true solid strength that might be depended on for the support of government. That therefore His Grace was the most necessary person for the King to cultivate.' But to George the very name Pelham smacked of ministerial control through corruption and recalled the discomforts of his grandfather. Under the circumstances it is notable that Newcastle survived Pitt. George's determination to recover the patronage and initiative meant that his days were numbered. In the negotiations which led to the Peace of Paris Newcastle fought for recognition of the claims of Frederick without success; opposed in everything and edged out of power, he eventually resigned in May 1762.

Horace Walpole wrote memorably about Newcastle's performance at the funeral of George II: 'he fell into a fit of crying at the moment he came into the chapel, and flung himself back into a stall. The archbishop hovering over him with a smelling bottle; but in two minutes his curiosity got the better of his hypocrisy, and he ran about the chapel, with his glass to spy who was there, spying with one hand and mopping his eyes with the other. Then returned the fear of catching cold; and the Duke of Cumberland, who was sinking with heat felt himself weighed down ... and found it was the Duke of Newcastle standing upon his train to avoid the chill of the marble.' Other accounts show that it was fashionable to laugh at him. The target was irresistible. He was so very high in office, so inept in manners. It does not mean that he was not an astute politician. His most serious fault was his incorrigible meddling. He could not leave well alone. It was his mother, to whom he was devoted, who spoke of him 'perpetually fretting your friends with unjust suspicions of them'.

It was hard for him to be out office. Remarkably Grenville brought him back as Lord Privy Seal (1765-6). He had a high conception of public duty. If it was a fault that he thought himself indispensable, he had the means and capacity to be so. He devoted himself to pension and place but made nothing from it for himself. He died a poor man. He loved Claremont and his garden, nobly fashioned by William Kent, but allowed himself little time to enjoy it. His labours and patriotism deserve better from the historian than they received from contemporaries.

R. Browning, *The Duke of Newcastle* (1975).

Duke of Devonshire

WILLIAM CAVENDISH, 4TH DUKE OF DEVONSHIRE (1720-64) was Prime Minister for only eight months (1756-7). His story is essentially that of Pitt and Newcastle for it was during the period before they overcame their differences to form an effective ministry, with bad war news feeding the sense of a system in crisis, that he came forward to do his duty to the King. He was a Whig aristocrat first, a politician second. He expected to serve the House of Hanover, but had no desire to get involved in the electoral business that was meat and drink to Newcastle. There was no 'Cavendish interest' comparable to that of Pelham or of Grenville. It enhanced his personal stature but reduced his political impact.

He was the first son of the 3rd Duke and of Catherine Hoskins. In 1748 he married Charlotte Boyle, daughter and heir of Lord Burlington. He was close to the King as Master of Horse (1751-5). He was Lord Treasurer of Ireland (1754-5) before becoming Lord Lieutenant. He then had little time to show that he cared for more than the interests of landowners before moving to the Treasury (November 1756). His role there was to hold the fort until a more stable arrangement could be made. His main concern was with wartime preparation and supply. Against Pitt, he approved the execution of Admiral Byng (March 1757) for his failure in battle, leading to the loss of Minorca; to him a straightforward case of dereliction of duty. He was indifferent to the rumours, intrigues and calculations of Westminster. His task was not eased, however, by the erratic conduct of Pitt, planning operations of war for future years, demanding a free hand while withdrawing for days into depressed inertia. Since Pitt could not command a Commons majority the ministry's demise was only a matter of time.

Devonshire resigned at the beginning of July 1757 without regret; he had already said that 'he would retain the Treasury but till some new system be completed.' The compensatory office of Lord Chamberlain suited him well, affording some influence, and at times a strong voice. After the death of George II, his successor and Bute would have done well to listen to Devonshire more attentively. For the diary that he kept between 1759 and 1762, while revealing little of the man, is full of judicious, balanced comment. With standing in court and Cabinet, involved in decision-making yet detached in outlook, not unsympathetic to the King's position, he could have been a valuable moderating influence. Instead he found himself on the margin, exasperated by Bute, not prepared to align himself with Newcastle. Eventually, since he would neither resign nor attend Cabinet, in 1762 George dismissed him. It sent the wrong signal to the Whig world and did nothing to restore stability.

Devonshire died relatively young, leaving for debate what he could have achieved. He had already earned the tribute of the editors of his Diary to his character and career: 'a natural balance of judgement, prudence and patriotism and above all, a sense of service without self-seeking.' It was no mean legacy.

P.D. Brown and K.W. Schweizer (eds), *The Devonshire Diary* (Camden, 4th set, Vol 27).

William Pitt the Elder

WILLIAM PITT, 1ST EARL OF CHATHAM (1708-78) was twice
Prime Minister, from 1757 until 1761, and from 1766 until 1768. In the
first ministry as Secretary of State, directing the war effort, he
became an illustrious public figure. He was what he had long sought
to appear, 'The Great Commoner'. In the second, when he took
non-executive office as Lord Privy Seal, the power of his name was
not enough to provide coherence in government. He would be the
last Prime Minister until, exceptionally, Lord Salisbury not to be
First Lord of the Treasury.

He was the fourth child and second son of Robert Pitt and
Harriet, *née* Villiers. The family was already established by the efforts
and ambition of his remarkable grandfather, 'Diamond Pitt'. Indian
wealth was translated into property and influence, aristocratic marriages, land – and a rotten borough, Old Sarum. Afterwards William
was to declare that a sensitive boy at Eton would be cowed for life,
but he made friendships there, notably with the Grenville brothers
and George Lyttelton, which would serve him well. He went to
Oxford and Utrecht but without clear professional intent. A commission in Lord Cobham's cavalry regiment did not prevent his
making the Grand Tour. It did bring him into the circle of Palladian
Stowe, where the 'cousinhood', Lytteltons, Grenvilles, their relations
and dependants, talked opposition politics and plotted action
against Walpole. The views and language of dissident Whigs
matched his own and fired his ambition. Member for Old Sarum in
1735, he quickly revealed the talent for debate which raised him to
the leadership of 'Cobham's cubs'. He embarrassed the ministry and,
more dangerously, offended his King, by the zeal with which he
espoused the cause of the Prince of Wales. Frederick's Leicester
House became the focus for politicians counting on the reversion to
bring office. But George II would outlive his son. Meanwhile he
remembered the gibes of 'the terrible cornet of horse'. Walpole
deprived him of his commission; the King resolved not to have him
in government. It would be eleven years before Pitt held Crown
office, twenty-two before he had high office.

Pitt could be excluded. He could not be ignored. He was a striking figure, 'tall in his person, as Shelburne later described him, 'as genteel as a martyr of gout could be, with the eye of a hawk, a little head, thin face, aquiline nose.' In 1739 the affair of Jenkins' Ear gave the opposition the excuse to hound the ministry into war with Spain (1739). Pitt believed that he had found a clear difference of principle and expressed it in terms which lifted debate and appealed to those who believed that England's future lay in her pursuit of overseas trade. When he declared that 'the complaints of your despairing merchants – the voice of England – has condemned it' (Walpole's appeasing Convention of Pardo), he raised the hunger for trade and the opportunism of politicians to a level of patriotic principle. Pitt opposed Carteret's policy – looking for Continental victory in the Marlborough style – because he believed that England's war was concerned mainly with Spain and winning her trade. Knowing that Carteret's colleagues and many in Parliament were uneasy about the cost of subsidies, Pitt found an appreciative audience for his assaults on the high-handed minister. 'Neither justice nor policy required us to be engaged in the quarrels of the Continent ... the confidence of the people is abused by making unnecessary alliances ... This great, this formidable kingdom is considered only as a province of a despicable electorate.' Rhetoric, Shelburne judged, 'was the only discipline he ever mastered'. The man who would one day boast of his having 'won Canada on the banks of the Elbe' might come to regret such posturing. But when an ambitious man could make his name by declaiming to the largely silent country gentry, the temptation was great. When he aimed at domestic corruption, and pro-Hanover strategies, he could hardly miss. He also hit the King. George might wince but he could neither save his minister nor block the inclusion of Cobham and Lyttelton in the Pelham administration. After ministers' successive resignations in February 1746, George had also to accept Pitt: first as Vice-Treasurer for Ireland, then, in May, as Paymaster-General.

The use he made of the Paymastership sets him apart from other politicians. He displayed his patriotic credentials and image as 'honest Mr Pitt' when – with a typical flourish and eye on the public 'out of doors' – he renounced the investment opportunities that made other Paymasters rich and lodged his accounts with the Bank of England. By rejecting the idea and tactics of 'connection', so serviceable to Old Corps Whigs, so suspect to those of independent views, he enhanced his patriot credentials. With a foresight and seriousness that recalls the activity of Winston Churchill in the 1930s, anticipating another war, preparing for a vital role, he kept in touch with his agents abroad, studied commercial statistics, gleaned information about French colonies, read books about war and planned a strategy of empire. He agreed with his city ally William Beckford that trade could flourish by war.

A dynastic marriage to Lady Hester Grenville in November 1754 brought private happiness. She had faith in him and there was no faltering in ambitious purpose. After the removal of Henry Pelham's restraining hand he was increasingly disturbed by Newcastle's foreign policy. He turned with relish to attack the government, its German treaties, urging an alliance with Frederick of Prussia, even if it meant a break with Hanover, and a 'blue water' policy focusing on the defeat of France overseas in the interests of colonists, 'those long-injured, long-neglected, long-forgotten people'. His bold bid for power embarrassed Newcastle and infuriated the King. Newcastle wanted to bind him to government but could not offer him the Secretaryship he demanded. With hostilities starting in India and Canada the country drifted towards the general war which called for a decisive leader. The defeat of Braddock in America and the furore over Admiral Byng's failure to prevent the loss of Minorca brought Newcastle to resign (November 1756) and Pitt to office. He stipulated that as Secretary of State he should be responsible for the formulation of policy, but Cumberland, commander-in-chief of allied forces, refused to receive his orders. Parliament was wary. His rhetoric had been reckless; his policies were untried. There were no early victories to bolster him. Newcastle lacked the nerve to direct but not the appetite for office. In April 1757 Pitt was dismissed, but the weeks that followed, when the country was virtually without a government, proved that Newcastle could not form a ministry without him. With petitions pouring in a coalition was devised (in June). Newcastle, as First Lord again, was to manage Parliament and find the money. Pitt, Secretary of State, had a relatively free hand to direct the war effort. 'Relatively' only because the conventions did not allow him to oversee other departments whose heads were answerable to the King. Co-ordination of policy could only be achieved informally through dealing in closet and Cabinet. This was where Newcastle's role was so important. It was fortunate for Pitt, and the country, that Newcastle was so resolved to stay in office that he could endure the impatient, often overbearing manner of his colleague.

'Pitt, Pompadour, Prussia, Providence.' The 'four Ps' were offered by the *London Magazine* to its readers in 1766 as the reasons for Britain's success in the Seven Years War. They could choose in what order of importance to rate them: Pitt's forceful direction, his resolution in pushing war to the limit; weakness at the heart of French government; the heroic endeavours of Frederick the Great; sheer good fortune – like that of Wolfe at Quebec (1759), or the presence in India of a man like Clive, Pitt's 'heaven-born general'. They could not assume such a favourable outcome for a future war. Nor could men in 1757. In his first months of power Pitt remodelled the instructions to commanders, but new plans and new men could not mature at once: the pace of war was slow. For a time, with Pitt concerned to keep Frederick in the war and to protect the country against French invasion by close blockade, it was not apparent that much was being achieved. The policy of diversionary attacks on places like Rochefort was memorably described as 'breaking windows with gold guineas'. Cumberland was defeated at Kloster-seven in June 1757 and compelled to make his peace. But Pitt disowned his action as being authorised by the Elector of Hanover (for once the connection was useful) and put his army under Ferdinand of Brunswick, later victor of Minden. Fortunately in India Clive had needed no orders from England; his victory at Plassey (June 1757) enabled Pitt to concentrate on what he held to be the vital spheres, Canada and the West Indies. Questions were raised about his decision to recruit Highlanders for the Army and to raise a militia. But he sustained support for the war by his determination to be honest, even about defeats: 'I despise your little policy of concealments.'

Relishing responsibility, magnanimous, pugnacious, with some-thing of the Elizabethan about him in his lust for victory, he inspired trust in his chosen commanders by his indifference to rules of seniority – several of 'Pitt's boys', like Keppel, captor of Goree, were in their thirties – and by his clear orders. The victories of 1759 made his name a household word, excited the people and impressed the old King. News of Minden set the bells ringing yet again. But it was the victories at sea of Boscawen off Lagos and Hawke in Quiberon Bay, with their dividends in the capture of West Indian islands and

African trading stations, that brought most acclaim and stiffened Pitt in his resolve to maintain, and extend, the war effort.

Pitt's personal dominance was unprecedented. But it owed more to character than to political management, and underlying political realities were unchanged. Parliamentarians were prone as ever to mistrust a strong executive and to form connections to prevent it. The accession in 1760 of George III was at once destabilising; he was inclined to view politics in personal terms and taught to believe that 'Pitt had the blackest of hearts'. In March 1761 Bute became Secretary of State. Pitt could not work with a man whom he knew to be inexperienced and believed to be in office primarily to find means of ending what George III, in his first speech, had called 'a bloody and expensive' war. Pitt substituted for 'bloody' the words 'just and necessary'. When peace talks began in 1761 Pitt was primarily concerned with winning more counters for peace, or future possessions, like Dominica and Pondicherry. Over the Newfoundland fisheries, which the French demanded, he would not budge. When, in October 1761, he learned that Spain was planning to come into the war he decided to strike first. His fellow ministers demurred. 'Being responsible I will direct, and will be responsible for nothing that I do not direct,' said Pitt, and resigned his seals and his war. His judgement may have been astray here. Newcastle and Hardwicke knew the discontents of the squires who paid the Land Tax. There was reasonable concern about the National Debt: £74.5 million in 1755, it was £133.25 in 1763, the year of the Peace of Paris. But it was not only to Pitt that Bute's Peace of Paris appeared weak: the sugar islands were returned, with the trading stations in West Africa and fishing rights in Newfoundland. Pitt attacked the concessions in a three-hour speech. France, he urged, had been given the means to become once more formidable at sea, while England's ally Frederick had been betrayed.

He then commanded only 65 votes in the Commons, but the crowd shouted for him. Their hero had been dethroned but he hoped for a restoration. There were able men, like the young Shelburne, who saw him as patron and mentor. But political authority called for some readiness to work with the grain, to meet colleagues halfway. Pitt's physical and mental state combined to rob him of patience and tact. At times he could be a caricature of himself in his appearances in the House, gaunt, pale, legs wrapped in rolls of flannel. At Burton Pynsent, left him by a wealthy admirer, he directed extravagant projects of landscape gardening. At Hayes, his favourite house, he found domestic comfort with Hester and four children. But there was no serenity. Was his manner, strained, unnaturally histrionic, just the barely controlled face of an inner frenzy? Do days of retreat in darkened rooms, between hyperactivity, suggest manic depression? Did the ostentation of his household, his postilions in blue and white, armies of servants around his children, signify a deep need for recognition, or a still restless ambition? Exalted or downcast, he remained convinced that his country needed him. If his patriotism was egotistic it was also dutiful and sincere. He was resolved to come back but on his own terms, from the position of independence that had always appealed to him: 'unattached to any party I am, and wish to be, entirely single'. That he could rise to a great occasion was shown when he spoke (unsuccessfully) for the Repeal of the Stamp Act, and against the Declaratory Act. He was wise to urge Parliament not to provoke the colonists by unnecessary assertion of the principle that it had the right to tax them. For him there should be no taxation without representation.

His principle, 'measures not men', appealed to the King, to whom Pitt now offered fulsome loyalty. In July 1766 he got at last the sole, unconditional direction of affairs. The problems which faced the government he seemed specially fitted to tackle: the observance of the Treaty of Paris by France and Spain, tension between American colonists and the mother country, the status of the East India Company. Choosing for himself freedom from the routines of office, as Lord Privy Seal he made appointments without regard for connections, but for perceived merit. Charles Townshend to the Exchequer, Shelburne, as Secretary of State, to order American affairs. He set about his duties with tempestuous energy. Yet, in October 1768, he resigned after a catastrophic ministry, leaving such leadership as he could give to Grafton, his First Lord of the Treasury. What had gone wrong? He had embarked upon an experiment in rule, not only without party but almost without Cabinet: 'sole minister' indeed. Then he became really ill and so remained, sometimes verging on madness, for the rest of his ministry. If he had stayed in the Commons he might still have held together 'an administration chequered and speckled', in Burke's words, 'patriots and courtiers, King's friends and republicans; Whigs and Tories ... indeed a very curious show.' But he took an earldom, removed himself from the sphere where he could show mastery, and forfeited the sympathy of the people for the doubtful advantage of a title and approval of a King whom he proposed to serve by 'destroying all party distinctions'. He made a show of governing, from Bath where he wintered, then from his Hampstead house. When, in 1767, Townshend produced the duties, on tea, glass and paper, so offensive to the American colonists whom Chatham thought he understood, he was quite out of touch, so distracted that he would not see his wife, sunk in painful brooding, a prey to sudden whims such as pulling down a house that obstructed his view. 'His nerves and spirits were affected to a dreadful degree,' wrote Grafton, 'his great mind bowed down.' The King clung to the hope that he would recover while the ministry drifted rudderless. Eventually Chatham himself, emerging from his shadows, forced his resignation on the King.

As he realised the gravity of the American situation Chatham re-entered the fray, declaring that 'he would be in earnest for the public' and 'a scarecrow of violence to the gentler warblers of the grove'. They, moderate Whigs, found a prophet in Edmund Burk, who wrote of Chatham that he wanted 'to keep hovering in air, above all parties, and to swoop down where the prey may prove best'. Such was Grafton, victim of Chatham's swift swoop on behalf of 'Wilkes and Liberty'. Pitt had not lost his nose for the big issue, the smell of injustice, a threat to the liberties of subjects. But Grafton was followed by North, and Chatham went off to farm, his cows typically housed in palatial stalls. Money was of no concern and debts piled up. But India was – and he pressed warmly the case for reform of the East India Company's management. Still closer to his heart was America but his warnings went unregarded till the eve of war. Then brave efforts to present his case, passionate, deeply pondered, for the concession of fundamental liberties – no taxation without consent, independent judges, trial by jury, along with the recognition of Congress – foundered on the ignorance and complacency of Parliament. In his last years he found again words to express the concern for the rights of British subjects which had been constant among the inconsistencies of his political dealings. In January 1775 the House rejected his bill for reconciliation. After war had broken out he warned that America could not be conquered. In April 1775 he went once more to the Lords where the Duke of Richmond was pressing a motion to grant American independence. His mind wandered, he was incoherent; only phrases here and there recalled the passion and intellect of the statesman. It was a speech of hopeless resolution. His last words before he collapsed were: 'My Lords, any state is better than despair; if we must fall, let us fall like men.'

He was driven to Hayes where his beloved William read Homer to him: the passage about the death of Hector. There, to the tune of heroic words, he died. He was buried in Westminster Abbey with fitting pomp. In the Guildhall Burke's inscription summed up what he had meant to the City: he was 'the minister by whom commerce was united with and made to flourish by war'. He could not write the nobler epitaph, which Pitt would most have appreciated: that his supreme gift to his country was in securing the allegiance of the American colonists.

S. Ayling, *The Elder Pitt, Earl of Chatham* (1976).
J. Black, *The Elder Pitt* (1992).

Earl of Bute

JOHN STUART BUTE, 3RD EARL OF BUTE (1713-92), Prime Minister 1761-3, owed his ascendancy at the start of George III's reign to the favour of the young King. On previous showing he had been more courtier than politician. His short tenure of the Treasury was undermined by his personal unpopularity and his lack of adequate support in Parliament. He was vilified both as favourite and as Scotsman: each a term of opprobrium, together a serious handicap. He deserved better. In the process of preparing the young prince for kingship he had instructed himself thoroughly. In office he showed commitment and competence. More than most Prime Ministers he has benefited from recent reappraisal.

His father was the 2nd Earl of Bute, his mother Anne Campbell, daughter of the Duke of Argyll. Eton and Leyden laid the ground for his lifelong interest in art and science. He was a representative Scottish peer from 1737 to 1741. He might however have escaped the notice of history but for a series of fortunate strokes. He began a fruitful acquaintance with the Leicester House faction by making a fourth at cards when rain stopped a cricket match in which Frederick was playing. On Frederick's death in 1751 he became the leading personality in the household of his widow, Princess Augusta, and a model to the young heir-apparent of adult poise, decent living, and civilised accomplishment. George's letters offer insights into his feelings towards Bute, 'his dearest friend'. Official status came with appointment to be Groom of the Stole in 1756, effectively head of the household, and expected to be prominent in future government. George invested Bute with the virtues that he felt he lacked himself. Friendship and trust went with a political philosophy and programme more reactionary than radical: freedom from expensive commitments abroad, resuming royal control and patronage and attacking the faction and corruption that George saw as the conspicuous features of the political scene. Traditional 'country party' ideas were thus lifted from opposition to serve in government. Bute's role was to be honest minister to a patriot King.

In 1760 George II died: a new reign and a new political world was soon signalled (March 1761) by Bute's appointment to be Secretary of State for the Northern Department. Two other deaths advanced his fortunes. In 1761 that of Argyll left him to assume the leadership of the Scottish members; that of Edward Wortley Montague, father of his wife Mary, brought a fortune from property and coalfields. The marriage of his daughter to Sir James Lowther, another wealthy landowner and borough-monger, added further to his political weight. But it was the palace interest that would be crucial.

George had come to rely on Bute to help him in the crises of life. He consulted him about marriage, confided to him his failings, and practised on him the tentative ideas which had their origins in Bute's teaching: Leicester House with a modish dressing of current Enlightened thinking. With Pitt insisting on untrammelled powers and Newcastle sticking nervously to 'pure' – that is to say Pelhamite – principles, Bute had to be wary. Indeed it was not the presumed ambition that shook ministers but the combination of hauteur and naivete. Devonshire was shaken to find that 'they [Bute and the King] knew mankind and the *carte de pays* so little'. They had their own *carte* – but it lacked the features, political alignments, local contours, so familiar to Paymaster Henry Fox, whom Bute relied on to lead the Commons.

As the financial burden grew, the issue of the war took precedence over others. George, 'glorying in the name of Briton', felt, with Bute, that the war in Europe was irrelevant to British interests (in his opposition days it had been Pitt's view too). The war had been won; now peace should be secured. The view was realistic, and it fitted with Newcastle's concern about the size of the debt. But, in a climate warmed by good war news, it also looked mean and grudging, as if victories were more to do with Pitt's glorification than British interests. When Pitt proposed an extension of the war by a pre-emptive strike against Spain, Newcastle and Bute made common cause and Pitt resigned (October 1761). Spain, as he predicted, came into the war and the problem of securing a peace commensurate with the victories gained grew more difficult. Newcastle believed that the best course was to pile on the pressure. When he failed to convince his colleagues that subsidies to Prussia should be renewed he resigned (May 1762). Frederick was abandoned. Already Prime Minister in effect, Bute succeeded to the Treasury. The King was happy. With his support, could Bute fail? He had earned some good opinions from government insiders, like the veteran Under-Secretary Edward Weston.

What ensued was a harsh lesson in Westminster politics, the power of demagogy and of the popular press. He kept a majority in Parliament; it was in the clubs that he was undermined, in the streets that his name was mud. By contrast Pitt remained the people's hero. Still with some parliamentary support, he opposed anything that appeared to detract from his achievement. Newcastle had a large and hungry following. He underlined Bute's problem: should he declare that he would not oppose, 'my lord Bute's next *levée* would be twice as full as any he had yet had'. Bute was weak in Cabinet too, for Grenville, the new Secretary of State, was an awkward colleague. Bute relied on Henry Fox to secure support for the peace. He was hardly needed for it was greeted with relief and satisfaction. Negotiated principally by Bedford, approved by Parliament by the large majority of 319 to 65, it was proclaimed in March 1763. Britain gained from France the whole province of Canada, all Louisiana east of the Mississipi, Cape Breton; valuable West Indian islands; in West Africa Senegal; in the Mediterranean Minorca in exchange for Belle-Isle. In India the French had their trading stations back but were eliminated from Bengal. The score is impressive: it would later be seen as the real beginnings of an empire of commerce, conquest and acquisition by other means. To some extent it was Pitt's achievement and he could stake a pro-prietary claim and the right to carp. Cod, he claimed, was British gold: it was folly to restore Newfoundland fishing rights to the French. In high prophetic vein he denounced the treaty, less for the terms than for the way in which it had been achieved, with the alien-ation of an invaluable ally and the threat which isolation meant for the future security of the nation. Whatever the terms, it could have been foreseen that France would seek revenge. Less obvious was that their opportunity would come through the revolt of the American colonies, emboldened by the removal of the French threat from Canada. Bute meanwhile won support for an essential peace. The debacle that followed was a personal failure of nerve rather than a political reverse.

Taxes could not be reduced immediately for war costs persist after a war is over. Rather than continue to increase the debt, Bute saw a new tax on cider and wine as a logical extension of the beer tax. The Englishman looked forward to easy times; he was furious at having to pay 4s a hogshead on his cider. Moreover this was an excise, such as had been so embarrassing to Walpole, with its associations of inspection and arbitrary justice, a gift to opposition. Unfortunately, in Sir Francis Dashwood, Bute had a Chancellor of the Exchequer of memorable incompetence. While he fumbled with his figures Pittites and others made play with Bute's supposed plan to subvert the constitution and bring in the tyrannical regime that a Scotsman was supposed to favour. Wilkes fanned prejudice in the *North Briton*. Riots in the city were followed by a petition to the King to refuse his assent. Inside the Cabinet Grenville, thorough-going isolationist, was at variance with Bute over foreign policy. In the Commons he appealed for back-bench support by moving for an enquiry into the expense of the late war. The ministry rode the storm and the cider tax was pushed through by substantial major-ities. But Bute had had enough. He was an honourable and fastidious man, and mortified by the venom and slander. Was it not said that he owed his position to the favours of the Queen Mother? His oppo-nents hit crudely – but with the right instinct. Westminster politics required of the ambitious a bold front, a thick skin, and a willingness to intrigue. Bute shrank from the business. Perhaps this cultivated, European-minded Scotsman would have been more at home serving a Continental-style enlightened autocrat.

In April 1763 he resigned. He probably hoped to have some influ-ence as 'minister behind the curtain', to George III what Granville had been to George II. Grenville, his successor, expected it, for one of his first actions was to exact a promise that he would not inter-fere. He would still express views to the King, but to slight effect. After 1768 his life was spent mainly in the country, where he resumed his scientific studies. He was largely responsible for the develop-ment of the royal estate of Kew as a botanical garden. Also he had the discernment to secure for Dr Johnson the award of a pension. Unhappy in politics, he was very happy in his private life.

K.W. Schweitzer (ed), *Lord Bute: Essays in Re-interpretation* (1988).

George Grenville

GEORGE GRENVILLE (1712-70), Prime Minister 1763-5, owed his early prominence largely to the connection of his family with Pitt and to the debating skills displayed, with other members of the 'Cobham cubs', in opposition to Walpole and Carteret. However, with junior office in the Admiralty, then in the Treasury (1747-54), he displayed a talent for administration, particularly in the field of public finance. As First Lord of the Treasury, and author of the Stamp Act, he has been held responsible for initiating the train of events that led to the revolt of the American colonies. He should rather be remembered as a capable and decent politician who contributed robustly to George III's early learning experience in the scope and bounds of constitutional monarchy.

He was the second son of Richard Grenville and Hester Temple. From Eton, Christ Church and the Inner Temple he went into Parliament in 1741, as member for the family borough of Buckingham that he would represent for the rest of his life. With marriage to Elizabeth, daughter of William Wyndham, a touch of 'country party' Toryism was surely added to the independent spirit of the Grenvilles. They were, of all the political connections, the one most disliked by George III; of all the family the most obnoxious to the King was its head, George's elder brother, Lord Temple. Childless himself, he used his wealth to promote his relations and expected, as Shelburne saw it, 'a deference to his opinions and inclinations which was not consistent with their interests or dignity.' To his credit Grenville, as Prime Minister, showed that he would be his own man. That did not, however, endear him to the King who saw him as a Grenville: at bottom, stiff and haughty. Where Grenville avowed principle George saw faction, the exclusive clannishness that he thought was prejudicial to the well-being of the country. He was not alone in this. Temple and Grenville were both unpopular outside their own circle and found it hard to secure the wide support that was necessary for an effective administration.

Yet he had earned respect for his energy and honesty as Treasurer of the Navy, a key wartime post, held with two short intervals from 1754 to 1762. It should be recorded that he opposed the barbarities of the press gang and the fraudulent voucher system used to pay seamen. With unrivalled experience he was a natural choice to succeed Newcastle as Secretary of State. But George III urged that he be 'narrowly watched and sifted' for he was openly critical of Bute and Henry Fox and scornful of court influence. He also led the group in Cabinet that stood out for higher terms of peace. For his pains he was briefly demoted to the Admiralty. In March 1763, wearing his Tory wig, he bid for support in the House by calling for an enquiry into the way that money had been spent in the war. The prime target was Fox, blatantly enriched by the Paymastership and now spokesman in the Commons for the ministry and the peace. In April the King had to accept Bute's resignation and Grenville in his place.

No one was better fitted to deal with the economic problems left by seven years of war. No one had a sounder grasp of the business of administration. He actually enjoyed it. He read everything that landed on his desk. 'An act of parliament was in itself entertaining to him', wrote his cousin Thomas Pitt. First he had to assert his authority. With the Duke of Bedford as Lord President of the Council he had the support of the Russell connection. His brother-in-law Egremont was already a Secretary of State. But he died, in June. Boldness was needed. He knew that he could expect to be undermined by the King and devised a novel kind of check. He insisted that nobody should consult with the King unless he knew about it beforehand. There was to be no second channel of favour: 'he must be known to have the patronage or the whole must break.' His own Secretary, Lloyd, handled this patronage, rather than Jenkinson who had worked for Bute. Fellow ministers were also to be denied any part in this crucial activity of political management. In his disciplinary zeal not even the family was sacrosanct, as Temple found when he supported Wilkes in the matter of the *North Briton* and was deprived of his Lord-Lieutenancy of Buckinghamshire.

In 1762, with Temple's encouragement, John Wilkes had launched his paper, the *North Briton*, outspoken, salacious and hostile to the court. Number 45, in April 1763, stigmatised the phrase in the King's speech about the peace, 'honourable to my crown and beneficial to my people', as a falsehood. The ministry chose this point to attack with a General Warrant authorising the arrest of all concerned in the affair. Wilkes looked beyond the courts to the radical instincts of that almost unknown political force – 'the people'. It became a constitutional test case, and the opposition – not all, as Dr Johnson insisted, having 'minds as narrow as the necks of vinegar cruets' – took up his cause. Grenville thought that it was a matter for the courts to settle. Lord Chief Justice Pratt ruled against the legality of General Warrants and Wilkes secured damages from the Under-Secretary of State, Robert Wood. London radicals celebrated. Grenville waited for Wilkes to overplay his hand while his political support faded away. When Wilkes failed to find a printer brave enough to reprint the offending articles, and set up his own printing press, the government counter-attacked. The Commons voted No. 45 a seditious libel, to be publicly burned. It later voted that parliamentary privilege did not cover his case. In December 1763 Wilkes slipped away to France. He was expelled from the House. In February 1764 his trial for seditious libel came on. He did not appear, so he was outlawed. The opposition returned to the question of General Warrants, and government only just survived the subsequent division upon the question. But to show that coercion, not conciliation, was the order of the day, General Conway was dismissed from his posts in the Bedchamber and in the Army for voting against the ministry.

Given the weaknesses of governments before and after him, Grenville's ruthless approach was justifiable. He sought a greater degree of centralisation than had been attempted before, even by Walpole. He kept his Cabinet small; normally only four or five were present. He looked to meet and punish demagogic disturbance before it could damage him. He had survived the Wilkes affair and won time – not enough it was to prove – to win over independent members by financial reforms.

Unfortunately – and this was the prime reason for the failure of his experiment in strong government – his methods were such as to stir opposition. So far from being the 'gentle shepherd' of Pitt's scornful phrase he was heavily and fussily dictatorial. Yet he was listened to attentively by the country gentlemen to whose interest he appealed by his drastic economies. He was in his way a good House of Commons man, for his memory was good and he was knowledgeable about procedures. His main hope of survival lay in the approval of the mass of uncommitted Members of Parliament who wanted the King's government carried on as efficiently and cheaply as possible.

Grenville was not alone in being alarmed by the size of the National Debt. The annual charge on it had risen to £19.5 million, three times the pre-war rate. To reduce it became his first object. Within a year of his coming to power supplies were almost halved. The Army was reduced from 120,000 to 30,000; the Navy was cut down even more severely. In April 1764 the First Lord was complaining that there were no more than seventeen serviceable ships of the line. In the long term the cost of this dismemberment was to be the poor military and naval performance in the first years of the American war. Meanwhile experienced naval officers moped on half pay; 'the bravest men the world ever saw', said Pitt of the Army cuts, 'sent to starve in country villages and forget their prowess.' Grenville's measures received support nonetheless. He pegged the Land Tax at 4 s and looked forward to when it might be reduced.

His American policy should be viewed in the context of wider imperial concerns. It is alleged that 'he had no sense that there was more to government than rules and regulations' (Langford). His legal training may indeed have led him to place too much reliance on legislation. Edmund Burke held that 'he conceived ... that the flourishing trade of this country was greatly owing to law and institution, and not quite so much to liberty'. Yet the context of his actions should be considered. With new acquisitions in America, the Caribbean and India had come great financial responsibilities. No one was better fitted to overhaul the financial structure of the country. Nor, he reasoned, should the colonies be excluded: each should contribute its share. It can now be seen that this was a dynamic period in the evolution of Britain's Empire. At the time the revenue problem was more obvious. He added considerably to the list of enumerated goods, those from the colonies that had to be re-exported from Britain. Finding that the Molasses duty was being evaded, his Sugar Act (1764) sensibly halved it, while tightening up the system of enforcement. Grenville also looked to secure Indian revenues through the energetic governorship of Robert Clive. Finally, he decided that Americans should be made to contribute more to the expenses incurred by the motherland. His Stamp Duty of March 1765 raised the issue of sovereignty hitherto dormant: it was a direct tax. Some colonists found a principle to justify their reluctance to pay tax. The followers of Rockingham and Pitt opposed the duty in terms that bound them later to repeal it. Is it not possible that more damage was done in relations with the North American colonies through the inconsistency of later policies – encouraging colonists to think that they could win by threats and gestures – than by the initial, and modest, levy?

Grenville was a reluctant but consistent imperialist. As to Europe, he was 'a little Englander'. He refused to countenance a policy that involved the payment of subsidies to foreign monarchs; he extracted payments from France for the upkeep of French prisoners in the war; and he refused to help the Corsican patriots who were in revolt against Genoa. Inevitably this meant that Britain drifted towards isolation. In 1764 Prussia and Russia came to terms in a treaty which emphasised Britain's withdrawal from Continental commitments.

Sandwich, in particular, was out of sympathy with Grenville's foreign policy. But the ministers lacked an underlying principle of unity or common interests. Grenville could not, by his personality, supply the deficiency. The King fretted under the restraints placed on him, and became ill with what may have been the first onset of porphyria. He decided to have a Regency council. Grenville rebuked him for not discussing the matter with him first. He was mortified too by being placed in a false position over the composition of the council. The ministers urged the King to exclude his mother; then two opposition members moved that she be appointed. The King was made to feel undutiful and ridiculous. He wriggled in several directions to find a successor to Grenville but for a time it seemed that the only alternative would be anarchy. Eventually, in July 1765, he fell back on Rockingham, with Grafton and Conway as Secretaries of State. Grenville remained active in opposition and was effective and useful in scrutinising the minutiae of government. A good House of Commons man to the end, he relished his chance to ride his old hobby-horse of economies. Indeed he died in harness, earning Burke's salute: a man 'to whom this country owes very great obligations'.

P. Lawson, *George Grenville: A Political Life* (1984).

Marquess of Rockingham

CHARLES WATSON WENTWORTH, 2ND MARQUESS OF ROCKINGHAM (1730-82) was twice Prime Minister (1765-6 and 1782), but for only sixteen months in all. He was a more important political figure than that suggests. His large estates, his calm, largely disinterested approach, and his ability to command loyalty, enabled him to lead for nearly twenty years a distinct party, the largest group of parliamentary Whigs. More brilliant men than he were willing to serve under him. When party ties were so loose, much was asked of a political leader. He had to have the personal qualities to maintain and head a connection that would be close enough, given the chance, to form a government. He must either be conciliatory to the point of negation, like North, or seen to stand for a set of principles acceptable to the King as well as to the mass of independent members. Since by 1760 Toryism no longer had any kind of party organisation, or even recognisable creed, they would either call themselves Whig or country gentlemen. They could be simply defined as not being 'the king's friends' or having some office or pension. Leading a more coherent body than any other group, Rockingham found supporters across the board. The more his principles were affirmed in opposition to the King's minister, from 1770 to 1782 Lord North, the more unpalatable the Rockingham Whigs became to the King. As the colonial revolt became the War of Independence their opposition came to seem unpatriotic and subversive. It was only the failure of this war that gave them, at last, the chance to put their principles into action.

He was the eighth child, and only surviving son, of Thomas, 1st Marquess, and Lady Mary Finch. He went to Westminster and Cambridge but it was family relationships that accounted mainly for his influential political allies, like the Dukes of Newcastle and Devonshire. He inherited the marquessate in 1750 and married Mary Bright in 1752. Arthur Young later praised the management of his estates, saying that 'he never saw the advantages of a great fortune applied more nobly to the improvement of a county.' Rents, rising to £40,000 a year, were enough to fund political activity. But his reputation was grounded in valuable work for his county. Early efforts in Parliament were concerned with promoting the county interest in wool and iron, coal and canals. He was a keen racing man, a member of the newly formed Jockey Club, and active in promoting meetings at Doncaster and York – like mediaeval tournaments, a chance for politicians to meet and plot. To be a county grandee, Lord Lieutenant, might have been enough for Rockingham. He did not promote himself. But his father had owed his advancement in the peerage to the Pelhams and it was natural that Rockingham should succeed, in the years after Newcastle's resignation in 1762, to the leadership of the attenuated Newcastle interest. He offended the King by his opposition to Bute and lost his Lord-Lieutenancy. The 'Bute myth' of the backstairs minister had its origin in Rockingham's dislike of the favourite.

It was Yorkshire that provided him with his political base and prepared him for a life of larger service: 26 out of 30 Yorkshire MPs were committed supporters. He was, however, a diffident politician when, aged thirty-five, in July 1765, he succeeded Grenville as First Lord of the Treasury. He had only been a Lord of the Bedchamber for a short period. He had no illusions: 'Howsoever unsuitable I might be for that office from my health and inexperience in that sort of business, yet I thought it incumbent upon me to acquiesce in the attempting it.' But the ministry had assets. The King had been chastened by his experience with Grenville and found no acceptable alternative. Bute was out of the question and Pitt would not serve except in a dominating capacity. The alternative to Rockingham was anarchy. Cumberland spoke for him and acted as intermediary with the court. He remembered the young Rockingham – then Lord Malton – in the '45, riding to join his army at Carlisle. It was not only his Secretary Edmund Burke who saw him as 'a man of honour and integrity'. He approached his task in a spirit of fairness. The ministry was a party one in that the main posts were filled by his candidates: it was the essential Pelhamite Whig principle that had to be reaffirmed against George's determination to select his own ministers. But Rockingham tried to rebuild the Pelham system on a broad base and looked for new recruits. There was insufficient talent. Conway, one Secretary of State, was a soldier, no match for experienced parliamentarians. The other, Grafton was only thirty, devoted to Pitt and half-hearted in support of Rockingham. When he resigned in 1766 he was replaced by another Duke, Richmond, aged thirty-one, impetuous, hot for reform, but without political experience. 'An administration of boys' the King called it. Few thought it could last.

Yet the ministry made a promising start. Objectionable elements in the cider excise were abolished and replaced by further window duties; general warrants were declared illegal and with them some of the debris of the Wilkes case. Almost at once Rockingham was faced by an imperial crisis. From Virginia to Boston colonists defied Grenville's Stamp Tax. Their mood was violent. A congress met to co-ordinate an embargo on trade with Britain. Opposition spread to the West Indies. Cumberland and many in Parliament wanted to take prompt military action. Fortunately it was impracticable since soldiers were few and widely dispersed. Rockingham took the pragmatic line he would always follow. If unworkable the tax should be repealed. He had to meet complaints about surrender before a colonial mob, the flouting of Parliament. The solution was to combine Repeal of the Stamp Tax with a statutory declaration of Parliament's right to legislate for the colonies 'in all cases whatsoever'. The case was prepared with care, Burke playing a leading part. Benjamin Franklin was called as a witness. More telling, though misleading, was the campaign in the country to connect falling trade and unemployment to the colonial quarrel. Influential in Parliament was the rhetoric of Pitt, who denounced the tax and colonial taxation altogether. After excited scenes in the Commons, repeal was carried by a large majority and Rockingham was able to tell the King that he had been vindicated by 'Publick Opinion'. This success was followed by some bold commercial legislation. The establishment of free ports in Jamaica and Dominica had limited practical results but challenged long-standing mercantilist principles. Grenville predictably denounced it as an attack on the navigation system.

Rockingham failed to build on his sound start. It was a time for compromise, not for further offending the King. His inexperience, and over-reliance on his solid party support, was shown when he attacked the 'King's Friends' who had voted against him. When George turned to Pitt, and Pitt made abundantly clear that he was keen to serve, Rockingham's position became untenable. In July 1766 he resigned, with the dignity and good humour of a man who expects to retain some influence, or to be recalled. He took with him Richmond and some others of his party. But he would have to wait for sixteen years and an American crisis far more serious that that of the Stamp Tax. Did he think that he could have managed matters better, with his policy of 'sleeping sovereignty', echoing Walpole and calmer times? Meanwhile it was North, not he, that benefited from Chatham's collapse and Grafton's incompetence.

Burke's *Thoughts on the Present Discontents* (1770), was a *livre de circonstance*, a piece of propaganda, a re-statement of a familiar theme. But it was precise in analysis and eloquent in expression. Burke claimed to find in the behaviour of the King's friends the influence of the Crown and the existence of a 'double cabinet', an undermining of ministers' authority. He argued for party and for a Cabinet united by collective responsibility. He was happy to take the moral high ground: 'When bad men combine, the good must associate.' He now appears far-sighted, but to many then 'the political creed of our party' was a cynical argument for the return of Rockingham. It certainly made for the cohesion of Rockingham Whigs but did not ease their return to power. Hostility to the King might unify aristocratic interest with country spirit, but North's skilful political and financial management blunted attacks and attracted some Whigs. That there were not more testifies to Rockingham's hold, his appealing image of probity. He ever doubted the wisdom of asserting legislative supremacy, preferring 'salutary neglect'. He objected to the use of troops because 'every town at which they were stationed would be turned into a second Boston.' North was not seriously vulnerable even in the opening stages of the war. Rockinghamites were jeered at when they called for peace. But consistency told eventually in their favour. They believed that victories only delayed the inevitable and they cheered at the news of the surrender at Yorktown. When George III clung to North, Rockingham turned again to the question of royal influence and planned to reduce it.

When the movement for parliamentary reform swelled with county resolutions and petitions, Rockingham made contacts with it. Savile's Yorkshire Association seemed to be a natural ally. But Rockingham's main concern was to increase aristocratic independence, and a better means to this end was to attack the bloated establishment through which the Crown exercised its patronage. It was Burke's programme of 'eoconomical reform'. For him the power of the pen; for his master parliamentary pressure. He was chary of popular excitements: 'There are so many visionary schemes and expedients by way of reform on float that general confusion and disagreement will ensue.' His bill of February 1780 'for the better regulation of His Majesty's civil establishments' was rejected, but he was encouraged to persist in this weapon of opposition – safer, as the Gordon Riots were to show, than direct appeal to the people.

In March 1782 North resigned and Rockingham took office with a strong hand of cards. He had held back to the point at which George virtually surrendered to him: as Richmond put it, 'all at your feet in the manner you would wish, and with the full means to do what is right.' The King, personally hurt by events in America, had even considered abdication before accepting Rockingham's conditions – to be at the Treasury, to have a free hand with regard to the choice of ministers, American independence and economical reform. It was some compensation for George that alongside Fox, whom he detested, there was Shelburne, whom Fox detested. Only Rockingham's genial authority, long tested by stubborn Yorkshiremen, could prevent the open breach between the two Secretaries of State which followed his death.

Starting at a dark time, lasting only four months, this was still a notable ministry. In Ireland, where he had an interest as a landowner in County Wicklow and supported Savile's Catholic Relief Act of 1778 (Savile's house was attacked in the Gordon Riots), he tried to counter critics who said that North's trade concessions were illusory by giving greater constitutional independence. With the abolition of the Irish Declaratory Act and Poyning's Law, the Dublin parliament enjoyed more freedom than for three hundred years. Following the advice that Burke had expressed often in speeches, the government tried to build upon goodwill at the cost of formal ties. The right of the British parliament to legislate for Ireland was abrogated, as was the right of the Privy Council to alter Irish legislation. The Lord-Lieutenant was a member of the British Cabinet and Acts of Parliament required the Great Seal. Otherwise for a brief period Ireland enjoyed virtual independence.

At home something was done to answer charges of corruption in public affairs: committees inquired into the methods whereby loans had been raised and contracts granted, salaries were introduced in certain grades of the civil service who had hitherto been paid, or had paid themselves, out of fees. Crewe's act disenfranchised revenue officers supposed to be directly amenable to pressure from the state, their immediate employer. Clark's act removed government contractors from the Commons. In the midst of all this activity, on 1 July Rockingham died of influenza. If he had lived, the split that led to the brief administrations, first of Shelburne, then of Fox and North, and subsequently the emergence of Pitt, might not have occurred. Fox, for one, might have had a more constructive career. Rockingham was not the last nor the least of those Prime Ministers whose task it has been to create a harmonious group in which more brilliant men can work. His was not a combative nature. Drawn by circumstances to be a reformer, he was counselled by instinct to avoid the extreme in language or action. A loyal Anglican, he was typically sympathetic to Irish Catholics, a friend to John Wesley. A decent restraint in opposition, principled action in government, were the examples he offered to the future. For all his limitations Burke's epitaph rings true: 'his virtues were his means'.

R. Hoffman, *The Marquess: A Study of Lord Rockingham 1730-82* (1973).

Duke of Grafton

AUGUSTUS HENRY, 3RD DUKE OF GRAFTON (1735-1811) attained high office under Chatham at the age of thirty-one, found himself virtually at the head of government the following year, and more formally Prime Minister (1768) after another year and Chatham's resignation. Two years more and he had resigned, 'being released from business and from an office which was peculiarly irksome to me'. He was twice in office again, as Lord Privy Seal from 1771 to 1775 and again from 1782 to 1783. He might have done better if he had not inherited his title at the age of twenty-two after only a year in the Commons, and if he had had time to learn the grammar of politics before aspiring to the prose. Having become Prime Minister by default, and with uncertain support, he had the particular misfortune of facing the demagogic challenge of John Wilkes and the deadly satire of 'Junius'. That the predicaments were to some extent his fault did not lessen his discomfiture nor the damage done through neglect or mishandling of vital issues, especially that of America. There had been enough ambition to fill his sails, but his guns were too light, his navigation unreliable.

He was the second son of Lord Augustus Fitzroy and Elizabeth Cosby. He received more enlightened teaching at the then fashionable Unitarian Hackney School than at Peterhouse, Cambridge. He was drawn into politics through fervent admiration of Pitt and corresponding dislike of Bute. It was at his London home that the Duke of Newcastle's 'young friends' met in 1762 to concert opposition against Bute's negotiations to end the Seven Years' War. Between Newmarket and Westminster he enjoyed the stir and self-importance of Whig politics – and perhaps its gambling edge. He may not have minded much being a victim of 'the massacre of the Pelhamite Innocents' when the King dismissed him from the Lord-Lieutenancy of Suffolk.

He joined the administration of Rockingham in 1765 on the understanding that Pitt would be brought in as well. When that proved impracticable Grafton was a restless colleague before resigning; but he was well placed when Rockingham fell in July 1766 and Pitt, now Chatham, formed his ministry. With little knowledge of the workings of patronage or expertise in finance, he was an unconvincing First Lord of the Treasury. The Chancellor of the Exchequer, Charles Townshend was, however, able, and with firm leadership from Chatham the ministry need not have been disastrous. Chatham became ill and the ministry fell apart. To Grafton fell much of the responsibility, without the authority, of Prime Minister. Drawing on the Bedford party for support only exacerbated the essential problem: the lack of guiding principles, agreed policies and Cabinet unity. When Chatham at last resigned, in October 1768, he did have more authority, but lacked the experience and character to impose his will to firm effect. His ordeal provided the strongest possible argument for Burke's theory of the necessity of party and collective Cabinet responsibility.

It was after Pitt's collapse, in June 1767, that he was left to deal with the Indian problem arising out of Clive's success and the resulting extension of the East India Company's activities. His solution, annual tribute to the state and a statutory limitation of the Company's dividend, would prove historic: the first response of government to the problem of control in what would prove, for eighty years, to be among the hottest of political potatoes. It was also a face-saving compromise. Nor did the ministers show resolve over the transfer of Genoese sovereignty over Corsica to France. Choiseul had experienced the effect of British seapower and expected the British to dispatch a squadron. Would it have warned him off? Probably – but the judgement is easier to make now than at the time. The next year Napoleon was born – a French citizen.

When Chatham resigned, in October 1768, it may be that Grafton would have been wise to follow him: his last action had been to speak in the Lords denouncing his own ministers' policy towards Wilkes. Grafton had been happy before to take advantage of Wilkes' demagogy, supporting him against Grenville's ministry. Did he now think that he was a spent force when he returned from exile to fight an election? On the ground that he was an outlaw his election for Middlesex was quashed. With popular partisanship turning to dangerous riot, he was re-elected. Logic rather than common sense led ministers into an embarrassing situation. After a further election had been quashed Colonel Luttrell was persuaded to stand, then deemed to be the member after polling 216 votes against Wilkes'

1,143. Yet Grafton was supported, at first by the whole ministry, the King, and by some of the liberal-minded, like Fox, who thought that the House must have control over its own membership if it were to be an effective safeguard against arbitrary powers, whether of King or people, and by the majority of that House. Against that view the 'popular party' stood for the rights of the electorate. Important business was held up while Wilkes' supporters kept his case alive before a crowded, sometimes exasperated House. A quarter of the electorate signed petitions calling for a dissolution of Parliament. Horne Tooke's Society for the Supporters of the Bill of Rights campaigned for electoral reform. A new kind of politics was coming alive. The bad harvest of 1768 had caused a drop in demand, with unemployment and misery. The grievances of Spitalfield weavers and Wapping coal-heavers exploded in violence; harnessed for Wilkes it could also alarm moderate men into supporting government.

Of more significance for the future was the nationwide interest centering on the very nature of parliament. Grafton came to epitomise the supposed evils of the system. This was the situation which the pen of 'Junius' was able to exploit. With what seemed to be a deadly personal animosity towards Grafton, Junius denounced the government for its weakness and venality. Grafton's private life certainly lent itself to a picture of sleaze. It would be a recurring pattern, no less damaging in democratic times: personal faults and lapses lending a flavour of scandal to political issues. It was recalled that 'Black Harry' was descended from Charles II and Barbara Villiers. Indeed there is something of Restoration indecency in the way he defied the code of fashionable London – more to do with appearances than with morality. He had left his wife Anne to live with his Nell Gwynne – Anne Parsons. He caused outrage by taking her into society. He was then publicly shamed when his wife eloped with the Earl of Upper Ossory. He divorced her in 1769 and married Elizabeth Wrottesley: all meat and drink for the radical press, distractions for a Prime Minister with American business on his desk.

His handling of Ireland shows Grafton at his most sensible. He insisted that the Lord Lieutenant reside in Dublin. His Octennial Act (formerly elections were held only on a monarch's accession) aroused a healthier political interest, though encouraging nationalist sentiment. Over the colonies Grafton did have positive views. He had not approved of Townshend's duties and he abolished them – except for tea. That too he would have liked to abolish but he was out-voted in Cabinet – Bedford men tipping the scales. Hillsborough, one of them, drafted the letter to the colonial governors in which the government's intentions were outlined; he omitted the passages about conciliation, to which the Cabinet had assented, and stiffened those which referred to 'execution of the laws' and 'legislative authority'. It was bound to offend the Americans. But Grafton would not resign upon this act of indiscipline because he felt that it would seem that he was surrendering to Wilkes; a show of strength belying his real weakness. So the good effect of his policy of friendship was lost and the government lurched towards disaster.

Hillsborough's attitude was shared by others in the Cabinet. It fatally lacked common purpose because it was based on no recognisable connection. Chatham's ideal of party-free patriotic government simply failed, first because Chatham collapsed, then because Grafton commanded no confidence. On top of other embarrassments he further lost credit over a legal case – a dispute over estates (and borough patronage) – between the Duke of Portland and Sir James Lowther. The Treasury seemed anxious to find flaws in Portland's claim. Junius pointed out that Lowther was Bute's son-in-law and favoured at court.

Grafton was opposed by a triple alliance of convenience between followers of Rockingham, Chatham and Grenville. But his ministry did not so much fall as fall apart. Lord Camden, who had supported the policy of conciliation with America, attacked the official policy and was dismissed. Lord Granby followed him out of the government, under pressure from Chatham. Charles Yorke, Hardwicke's son, was prevailed upon to accept the Chancellorship but, in an agony of uncertainty about his merits and responsibilities, he cut his throat. After this tragedy, Grafton had had enough.

George III looked to him as a possible successor to North. He was Lord Privy Seal from 1771 to 1775, again briefly under Shelburne (1782). He resigned then, for reasons worth study as comment on his political career, in protest against the First Lord of the Treasury 'becoming Prime Minister as distinct from holding the principle [*sic*] office in the Cabinet'. He was never again of any consequence in politics but came to enjoy more respect than he had had when in power. He wrote his autobiography which, being edited later with his letters, offers a largely favourable view. He became Chancellor of Cambridge University. The younger Pitt thought well of him and tried to enlist him for his first ministry. He preferred to be free to enjoy his Suffolk estate of Euston and pursue the interest in religion which led him back to the Unitarianism of Hackney days. After the French Revolution, he attacked the government for its repression of radicals. It was the liberal side which the American colonists, unfortunately, had not been allowed to see.

Lord North

FREDERICK NORTH, 8TH LORD NORTH and (1790) 2ND EARL
OF GUILFORD (1732-92) was Prime Minister from 1770 to 1782. He
owed his long tenure to the support and friendship of the King,
to marked administrative ability, and to his hold over members of
the House of Commons. He faltered sometimes in the face of the
serious challenges of his later years in office, discontents in Ireland,
the reform movement, and, unfortunately for his reputation, the
revolt of the American colonies and subsequent war. He felt that he
was unsuited to the demands of war, and posterity has confirmed his
estimate. He has been, for too long, 'the minister who lost America',
with caricature to match – the plump, lolling figure on the Treasury
bench, indolence and procrastination in the face of national disaster.
He should be remembered rather as among the most successful of
peacetime ministers.

He was the eldest son of Francis, Ist Earl of Guilford and of Lady
Lucy Montague. After Eton and Trinity College, Oxford, in 1754, he
entered Parliament for Banbury. It usually deferred to the head
of the family at neighbouring Wroxton; unusually he remained its
representative for his remaining thirty-six years in the Commons. In
1756 he married Anne Speke. Without aid from the family estates
and with a growing family, he remained relatively poor; indeed he
had on occasion to be helped out by the King. His palpable honesty
and a pleasant, amusing, sometimes self-deprecating manner
endeared him to MPs. With Grafton's recommendation that his successor should be in the Commons 'as the most fitting place for a
prime minister', and general expectation that he would be the man,
he came in on a wave of goodwill, and retained much of it to the end.

North's ability received early recognition: he was a Lord of the
Treasury, 1759-65, before Rockingham removed him. Chatham made
him Joint Paymaster-General (1766) then, following Townshend in
1767, Chancellor of the Exchequer. He retained the office when he
became First Lord of the Treasury in January 1770. He was perhaps
fortunate in Grafton's embroilment in the Wilkes affair, and the

collapse of his vote in the face of satire and opposition from both Chatham and Rockingham. Chatham was unfit and Rockingham bound by party ties and suspect to the King. George III had faith in him. Typically he wrote: 'Believe me a little spirit will soon restore a degree of order in my service.' His being evidently the King's man did not upset the independent members on whose votes he would rely. Indeed it was a positive advantage that he started with only a small personal following. He was able to enlist men from all connections. Grenville men felt free to return to office; one of them, Suffolk, became Secretary of State in 1771. Grafton himself was Privy Seal, Dartmouth, a Rockinghamite, became Secretary for the Colonies, and Sandwich, who had been associated with Bute, went to the Admiralty and set about reforming its dockyards. The administration inspired respect; government majorities well above 100 recalled the Pelham years; so did his financial expertise and deft management of patronage. He amused the House when he explained that 'when he only nodded, or squeezed the hand, or did not absolutely promise, he always meant No'! It added, if anything, to his reassuring image that he appeared reluctant to intrude on others' departments, seeing himself as one of several ministers under the Crown rather than 'sole' or even co-ordinating minister. In Cabinet he did not press his views. But his office, with control both of finance and much of the patronage, assured him the primacy. He was remarkably diligent and rarely missing from the chamber. In the first five years he made 800 speeches or interventions.

The prime concern of merchant and landowner was the return to what they would see as normal budgeting, with the reduction of debt and taxes. That it meant also reductions in the Army and Navy, and pain for half-pay officers and discharged men, did not generally concern them. North sought to avoid entanglements abroad and to find a million pounds a year for the reduction of the debt. Eventually this would have led to the reduction of the Land Tax; meanwhile he pegged it at 3s. When annual spending rose from £8 million to £20 million his skills were tested. New taxes, as on carriages, servants, auctions, fell mainly on the rich, as he thought right, though later it had to be sugar, soap and salt. He incurred suspicion by his dealings with cronies in the City to secure loans at favourable rates sugared with lotteries and premiums. He had to make concessions but held to his conviction that what mattered was the rate of interest, not the capital sum of the debt. The finances were in reasonably good shape at the end of the war, ready to benefit from industrial growth. Meanwhile, at the height of the war North's lucid speeches, made with reference only to a few notes, commended his budgets to MPs and sustained their confidence. After losing the war Britain would not lose the peace.

North's talent for the conciliation of interests was revealed in his handling of the Indian problem. Bold action was called for because of the boom and subsequent slump of East India stock, caused by widespread buying for influence in the Company. Stakes were high as the return of wealthy nabobs made enviably plain. But the Company slid into deficit because of the rising cost of defence and the falling sales of tea. Moreover, as it waded deep into Indian politics and lands, it had to be brought under some control. From inquiries which exposed corruption among Company officials, and a vote on the specific case of Clive (North voted against him but seems to have been relieved that the subsequent motion was lost), emerged the Regulating Act of 1773. It secured the immediate future of the Company by a compulsory loan and by freeing the tea trade from duties payable on re-export. There was to be a Supreme Presidency, Bengal being elevated over Madras and Bombay and placed under a Governor-General and council of four, appointed by Parliament. Meant to be temporary until the renewal of the charter in 1780, the scheme represents a typical compromise between the extremes of commercial independence and state control. But it was a significant extension in the responsibilities of government, seen at the time as bold, even 'Cromwellian'. Because of the value of the patronage and persistence of problems inherent in the Company's expansion, India was to be the subject of further legislation in 1783 and 1784 and to have a critical impact on the careers of Fox and Pitt. Meanwhile North achieved his object: the stability of the Company and therefore of Britain's position in India, more beneficial to the natives than it would have been if left to the merchants and Company agents.

North reaped the American harvest of earlier and reckless sowings, notably Townshend's duties of 1767. But the unloading of tea in America to help the East India Company's trade balance, and the subsequent dispute with Boston in December 1773, must be laid at his door. Should he have realised that it would be seen by Americans as an attempt to force the issue of sovereignty? The closure of the port of Boston merely served to unite that town with other colonies not hitherto sympathetic. The coastal colonies resented the Quebec guarantee of land down to the Ohio which barred their westward expansion. New England lawyers and politicians convinced themselves that North intended to enslave them. He believed, with many, that he had only to coerce Massachusetts for the disturbances to subside. His resolve was stiffened by the uncompromising mood in Parliament and country. But he would neither dictate a policy nor prevent ministers pursuing several lines of action at once. Lord George Germain wanted swift military blows; Sandwich, concerned about invasion from France, wished to keep the fleet at home. North hoped for effective action by loyalists. In reality, from the meeting of the pan-colonial congress of 1774 to the skirmish of Lexington in April 1775, the Battle of Bunker Hill in June 1775 and the Declaration of Independence in July 1776, he seems to be but a spectator of events. Yet, defying colleagues' protests, he did offer a way to peace; but his proposal to waive tax in any colony in return for a contribution to its defence was spurned by the colonists as an attempt 'to divide and rule'. Committed to war, the administration discovered too late the cost of peacetime economies. Gage advised the government to send large forces at once, but they were not to be had, and the Navy was short of commissioned ships. Howe demanded 20,000 troops for 1777, received only 2,500, so missed his chance of acting decisively when the Americans were weak. In October Burgoyne had to surrender at Saratoga, victim of over-optimistic planning. A big effort was planned for 1778; at the same time commissioners were sent to treat with Congress. But in that year French forces came to tilt the scales; in 1779 Spain entered the war and Gibraltar was besieged. The recriminations which followed the indecisive Battle of Ushant between Keppel and Palliser, and the former's trial, weakened the ministry. By 1779 Howe was pessimistic and urged peace. But George III was convinced that a principle was at stake in what had become a global war.

North's political survival became the King's obsession. At times he wanted to resign, at others appeared convinced that he must stay. Robinson was palpably unfair when he said that North was 'the original cause of the bad situation of everything'. But as Secretary to the Treasury he was well placed to judge. North knew his shortcomings and was accurate in his analysis of the weakness of 'a government of separate and squabbling departments'. Of course the buck stopped at his desk. 'Nothing can goad him forward, said Lord Chancellor Thurlow, 'he is the very clog that loads everything.'

The times were certainly critical. Ireland simmered, reform movements took heart from American rebels; in June 1780 demagogy's frightening power was revealed in the Gordon Riots. Yet North's majorities held up. To the country gentleman America was not everything. Whether it came from French invasion, apparent weakness of the Navy, radical challenge to traditional rights, or drunken incendiary mobs, the threat to property was more immediate, and the instinct was to support the government. It was through North's alleged subservience to the court that opposition Whigs could best exploit popular concerns. The argument that the influence of the Crown, in the words of Dunning's famous motion, 'has increased, is increasing, and ought to be diminished', struck home and has survived to leave a false impression of North's relations with the King. Radicalism had its constructive side. In Yorkshire, Christopher Wyvill's Association became the prototype of similar movements for franchise reform all over the country. To many North remained a reassuring figure, the main hope for sound finance; and it was here that character told in his favour – as it didn't for Fox. The violence of Fox was more than most could accept. If North could keep his nerve independent members would still support him.

In Ireland the Protestant gentry formed volunteer associations to take over home defence and release regular troops for service abroad. The force became a weapon for nationalists like Flood and Grattan, no less patriotic for being Protestant. They were encouraged by Fox's Whigs to voice demands for more freedom of trade, and for constitutional independence, in the language of liberty from the oppressor. In 1780, after the Irish boycott of British goods, North made necessary concessions, notably the right to trade freely with the colonies, and freedom of wool and glass exports. Englishmen grumbled at North's apparent weakness, Irishmen yearned for legislative security. Meanwhile they had learned how to turn Britannia's woes to Irish advantage.

For Britannia did not rule the seas. It was this, until Rodney's decisive victory of the Saints in April 1782, more than French volunteers, more even than Washington's tenacity, that enabled the American colonists to win. Clinton would win battles in the south but, when Howe was forced to surrender at Yorktown (1781) and Foxites cheered the news, the issue was effectively decided. North clung on till March 1782. In the end, as Rigby put it, 'he had to give the thing up' because peace in America was necessary if England were to defeat her foes in Europe, reinforced now by Holland; and North was compromised by his record. His loyalty was to the King; for duty and direction he always looked to Parliament. George was powerless to refuse Rockingham and Fox and their programme of 'economical reform'.

Early in 1783, after the death of Rockingham and Shelburne's failure to muster enough support, North joined Fox under the nominal prime ministership of Portland. It was a surprising volte-face. Nine months as Home Secretary suggests more the call of duty, and an effort to bring stability, rather than the office-hunger suggested by critics. North was no cynic. But it did his reputation no good. To the King his conduct was unforgivable: first defection, now desertion. He waited for his chance to destroy the coalition. Ministers claimed that their India Bill secured public control, free of executive corruption, but their enemies pointed out that it meant an extension of Whig patronage. To the cartoonists' North, bulging eyes, pouting lips and full belly, was now added 'Carlo Khan', monstrous and greasy. Encouraged by the King, the Lords voted against the bill. In December 1783 Fox and North resigned and Pitt became First Lord of the Treasury. He would find that he had much to thank North for. The reports of the Committee of Public Accounts, set up in 1779, would be the basis of his reforms. It was North's fate to have the blame for abuses rather than the credit for tackling them; to be associated with a humiliating defeat which he was powerless to prevent. Meanwhile, slowly going blind, did he ever reflect how differently he would be perceived if he had resigned in 1776, when his first overtures for peace were rejected? Or even in 1779, if he had followed the logic of his own perception, when writing to his master: 'In critical times, it is necessary that there should be one directing minister'? A 'directing minister' he was not, and could not have been. Having the worst of both worlds, he was blamed as if he had been.

P. Thomas, *Lord North* (1976).

Earl of Shelburne

WILLIAM PETTY, 2ND EARL OF SHELBURNE, 1ST MARQUESS OF LANSDOWNE (1737-1805) did not for long enjoy the high office that he might appear to have deserved. He was Prime Minister for only nine months (1782-3). Intellectual in tastes, original in views as in his choice of friends outside Westminster, ambitious to succeed and brave in policies, it was his fate to arouse suspicion of motives and methods. So he saw promising plans miscarry or come to fruition under another man's direction. Patronised by the elder Pitt, he promoted the younger – who became the Prime Minister and reformer that Shelburne wanted to be.

He was born in Ireland, the eldest son of John, 1st Earl, and Mary Fitzmaurice. In their semi-feudal household tutors fostered an independent spirit that might have been constrained by more formal schooling. After two unsatisfactory years at Christ Church, Oxford, he pursued a military career. He served in Germany with distinction and was appointed, in 1757, *aide-de-camp* to the King. With only a year as MP for High Wycombe before inheriting the earldom (1761) he missed the training in practical politics and tactics that the Commons could provide. In the Lords he tended to devise plans without testing them in debate, and to neglect the informal soundings that might ease the way to legislation. Influence at court secured early promotion to be President of the Board of Trade (April 1763). He had accepted it on the typically Chathamite condition that he should have 'equal access to the king with other ministers'. Finding that he did not, he resigned within a few months. He had already fallen out with the Paymaster, Henry Fox. As a soldier, he scorned Fox for profiting from the war. Fox's influential family, arrogating to themselves the guardianship of the constitution, according to their Whiggish interpretation of it, would not forgive or trust the outsider, the Irish colonel and courtier, with his own agenda of reform. Meanwhile Shelburne enlarged his political connection by marriage to Lady Sophia Carteret (1765). He picked promising young disciples like Dunning and, typically, the soldier Barré, with

American experience behind him, to voice his ideas in the Commons. Horace Walpole describes him holding 'a little knot of young orators at his house'. Most important, he courted Pitt. The liaison never ripened into friendship, but Pitt respected his ability and wide-ranging mind. Forming his second administration in 1766 he made Shelburne Secretary of State for the Southern department. He conceived its colonial responsibilities to be important and America paramount. Pitt's collapse left Shelburne free to devise policies but hampered by divided responsibility with the Board of Trade. Optimistic proposals for resolving the financial problem were abandoned while Townshend's duties ran counter to his conciliatory policy. It did not help him in Parliament that Benjamin Franklin was a frequent visitor and that he was regarded as the colonists' friend. He did little to help himself. As early as 1767 Grafton thought him too isolated to remain in office, 'considering the little cordiality shown by his lordship towards myself and others of the Cabinet of late'. When the American affairs were hived off to a separate ministry Shelburne kept his department without 'the American business', the confidence of fellow ministers, or of the King. In October 1768 he resigned, to be followed by Chatham.

He held no office again for fifteen years. Though he did not see active service he rose steadily in rank, to that of general. He gave up his correspondence with Chatham and could only protest as the colonists moved towards defiance. Though they opposed the war Burke and Fox refused to collaborate with him. Until the defeats of Saratoga and Yorktown brought reluctant reappraisal Shelburne's was an eccentric voice. He eventually declared that the right of taxation had been 'from the start chimerical'. Meanwhile he hoped for 'a fair, honest, wise and honourable connection, in which the constitutional prerogatives of the Crown, the claims of Parliament and the liberties, properties and lives of all subjects of the British Empire would be equally secured.' He was trusted by leading Americans as a disciple of Chatham and was not inhibited, as was North by his previous record, from an open-minded approach. So political differences were sunk when, under Rockingham, in March 1782, he became Secretary of State for Home, American and Irish affairs with a mandate to end the American war. With Fox, the other Secretary of State, in charge of negotiations with France and Spain, working through separate agents, the arrangement was precarious. It was made worse when Shelburne supported Lord Chancellor Thurlow's wrecking tactics to undermine the credibility of the administration, already weakened by Rockingham's debility and quarrels in the Whig camp. When Rockingham died, in July 1782, and Shelburne took his place as First Lord of the Treasury, he became openly what he had been covertly – the King's minister. Fox resigned.

His prime ministership was dominated by negotiations for peace, challenged throughout by a frankly factious opposition. Fox admitted that he could have done no better but in April 1783 he joined forces with North to defeat the peace terms and compel the reluctant King to accept their coalition of convenience. Shelburne might still have carried on, but he believed that George had let him down, and resigned. The subsequent peace of Versailles reflected his ideas and terms. In the circumstances he achieved a tolerable settlement, and in a way, notably generous to the rebels, that went some way to assuage old wounds. He had to abandon his dream of a federal union. Instead, he tried to link the idea of mutual trade benefits with a peace that, otherwise, could be no more than recognition of defeat. In the event Britain recognised American independence and ceded much of the disputed territory in the north-west. Loyalists were sacrificed since the request to individual state legislatures that they should compensate for confiscated properties was not given proper sanctions. France and Spain were left with gains incommensurate with their expensive efforts: to France Goree and Senegal, Tobago and St Lucia; to Spain, Florida and Minorca.

In 1784 Shelburne was made Marquess of Lansdowne. He played little further part in active politics but remained a keen observer and trenchant critic. His wide-ranging views distanced him from the main body of political opinion. In 1791 he was praising the French National Assembly for declaring that the right of making peace and war belonged to the nation, not to the Crown. In 1793 he protested against war with France. He kept pressing for parliamentary reform. Pitt was necessarily pragmatic and cautious and kept his distance from the man who had first brought him to office.

It is common to assess Shelburne in terms of flaws, inconsistencies, the widespread mistrust of fellow politicians, and his ultimate failure. He deserves to be judged by his own high standards and aspirations. He was a subtle, thoughtful statesman, impressive in intellectual range. Patron of Bentham, Priestley and Price, correspondent of Mirabeau, Romilly and Adam Smith, visionary about empire and champion of free trade and administrative reform, he belongs in interests and style to the European Enlightenment as much as to the domestic political scene. One can envisage him as a reforming minister in an absolute monarchy, a Turgot or a Tanucci. He was committed to political causes without the connections or patience to implement them. So he tried unconventional ways. With only a handful of followers in Parliament he used agents in the city, like Alderman Sawbridge, to work for him. He secured influence in the East India Company through purchase of stock through agents. Significantly – though wrongly – he was credited with the authorship of 'Junius'. He pioneered some modern methods. In 1780, frustrated by the exclusive claque of Rockingham and the wild oratory of Burke and Fox, he employed Price, Priestley and Jebb to prepare a programme of economic and administrative reform. His ideas were more thorough-going than those of the Rockinghamites. Where both saw reform as a way of curtailing the power of the King, he also saw it as the means of remodelling administration. In that, as in his forward-looking approach to Irish questions (he favoured remission of tithe to Catholics), he is impressive. Yet his free, adventurous thinking offered no advantage in the close political world where personal relationships counted for so much.

For all his faults men could understand Fox and could love him; for all his virtues they did not love Shelburne. With all his ideas and interests, clients and correspondents, he found it hard to relate to people except in the capacity of minister, patron or intellectual enquirer. He could be a generous patron, even a good friend, but he was not a clubbable man. His sharp comments on fellow politicians are often revealing, as much of him and his frustrations as of the subject. With polished objectivity one sees a lack of sympathy, a tendency to decry and suspect. The political world responded in kind. His was a temperament basically unsuited to the political game.

As a young man he had said: 'the only pleasure I propose by the [political] employment is not the profit but to act a part suitable to my rank and capacity such as it is.' The part had been more valuable than contemporary verdicts suggest. Deprived of such employment he could find compensation in his library and pictures at Bowood and Lansdowne House, with his second wife Louisa, *née* Fitzpatrick. Besides great houses and their treasures he bequeathed a political tradition: the 3rd and 5th marquesses both became Cabinet Ministers.

J. Norris, *Shelburne and Reform* (1963).

Duke of Portland

WILLIAM HENRY BENTINCK, 3RD DUKE OF PORTLAND (1738-1809) was twice First Lord of the Treasury (1783 and 1807-9), but in neither case an effective Prime Minister. There is as much interest in the reasons for his elevation as in his performance at the Treasury: they show that he was a significant figure because of the faults or failings of others, and of the role he was required to play. A cartoon of 1807 shows an irascible John Bull surveying a figure, upright and rigid in a chair of blocks of Portland stone; on his chest is hung a placard, 'repaired and whitewashed in the year 1807'. In this year Portland became First Lord for the second time. He was then the nominal leader of a ministry of discrepant talents at a dispiriting juncture of the Napoleonic Wars. He had played a leading part in politics for thirty-five years but few men who have enjoyed such eminence are less known. He may indeed be seen as a type already met in Rockingham, one that will reappear: the English aristocrat who comes to high office as much by virtue of honesty and conscientious application as by the influence of broad acres. Here was the safe man who could be relied on to lead brilliant ministers less steady, more factious, or – crucially in George III's reign – less acceptable to the King.

The eldest son of William, 2nd Duke, and of Lady Margaret Harley, he went conventionally to Westminster and Christ Church, predictably to Parliament, and, after probationary time in the Commons, representing the few voters of Weobley (1761-2), followed his father to the the House of Lords. Portland joined the following of Rockingham, whose career in some respects resembles his own. Marriage to Lady Dorothy Cavendish added the Devonshire interest to his political weight. Impeccable Whig credentials were enhanced in 1768 by a spirited defence of family rights over an estate in Cumberland, granted by William III but challenged by Sir James Lowther. Since Lowther was Bute's son-in-law, and since arbitrary government was a sensitive topic in the climate created by the Wilkes affair, the Crown's support for

Lowther made it a national issue and brought Portland to prominence.

In 1782 he was Lord Lieutenant of Ireland in Rockingham's second ministry when legislative independence was given to the Irish parliament. He had too little time to bring his sympathy and good sense to the desired re-definition of the Anglo-Irish relationship, but enough to appreciate the strength of nationalist feeling that would soon bring rebellion. After Shelburne's short, unpopular administration he found himself nominal head of the Fox-North coalition (April 1783). The choice was owed largely to the awkward position of Charles Fox. He would not serve under Shelburne, the still powerful Rockinghamites did not want him as official representative of an aristocratic party – and George III detested him. Portland he could accept, at least provisionally. So the duke 'stormed the closet' with Rockinghamite terms: the King had to approve the Cabinet altogether before discussing minor offices. It was a pragmatic solution but it could be justified in terms of national interest. There was an urgent need for a working majority for a government confronted by serious post-war problems. George would have been under no illusions, however, as to the location of power. Fox was Leader of the Commons as well as Foreign Secretary. Some openly called him 'the Minister'. Portland's position was weakened at the outset because, as a peer, he could not have the Exchequer.

The King made difficulties from the start, refusing to grant any British peerages, and objecting to the generous financial settlement for the Prince of Wales. His opportunity for more serious damage came with the India Bill, seen by the ministry as a necessary move to secure greater control over the East India Company, and reduce Crown patronage by parliamentary oversight, but by its opponents as a means of increasing the patronage of ministers. When George III told members of the Lords, through Lord Temple, that any peer voting for the bill would be regarded as his personal enemy, its fate was sealed. Portland failed against these tactics and had to accept dismissal (in December), and watch, from the relative quiet of the Lords, the young Pitt holding his own against ferocious attacks, until he was strong enough to go to the country and secure a majority.

Portland emerged from the Whig debacle with some honour and without undue blame for the loss of the India Bill. He might have become the head of a greater partnership, between Fox and Pitt, if his terms had been less binding or Pitt's independence less proud. It could not have been foreseen that Pitt would remain in power for seventeen years, that the reputation of Fox and his followers would decline with his hope of office, or that the impact of the French Revolution would bring about a new political alignment. In that Portland played a pivotal role. In opposition, working diligently from his town base, Burlington House, against Pitt's astute management, Portland had a thankless task. Fox was indolent, and avowed Foxites a reduced band after the election of 1784. Other supporters were commonly called 'those attached to the Duke of Portland's interest'. In January 1794, a year after the outbreak of war with revolutionary France, he announced his break with Fox and support for the war. Burke's earlier and dramatic conversion to conservative principles had not appealed at once to Portland. Burke's language was rather extreme for his taste. He was drawn away from Fox less by any clear sense of differing ideology than by concern, shared by other aristocratic Whigs, about Fox's reformist rhetoric and negative attitude towards the war. For Portland there need now be no distinction between the interests of class and country. The priority was to show willingness to rule, to hold steady in the face of a dangerous enemy and subversive activities at home. It would be the unifying spirit that would make possible, through the long years of endurance, the prosecution of war without serious political opposition.

Later, after the breakdown of the Peace of Amiens and the death of Pitt, it would make possible the creation, out of Pitt's personal following and other disparate groups of coalitions strong enough to carry the fight on to victory. In the process was forged a new alignment along a broad front of anti-Jacobin and anti-reform principles, a new Toryism which was to survive until the Great Reform Bill. Its principles and concerns can already be discerned in the seven years, 1794 to 1801, in which Portland as Home Secretary was responsible for domestic security. Portland provided stability and soundness of administration. He was a realistic patriot but no zealot. The relatively mild action of the government against subversive elements reflects his calm approach. He was not sufficiently moved by the distress caused by periodic food shortages to argue for peace. He was opposed to the concessions to Irish Catholics proposed by Fitzwilliam, Lord Lieutenant. The rift destroyed an important Whig alliance. After the Irish rebellion of 1798 he facilitated the use of British secret service money to smooth the passage of the Act of Union. Since he did not care about Catholic Emancipation, he did not resign with Pitt on the issue, but stayed in Addington's Cabinet. In January 1805 he served Pitt again, though without office.

On the fall of the 'Ministry of All the Talents' (March 1807), again on the Catholic issue, he emerged to head a government which was torn apart by the mutual hostility of Canning and Castlereagh, its ablest members. 'It is not', said Perceval, 'because the duke of Portland is at our head that the government is a government of departments but it is because the government is and must essentially be a government of departments that the duke of Portland is our head.' 'Head', he might have added, because he had the experience to make powerful individuals work together for the good of the state. He was not thought of as a weak man. He was, unfortunately, a sick man, and his grasp was faltering. He was much weakened by gout. He spent much time asleep. He only attended the Lords fifteen times. Hansard does not record a single speech in two and a half years. In the months before his death he could read nothing and transact no business. Perceval meanwhile gained authority. For months Canning intrigued against Castlereagh. Portland sought to placate him by offering to replace Castlereagh at the War Office by Wellesley, but failed to inform Castlereagh, leaving him to discover Canning's intrigues. He was fettered, in any case, by Perceval's threat to resign if Castlereagh were humiliated. Matters were brought to a head by news of the failure of the Walcheren expedition. Portland then resigned himself (6 September 1809). Castlereagh discovered what had been going on, and called Canning out to a duel. Shortly afterwards Portland had a fit and died.

A stronger or fitter man might have found it hard to retain loyalty and unity. This quiet man failed hopelessly. 'A perfectly amiable man with an honourable mind', recorded one diarist. But he added: 'his death is not likely to create any sensation in the state of parties.' They continued fragmented. Another coalition was cobbled together. It was fortunate, at a dark hour, that Perceval was there to give it a strong lead, showing up, in the process, what had been lacking in the previous administration.

William Pitt the Younger

WILLIAM PITT (1759-1806) was Prime Minister from December 1783 to February 1801, and April 1804 to January 1806: the second longest time of service. At twenty-four he was also the youngest to take office. The kingdom was then 'trusted to a schoolboy's care'; it would be a 'mincepie administration', demolished by Christmas. Those who scoffed would stay to praise.

He was born on 28 May at Hayes in Kent, second son of William Pitt and Hester Grenville. It was the 'year of victories'. Later failures would not diminish the prestige of his name. Resolute, efficient, devoted, Hester provided her son with a more stable inheritance than that of Pitt and Villiers – sometimes brilliant, sometimes mad. William was notably sane. At seven he announced that he was glad that he was the younger son so he could follow his father in the Commons. He seemed to know that he must do great things.

The elder Pitt trained him for statesmanship, as if a prince for a throne. The future orator learned to think on his feet by reading aloud in English from foreign texts, pausing if necessary for the right words. Edmund Wilson taught him intensively; it invited reaction. At the age of fourteen he went to Pembroke College, Cambridge, in Wilson's words 'to be admired as a prodigy; not to hear lectures but to spread light.' There his tutor and lifelong friend Tomline enthused: 'his parts are astonishing and universal.' But Pitt fell ill. For convalescence the doctor prescribed early rising, daily riding and port. For many years his health was sound – but he came to rely on the port. In 1776 he took his degree by privilege, but stayed at Cambridge. By now he was an accomplished mathematician and linguist, steeped in Newton, Locke and Hume. Paley's *Principles of Moral and Political Philosophy* accorded well with his sanguine temper and rational mind. Soon immersed in politics he would not aspire nor explore beyond these masters. His was a very English kind of Enlightenment.

After Lincoln's Inn he practised on the Western Circuit but without enthusiasm. In 1780 he finished bottom of the poll at Cambridge but was offered Appleby by Sir James Lowther. He was poor and would remain so. Power and its responsible use were all his aim. Patriotic service was inborn. With his strict upbringing and purposeful preparation, Pitt differed conspicuously from Charles James Fox, heir to another political tradition: their rivalry would help define his career – and Fox's. Each man called himself a Whig; each opposed Lord North. Fox was high in the counsels of Rockingham but Pitt attached himself to Shelburne, and to his father's conception of colonial policy and administrative reform. In February 1782 Rockingham came in, but offered Pitt nothing. He had declared that he would not accept 'a subordinate post'. After Rockingham's death (July) Shelburne made him Chancellor of the Exchequer.

'Not a chip off the old block; it's the old block itself,' said Burke. His mature reasoning impressed the House. Fox could dazzle. It was the architecture of Pitt's speeches, his grasp of a brief, which compelled attention and, crucially, impressed the King. He was soon free to take his own line. In March 1783 the ministry was destroyed by Fox's alliance with North. Their ministry was resented by the King but too strong in Parliament to be defied at once. Pitt's experience of an unstable ministry had reinforced his pragmatism; he now awaited power on his own terms and won attention with proposals (both rejected) for parliamentary and administrative reform. He travelled to France and met Necker, whose wife tried to arrange a marriage with their daughter. Pitt seems to have been unaware of her intentions and the future Mme de Staël was left to look elsewhere. He never again went abroad.

On 17 December Fox's India Bill was defeated in the Lords. George III ordered ministers to surrender their seals – and summoned Pitt to be First Lord of the Treasury and – denoting his central concern – Chancellor of the Exchequer. 'Royal tyranny' cried the Foxites. Some just laughed. 'Billy's painted galley', opined Gibbon, 'will soon sink under Charles's black collier.' But Pitt was heartened by Robinson's estimate of electoral prospects. Without Shelburne, potentially disruptive, and Temple, his uncle, who soon resigned, his ministers were an unknown quantity: Dundas and Grenville, staunch allies, had yet to prove themselves. But Pitt stood firm. The opposition weakened their case by their vehemence; he strengthened his by his conduct. He refused the Clerkship of the Pells, a profitable sinecure. He must appear independent of the court when, in reality, he relied upon it. He presented his own India Bill, providing for the public control proposed by Fox, without its objectionable scope for patronage.

The bill was narrowly defeated. Meanwhile Robinson prepared the ground by discreet mention of the King's favour. On 24 March Parliament was dissolved. In the ensuing election Pitt won a famous triumph. It reflected growing respect for the man, a surge of popular feeling; especially, careful political management. 160 supporters of Fox and North lost their seats. Returned head of the poll at his beloved Cambridge Pitt remained its member for life.

The next five years, his most satisfying, saw a series of measures designed to restore England's reputation and finances. Post-war debt was £231 million. There were discontents in Ireland, disorder in India. Abroad England had no friends. Yet there were economic forces working for government. Technical advances were creating industrial strength; leading to increased trade, it would enable Britain to survive a prolonged war. Nonetheless Pitt's part was significant. 'So perfect a knowledge of the Commerce, Funds and Government of the country', wrote Lady Gower, 'that one must imagine that he had the experience of fifty years.' He went some way to implementing the free trade advocated by Adam Smith. At dinner he complimented the author of *The Wealth of Nations* thus: 'Nay we will stand until you are seated, for we are all your scholars.' He showed also a Walpolean grasp of political realities and eschewed the grand projects of the more doctrinaire reformer. He hit smuggling by reducing duties, simplifying the method of collection, and empowering officials to search at sea. The yield on such dutiable goods as wine, spirits and tobacco rose sharply. In additional duties on goods ranging from hats, ribbons and hair powder to horses, even servants, we see the future: a government seeking profit from consumer growth in an expanding economy.

The fashionable process of 'economical reform' was carried further by an enquiry into 'fees, gratuities, perquisites and emoluments'. Pitt's statutory Commission for Auditing the Public Accounts started the reform of archaic procedures. Government loans went to tender. An annual deficit was turned into a surplus and the means found for the reduction of the Debt. To this end Pitt instituted a Sinking Fund (1786). Though different in method it was Dr Price's project which had 'the effect almost of magic' and drove him 'half-mad' to create it. In seven peacetime years his commissioners were enabled to buy up a substantial amount of stock.

It restored confidence in the government's solvency that would last through war – though Pitt was then criticised for borrowing at high rates in order to maintain the fund. His triumph of financial grasp and parliamentary stamina was the Consolidation Bill of 1787 containing 2,537 resolutions. National book-keeping was vastly simplified. He could claim that 'the public accounts are freed from that obscurity and intricacy in which they were formerly involved'. On the eve of war he could forecast a continuance of surpluses. It had been an astonishing achievement.

Fox and his friends roused prejudices when they attacked the Free Trade Treaty of 1786 but Pitt carried it through in his loftiest style: 'to suppose that any nation could be unalterably the enemy of another is weak and childish'. The French would come to deplore a treaty which reduced duties on the main French and British exports; indeed Robespierre would claim that Pitt had deliberately precipitated the Revolution.

Pitt was less resolute in pressing schemes which promised no material advantage. Early experiences reinforced his natural pragmatism. In 1785 his scheme for the reform of Parliament by the disenfranchisement of thirty-six boroughs, and the distribution of seats between the larger counties and the cities of Westminster and London, was defeated by 74 votes: reform was dropped. Since Wilberforce was ill, Pitt himself introduced the motion for an inquiry into the slave trade (May 1788). In 1792 he spoke eloquently for total abolition but the House preferred the compromise of Dundas – regulation. There the matter was left until 1806.

Pitt was not at heart a radical. Reforms, however desirable, had to be placed in the balance with all the needs of government. He was not, it seemed, a minister prepared to jeopardise government for a single principle. Abolitionists and Reformers had to make their own way as best they could. Although he consciously tried to lead ministers, Pitt was forced, perhaps content, to accept the system of his time. There was no unanimity in his Cabinet about reforms, nor party discipline to enable Pitt to impose his personal view. He had only some fifty personal adherents as against twice that number who could be called Foxites. His authority in Parliament rested on respect for character and competence. Ireland put it to the test.

Quarrels about the emancipation of Catholics divided the legislature; the people suffered from poor trade. Pitt saw free trade as one solution and precursor of inevitable union. Whigs opposed it and Fox was fêted in Manchester. When Pitt modified his proposals Irishmen felt betrayed. The distresses festered for want of intelligent, enforceable legislation. By contrast in Canada, in 1791, far-sighted action was taken to avoid racial dispute by the division into Upper or British, and Lower or French provinces, each with its elected assembly. The French community remained, however, obstinately separate; and problems remained to be solved by Durham and the act of 1840.

When, in 1784, Pitt secured the passage of his India Act, Whigs felt cheated – and made Warren Hastings the target of their revenge. They hoped that Pitt would become involved. He, however, voted for indictment on the Benares charge. Justice could take its course without reflection on the government. As Pitt hoped, Hastings was eventually acquitted upon all charges. Human sympathy subdued by political calculation – it recalls a time when he upheld an election scrutiny against Fox: technically right, but ungenerous. Pitt stood habitually on the moral high ground; but even his friends wished that he would sometimes glance down.

Pitt's style of leadership was detached. In Cabinet he was uncommunicative. He entertained little. In the Commons he seemed scarcely to acknowledge the existence of his back-benchers. He detested the business of patronage that had been meat and drink to Newcastle and North. His integrity and commanding air earned loyalty, if not love. His lavish creation of peers (119 in his time) raised eyebrows. They included a number of soldiers and sailors, also his banker, Smith. He was also largely indifferent to the idea of nobility as a caste. We may see the process as part of the consolidating of an elite; under war conditions tending towards the conservative. He was concerned to balance the Whigs and compensate for the abolition of some other forms of patronage.

Under his armour there was a good-natured man, gentle and sometimes thrown when met by a contrary opinion. Dundas once warned him of 'the unyielding nature of your temper when you are anxious upon a subject.' His instinct for perfection was constantly challenged by his realisation of what was possible. He laboured, however, to master subjects held to be important. During the Hastings case he shut himself up with Dundas for ten days to study the intricacies of the Bengal revenues.

Pitt devoted himself to altering Britain's condition of isolation. In 1783 the Emperor had voiced a common opinion when he said that the country had 'descended forever to the rank of a second-rate power like Sweden or Denmark.' Isolation could indeed be mistaken for impotence. A crisis rose in 1787-8 from the quarrel in Holland between the Republican Party and the Stadholder. Pitt backed him with a subsidy and held the fleet in readiness, while Prussian troops marched to defend him. The French had to accept the defeat of the Republicans whom they had formerly upheld. Spain too yielded to British power. After arresting British ships in Nootka Sound (1790) they subsequently admitted the British right to navigate the Pacific. The Eastern Question cast a longer shadow. After Suvaroff's victories over the Turks in 1791 Pitt became alert to the danger of Poland and the Turkish Empire being dismembered between Russia, Austria and Prussia. He demanded that Russia should restore her conquests, notably Okzakoff, but the Whigs protested, the Cabinet was divided and Pitt had to retreat; the price paid was the second partition of Poland.

George III's precarious health balance was a problem. Between October 1788 and 1789, when he recovered from apparent madness, Pitt conducted a delaying action in his search for precedents and for a formula to limit a regent's inherent right. Fox called for full powers but spoiled his case by careless preparation. When the King recovered the Regency Bill had not become law and Pitt could justly claim that he had stood for the rights of the Crown and the privileges of Parliament against a prince whose gross and unfilial conduct affronted sober citizens. As a gesture of independence Pitt returned the offer of £100,000 from the merchants of London – though short of money as always. Around now a note of awe tinged contemporary accounts of 'the good minister'. His slender figure, the long, haughty nose above a disdainful mouth, his absorbed public manner, and simplicity of life were all so different from the lavish style of Fox. Pitt's friends knew a more spontaneous person, one who loved children and read the poems of Burns, went dutifully to church but liked to argue points of doctrine; a delightful companion at table. Richard Wellesley described his manners as 'perfectly plain' and thought him endowed 'beyond any man of the time ... with a gay heart and a social spirit'.

Appraising the French Revolution Pitt sympathised first with the creation of a limited monarchy, as if a dose of British medicine would be good for the French patient. He soon shrank from the extremes of violence. Essentially he judged what was happening in France by

9   William Lamb, 2nd Viscount Melbourne
(Artist: Sir Edwin Landseer)

10 Sir Robert Peel, 2nd Baronet
    (Artist: Henry William Pickersgill)

11   Henry Temple, 3rd Viscount Palmerston
      (Artist: Edward William Wyon)

12   Benjamin Disraeli, Earl of Beaconsfield
(Artist: Sir John Everett Millais)

13 William Ewart Gladstone
(Artist: Sir John Everett Millais)

14   Robert Gascoyne-Cecil, 3rd Marquess of Salisbury
(Artist: George Frederic Watts)

15   Herbert Henry Asquith, 1st Earl of Oxford and Asquith
(Artist: Andre Cluysenaar)

16 David Lloyd George, 1st Earl Lloyd-George
(Photo: Alvin Langdon Coburn)

its effect upon England. He welcomed Burke's defection from the Whigs but remained unimpressed by his flights of rhetoric and prophecy. The effect of the Revolution was to create a new Toryism, working against change. He would not own the name of Tory, nor care about the role envisaged by followers like Canning: Mr Pitt the champion, even crusader, for Church and King against intellectual, social and political revolutionaries. As war developed, after 1793, Fox's attitude became increasingly unpopular. For some years the opposition virtually withdrew from Parliament. As a war leader Pitt could count on patriotic sentiment and generous loans. The price was heavier than even the mounting figures of the National Debt could show. Schemes of reform wilted in the prevailing mood of anti-Jacobinism. Pitt could express this spirit but seldom gave way to its excesses. He was little suited, however, to the demands of 'this war of armed opinion'. It was Pitt's tragedy no less than Fox's. It consumed his spirit.

Pitt upheld the Scottish judiciary in 1793 after treason trials of notorious severity with biased judges. He seems for once to have capitulated before public opinion. But he panicked less than his associates before the disturbing symptoms of social revolution and his 'reign of terror' was relatively mild. There was widespread acquiescence in the anti-Jacobin agitation of 1792-9 – the Aliens Act, the Seditious Meetings Act, the Treasonable Correspondence Act, the suspension of habeas corpus and the anti-combination laws. Each can be justified by the conditions of the day. In the absence of a police force the state could not rely on a general enforcement of laws but had to hope for an effect on the popular mind of punitive legislation selectively but severely applied. 'No war, no Pitt' yelled the London mob in 1795 – but it was the high price of food that they complained of. A bad harvest then was today's hike in oil price: a significant factor in economic performance, and national well-being – and beyond ministers' control.

Pitt always kept negotiated peace in mind but unfortunately the British did not achieve enough success to give them a strong hand. Pitt never seemed able to devise an overall strategy. He can be criticised for failing to appreciate the ruthless mentality of revolutionary governments who were unconcerned by the loss of sugar islands and trading posts. Their acquisition was, moreover, of doubtful benefit to England. In the West Indies 40,000 British troops died of disease. Nor did economic warfare bring the success expected; only slowly did Pitt accept that France would not be destroyed by inflation.

Pitt was ill-served by his Continental allies, who accepted his subsidies but could not match the spirit of the French armies, the administration of Carnot or the genius of Napoleon. Successive coalitions were bedevilled by the failure of the powers to act together. English military intervention was also inglorious: the Duke of York's expedition to Flanders had to be withdrawn (1794), the Quiberon Bay expedition was a fiasco. In 1795 Prussia and Spain left the coalition; in 1796 Spain joined France. The campaigns of Bonaparte smashed the Austrians in Italy and in the autumn of 1797 Britain stood alone and consols fell to 48. Could 'the efforts of a free, brave, loyal and happy people', in Pitt's words, check France? France came to mean Bonaparte, First Consul in 1799, Emperor in 1801. Was peace possible with such a man, contemptuous of the old diplomacy? Between the iron obstinacy of Grenville and wishful thinking of Fox, Pitt had to steer a middle course, trusting in the Navy to bring Bonaparte to the table.

Pitt had exempted it from peacetime economies. In Barham at the Admiralty he had a great administrator. After the naval mutinies of 1797 the victories of St Vincent and Duncan restored confidence; in 1800 the brilliant success of Nelson at the Nile gave Napoleon a salutary lesson in the importance of sea-power; his victory at Copenhagen in 1801 demonstrated the new ruthlesness. Pitt spent hours poring over maps, consulting with ministers and commanders, wrestling with the problems of war finance. He had the moral stature to promote unpopular taxes, notably, in 1798, an income tax rising to 2s in the pound for all above £200 a year. He was hissed by the mob, but the burden was placed fairly on the better-off; as again when he raised the Land Tax.

Pitt bore the burden alone. His own affairs were oddly confused; creditors pressed. The master of the nation's finance could not manage his own. Did nothing matter but politics? He was fond of Eleanor Eden, but he decided against marriage. Did he foresee that his life would be one of cares and sickness? Was he unusually considerate, or unfeelingly cold? He remained a bachelor, living at Downing Street and Walmer castle (as Warden of the Cinque Ports) with his niece Lady Hester Stanhope as housekeeper. His health deteriorated, he drank deeply but without the gaiety of earlier years. Dundas claimed that he divided his time 'between cellar and garret'.

Ever a neglectful correspondent, he now became increasingly casual about political and personal affairs. In 1806 there were still odd documents from the 1780s in his room. He was usually calm but could crack: in May 1798 he fought a duel with Tierney on Putney Common after a tense exchange in the Commons.

The problems of Ireland did not wait upon the events of war. By the impetuosity of Earl Fitzwilliam, who introduced a bill (1795) in the Irish parliament for full civil equality for Catholics and Protestants, Pitt became – neither first nor last of Prime Ministers to be so – engulfed by 'the Irish question'. In a hysterical atmosphere calm measures were spurned. He offered a charter for Maynooth College – but Catholic feeling could not be assuaged. The United Irishmen planned a republic, but their title was a misnomer. The Catholic rising in Leinster and Wexford was less a republican movement than an agrarian jacquerie fortified by religious fanaticism and, belatedly, by French troops. Hideous atrocities embittered both peasants and soldiers before the rising was suppressed (1798). Pitt was roused by the threat (and cost) to the mother country.

In January 1800 he presented the case for the union of Britain and Ireland in a speech that was masterly, humane and comprehensive. Irish borough-mongers were persuaded to surrender their rights by cash, sinecures and titles. The resolution passed the Dublin parliament. Then Pitt hit the rocks. Alerted by Lord Chancellor Loughborough, George insisted upon his Coronation oath. Pitt felt that he was committed to the Catholic cause by previous transactions (though no formal promise). In February he resigned. George threatened insanity and Pitt worried about the prospect of a regency: so he promised that he would not again raise the question of Catholic Emancipation. Addington was left to negotiate the peace of Lunéville. Pitt continued to give support as a private member. He had never seen himself as head of a party; now he would not lead any systematic opposition. He was reticent to a point that exasperated his friends. They longed, in Canning's words, for the return of 'the pilot who weathered the storm'. Was he waiting for the unequivocal voice of public opinion? He suffered in health from sudden release from the tensions of high office and visited Bath to relieve gout and stomach disorders. Only a private subscription among friends saved him from his creditors, but he still had to sell Holwood, his country house.

In May 1803 war was resumed. As colonel of the Kentish Association and Warden of the Cinque Ports, Pitt drilled volunteers.

At first he supported the government. But the government's naval policy alarmed him. Then Fox joined him in voting against the Militia Bill and Addington's majority sank. At the end of April 1804 he resigned. George III resisted Pitt's request to have Fox in – and Grenville stayed out in sympathy with Fox. Pitt shouldered his burden with only Dundas close enough to be of much use. The latter's impeachment and disgrace was shattering. Pitt wept, but kept his head and planned for victory. The Navy's part, planned by Barham, was to annihilate the French and Spanish fleets while Austria and Prussia, partners in this Third Coalition, were to bring the French to action in Italy. In the event Napoleon's invasion plans were thwarted, but Trafalgar (October 1805) tempered glory with grief. Pitt, who admired Nelson intensely, could not sleep the night he heard the news. Napoleon was confined to the Continent; but there his triumphs of Ulm and Austerlitz spelt the destruction of Pitt's expensive design.

In November 1805 he went to the banquet at the Mansion House: the mob untied the horses and dragged his carriage themselves. To the Lord Mayor's toast to the 'Saviour of Europe' he simply replied: 'I return you many thanks for the honour you have done me; but Europe is not be saved by any single man. England has saved herself by her exertions and will, as I trust, save Europe by her example.' The frail figure seemed to embody the collective will of the nation. In December, however, came the bad news and Wilberforce spoke of his 'Austerlitz look'. He may not have said 'Roll up that map of Europe, it will not be needed these ten years', but surely believed it. In his last delirium listeners caught the cry, 'Hear, Hear!' And later, 'Oh my country, how I leave my country!' He died in the early morning of 23 January 1806. His last thoughts seem to have been of the Parliament and of the country that he had most nobly served.

Lord Malmesbury vowed that in his whole future life he would always act as he believed Pitt would have wished. That was the Pitt effect. For his followers, more generally for a whole political class, Pitt became, more than a memory, an idea. Because his mind had been so open, his policies so pragmatic, his appeal was broad. It was that which had frustrated Charles James Fox; and it was he that said, after Pitt's death, that 'it seemed as if there were something missing from the world'.

J. Ehrman, *William Pitt* (3 vols, 1969, 1983 and 1996).
William Hague, *William Pitt the Younger* (2004).

Henry Addington

HENRY ADDINGTON, 1ST VISCOUNT SIDMOUTH (1757-1844) was
Prime Minister from February 1801 to April 1804. He made a peace,
which soon collapsed, then proved inadequate to the renewed
challenge of war. Over his ministry looms the great name of Pitt, his
predecessor and successor. It was unfortunate for posterity's view
that his name rhymed with that of a pleasant suburban village. No
reappraisal can make a great man of him, but his solid achievement
deserves a fairer perspective.

His father Anthony was a reputable court doctor, the elder Pitt
being among his patients; his mother Mary, *née* Hiley. He was
educated at Winchester and Brasenose College, Oxford, read some
law but decided on politics. In 1783 he was elected for Devizes.
That after only six years he was elected Speaker says much for his
reputation for Wykehamist manners, tact and good judgement. He
pleased many by his mild adherence to traditional forms and
conciliatory skills. In the crisis of 1797 Pitt seems to have considered
resigning in his favour, as a man without political baggage, therefore
acceptable as a peacemaker, though temporarily and under his direction. It is also revealing that George III used him as his emissary to
Pitt during the dispute over Catholic Emancipation.

When Pitt resigned, in February 1801, Addington was the King's
choice; sound on the big issue, Emancipation, acceptable to
'king's friends' and many independent gentlemen. He had a small
personal following, about a dozen; many more wanted him to make
peace. Grenville deplored 'a general want of dignity ... and a little-
ness of character' in Addington's ministry. But Whigs were in dis-
array, in several small groups with different views and loyalties,
unwilling to work together in effective opposition. Some Pittites,
like Canning, were scathing but restrained by respect for their
leader. 'Though I must not goad or pelt the doctor ... I am enabled
to put a thistle under his tail.' Canning was as scornful of those,
notably Liverpool and Perceval, who were willing to serve. As for
Pitt himself – as patriot and politician, he felt he should offer

support; also he was exhausted, and he feared for the King's sanity.

It was a moment in politics, not unique, when the overwhelming desire, stronger than party passion, was for economies and good order. The second coalition had collapsed. It was widely felt that the war against the Revolution had become meaningless. Nelson had dealt a shattering blow at the Battle of the Nile and Britain appeared to be secure. But the war could not be won, nor allies obtained. Addington himself is recorded as saying that there was not 'the least prospect of obtaining such alliances.' Gold payments to Continental allies had already exhausted much of the Bank of England's reserves; the pound had depreciated, trade was disturbed, bread was expensive. After Union without Emancipation, Catholic Ireland was inflamed; a second rising might be expected. If a lasting peace could not be hoped for at least a breathing space could be got, a chance to recuperate.

After a year's approaches and bargaining the Treaty of Amiens was signed in March 1802. Except for Trinidad and Ceylon, taken from Spain and Holland respectively, British conquests were handed back. France agreed to help obtain compensation for the House of Orange and to evacuate Italy. Wyndham, Canning and, more surprisingly, Grey criticised the peace and 'Britain's guardian gander' who signed it. But Pitt continued to back Addington. The peace soon started to crumble as France went from one provocative act to another. Napoleon accepted the 'presidency' of the Cis-Alpine Republic, annexed Piedmont and enforced control of Switzerland by military intervention. The British, concerned about the spirit in which Napoleon was interpreting the peace, held on to their Indian posts and to Malta (to be returned to the Knights of St John), as bargaining counters. War was resumed in May 1803 and 'the doctor', the minister for peace, had to contend with war – and the threat of invasion. The Navy had been reduced from 130,000 to 70,000; the regular Army establishment was reduced to 95,000. But Addington had done better than just cut and save.

Like Pitt before him, and later Perceval, he was both First Lord of the Treasury and Chancellor of the Exchequer. He was responsible in all for four budgets. A saving of £25 million in one year was accompanied by an important innovation. He introduced something comparable to the modern budget statement, with a review of the past year and projection for the next appearing in one statement. In 1803, with the prospect of renewed war requirements, he introduced a new version of Pitt's income tax, 'hinged on the same principles', he said, but taking from the defunct Land Tax the method of assessment, and collection at source.

War revealed Addington's limitations, though he carried on till April 1804. He wanted a defensive war; allowing that Napoleon would master the Continent, he relied upon the Navy to hold the Channel. He increased the militia but created confusion by appealing for volunteer companies, setting in motion a patriotic movement with only the haziest idea of how to control it. Priority was not given, as it should have been, to training a regular army to defeat the French on the Continent. Addington may have lacked vision but many still trusted him: Southey, Hastings, even Nelson. He was calm in crisis and he wisely made no fuss over Colonel Despard, a crazy officer who planned to murder the government – and was executed for it. He was also willing to negotiate with Pitt, but on terms which looked condescending. According to Macaulay he suffered from a delusion, 'not unlike that of Abou Hassan in the Arabian tale. His brain was turned by so short and unreal a Caliphate.' Pitt was not the man to condescend to. Now, disgusted with Addington's performance, he waited for him to resign and for the King to call him back.

When Pitt formed his new government in May 1804, several of Addington's followers, such as Hawkesbury and Eldon, were included. Addington himself returned in January 1805 as Lord President of the Council, with the title of Viscount Sidmouth. Too much bitterness, however, had been caused by the machinations of the last part of his ministry to allow for an easy assimilation of Addington men. The impeachment of Dundas, Pitt's friend and First Lord of the Admiralty, increased the strains, since Addingtonians voted with the opposition in a division which went, by the casting vote of the Speaker, against the First Lord. He resigned in May 1805, Sidmouth in June.

He reappeared in the 'Ministry of All the Talents' as Lord Privy Seal. He became Home Secretary in Liverpool's government (1812) and remained there until 1821. In the face of the hardships which followed the war, the social evils of industrialisation and widespread agitation, Sidmouth's policy was bleakly, unimaginatively repressive. The suspension of Habeas Corpus in 1817, the Six Acts of 1819, were the policy of the government, not his alone, and can be defended as appropriate under the circumstances. But his shortcomings during this period are exposed by the reforming activity of his successor, Robert Peel. Strong nerve, patience and staying power, Sidmouth undoubtedly still possessed. But the will and imagination to shake free of the reactionary straitjacket was lacking, as in others conditioned by the excesses of Jacobinism and the strains of total war. The doctor was less of a political lightweight than he has been depicted, but Canning may still be allowed the last word: 'Pitt is to Addington / As London is to Paddington.'

P. Ziegler, *Addington* (1965).

Lord Grenville

WILLIAM WYNDHAM, BARON GRENVILLE (1759-1834), younger
son of George Grenville and Elizabeth Wyndham, presided from
February 1806 to March 1807 over the 'Ministry of All the Talents',
which was distinguished for the abolition of the slave trade but for
little else. He was an upright man, clear and strong in adherence to
a principle, but known before all for his guardianship of the family
interest. As contemporaries recognised, he was a Grenville. The
family stood out like an island in the choppy sea of Georgian
politics. Frowning cliffs and rocky shores defended their privileged
base. Clannish and exclusive, they were willing to exert themselves
in the public interest: like his father George (Prime Minister 1763-5)
he did not shrink from the spadework. They also expected to be
well rewarded. In 1807 the family was drawing £55,000 a year from
public sources. They were unwilling to join any association except on
their own terms, which were always pitched high. Earl Temple,
George's uncle, damaged the Pitt administration at the outset by
a resignation never satisfactorily explained. His elder brother
Buckingham made demands which soon became demands on the
state. In 1806 Fox had to introduce a special bill to enable Grenville
to continue to hold the office of Auditor and Comptroller-General
concurrently with the Lord Treasurership: wearing one hat he was to
control and audit what, wearing the other, he was to spend.

Born to a great political family, with formidable influence, two
Prime Ministers in the line before him (the younger Pitt was his
cousin); after Eton, Christchurch and, in 1783, the family borough of
Buckingham, Grenville was well placed for advancement. Liberal in
economic views, a student of Adam Smith, he was serious and
professional in his approach to government. Family loyalty, common
interest and similar style in politics and personal life, bound him to
Pitt. The cousins even looked alike. For seventeen years, nine of
peace, eight of war, he served the Crown, Paymaster-General (1784-
9), Home Secretary (1789-91) and Foreign Secretary (1791-1801).
He was the chief author of the Canada Act of 1791, though Pitt saw

it through the Commons. Both parts of the country were given a legislative assembly on British lines, while council, executive and governor broadly represented the British institutions of Upper House, ministers and King. Grenville believed that 'the constitution of Great Britain is sufficient to pervade the whole world'. Such splendid Whiggishness made him an unbending opponent of Jacobin and Bonapartist extremes.

Splendid too was Grenville's wartime tenure of the foreign ministry. Financial affairs naturally concerned him less than they did Pitt. Where Pitt was willing to negotiate, he was for fighting on. This intelligent, steady man epitomised the stubborn will of his countrymen. Defeats, mutinies, deficits were brushed aside as of no importance. Peace on any other terms than those of Great Britain was unthinkable. When the French renounced the Scheldt treaties he declared that his government could not watch with indifference any nation make herself 'sovereign of the Low Countries or general arbitress of the rights and liberties of Europe.' He was relieved when French intransigence wrecked peace talks in 1797: 'it would be ten thousand times safer to face the storm than to shrink from it.' When Bonaparte, newly made First Consul, wrote to George III as one ruler to another, Grenville replied with a freezing memorandum: the British government saw no reason for departing from established methods and manners in diplomacy and 'the best way for the French people to achieve peace would be to restore their proper rulers'.

Not surprisingly Grenville opposed the terms of the Peace of Amiens in 1801: 'England has given up everything everywhere.' By then he was out of government, having resigned with Pitt over Catholic Emancipation. He now moved to Fox and Grey. Like Spencer and Windham he was impatient with Pitt's tolerant attitude towards Addington. When Pitt tried to form a National Government he refused to join it. Narrow partisanship, misplaced loyalty? Pitt certainly thought so: 'I will teach that proud man that I can do without him, though I think that it will cost me my life.' Grenville's loyalty was to Fox, whom George would not have as Foreign Minister, and to Catholic Emancipation, which Pitt was now prepared to defer at a time when invasion threatened. When Pitt died, shattered in health and hope, and his following splintered; with the Portland group now ready to support him, Grenville emerged, ironically, as the Prime Minister, without whose reassuring presence

George would not countenance the return of Fox and his fellow Whigs. In office at last Fox proved both competent and emollient – a valuable ally in a ministry which, despite the claim, did not represent 'All the Talents' and had no natural cohesion. His death in September 1806 was a serious blow. Even so there would have been sufficient support in Parliament for the government if they had not, in Sheridan's phrase, 'built a wall against which to run their own heads'. To secure a token victory for his ministers' principles Grenville sought to gain royal assent for further concessions to Roman Catholics. It could be argued in the interest of military efficiency that Catholic officers should hold ranks up to that of colonel – as they already could in Ireland. The old King was nearly blind but still sane and determined as ever to assert his prerogative. Ministers offered to drop the bill, with the proviso that they should be allowed to put the case to their followers. George acted with doubtful propriety when he demanded a pledge from ministers that they would never again raise the question. They took a risk when they refused. The King was ready with an alternative ministry. It would be twenty-three years before they returned to power.

Fox had hoped to make peace with France but he soon learned that Bonaparte was more interested in further control and conquest. Windham, Secretary for War and the Colonies, had already shown as a war minister, but under Dundas, a passionate will to win; but he had felt thwarted in the direction of operations. Now he put forward the scheme that embodied his thinking, the General Training Act. The volunteer system was abolished. The whole male population of military of age to serve was to be trained in batches of 200,000. They were allowed to enlist for a short period and offered higher rates of pay if they chose to re-engage. The conception may have been sound, the execution was certainly poor. To avert chaos Windham should have given all his time to the system. Instead, unfortunately he preferred to plan operations. The sorry failure of an assault on Buenos Aires did nothing for the credit of the government. Napoleon planned economic war by closing Continental ports. Grenville was not alone in coming to believe that the war could not be won. But he was true to the legacy of Fox, who had promoted a bill for the abolition of the slave trade, when he used all the influence of government to overcome the resistance of the West Indian interest and took charge of its passage through the Lords. At the height of war, at a time of mounting debt, the government found

time and resources for a Christian cause which was of no conceivable
relevance or advantage to the war effort. It was nobly done.

Grenville and Grey had further chances of office in 1809, 1811 and
1812. The best prospect was after Perceval's assassination. Grenville
demanded Catholic relief and a cut in public expenditure. Principle
and prejudice seem to have been at work to prevent them seizing
the moment. There was something else. Grenville was always drawn
to his beloved Cornwall, like Grey to Northumberland. 'Lord
Grenville's attachment to Boconnoc surpasses anything I have
yet seen,' wrote Auckland: 'Politics are no more alluded to than
astrology.' Weighing politics against the pleasures of gardening
and scholarship was he not tempted to stay out of the ring, saving
honour, through making demands that he knew would not be
satisfied? He shrank not from the work of office but from the fray:
long hours of debate, the disagreeable necessity to negotiate, the
whole fraught business of politics. He had seen what it had done to
his cousin.

In 1815 Grenville fell out with Grey over the future of Napoleon.
Grenville was for destroying him, Grey for coming to terms. In the
post-war years he voiced views about sedition with sufficient energy
to impress Liverpool, but he declined when offered a post. In 1823 he
formally retired, to spend his remaining years at Dropmore where a
magnificent library solaced his last years.

Another aristocrat's view of Grenville is of objective interest,
since Lord Derby was talking fifty years on (1862), and comparing
him with Pitt and Fox: 'He had less principle than either of them:
with him the leading idea was the importance of the family connection, and to this he was always ready to sacrifice the national
interest.' Indeed Grenville can be read as if modelling for the
Namierite idea of parliamentary politics as representing less
ideological conflict between Whig and Tory than a contest between
factions and families for place, pension and sinecure. 'Gorged with
places and pensions' was a newspaper's charge (1806) against the
Grenvilles. It was food for radicals and has left its mark. Namier's
view is overstated, if not wholly discredited. Meanwhile it is
ironic that Grenville, who plainly belongs to an older aristocratic
era than that of Lord Derby, proves to have been a significant
transitional figure. When he consented to be Prime Minister he
facilitated the homecoming of the Portland Whigs; by standing
firm for Catholic Emancipation he cemented their position; by

encouraging them to hold together against the temptation of coalition, he laid down the lines for their eventual revival under the banner of Parliamentary Reform. The Duke of Omnium would have much to thank him for.

P. Jupp, *Lord Grenville* (1985).

Spencer Perceval

SPENCER PERCEVAL (1762-1812) had been Prime Minister for three years (1809-12) when he was shot dead in the lobby of the House of Commons by a bankrupt merchant, John James Bellingham. His shocking end may be better known than his admirable life. Yet it may be that, but for a madman's bullet, he would have earned a larger place in political history as the Prime Minister who rode out the storm – and brought the ship safely into harbour. He was only fifty when he was killed, physically robust and active, politically secure and respected. Napoleon was preparing to march on Moscow, Wellington to take the initiative in the Peninsula. Indeed, in Fortescue's words, he had 'endured the dust and heat of the race without earning the immortal garland'.

He was the younger son of the second Lord Egmont, who was celebrated for his glum appearance, and of Catherine Compton. Egmont died when Spencer was eight. The boy was sent to Harrow, then entering its golden age as a nursery of politicians. He became a competent classical scholar and made lifelong friends, among them Dudley Ryder, the future Lord Harrowby and staunch political ally. At Trinity College, Cambridge, he became a confirmed evangelical, living in a set apart from the majority of undergraduates, a world of earnest manners and set opinions. He could be eccentric in his religious opinions, as when indulging in millenarian speculation, and pondering the identity of the creatures in the book of Revelation. He would not hesitate to promote legislation on moral questions such as divorce. Yet he was almost unmarked by the less attractive features of contemporary evangelicalism. There was little of the self-righteousness that men noted about 'the Saints'. For lack of means he had to go straight to a legal career. Decisive, tough-minded and methodical, he rose rapidly at the Bar. Most prominent politicians began their career, through patronage, in a proprietary borough. It was only after a fiercely contested election that he became member for Northampton (1796). He had the support of Castle Ashby but his constituency, with its thousand electors, had to be wooed. He learned from his experience in 'middle England' and kept the seat for life.

It was around then that Romilly spoke of 'his excellent temper, his engaging manners and his sprightly conversation'. Like many small men (little more than five foot tall) he was also thrusting and tireless. He married Jane Wilson against the wishes of her father who did not see a future Prime Minister in this impecunious barrister. He was helped by a sinecure, one that had escaped the reformers' trawl: the Surveyorship of the Maltship and Clerkship of the Irons. Orthodox on sensitive questions, he deplored the Revolution and revered the constitution. His elder brother, Lord Arden, was a junior minister and gave a helping hand. From the start he was a fervent Pittite and spoke effectively for the ministry in critical debates. At the same time he was entrusted with the prosecution in important state trials, such as that of Binns of the London Correspondence Society (acquitted after a brilliant defence by Romilly). Legal and political careers advanced together and, in 1801, he became Solicitor-General under Addington. He could take office under Pitt's supplanter, since he rejected Pitt's policy of Catholic Emancipation. In his immovable opposition to any concession to Irish Catholics he drew largely on the views of his intolerant brother-in-law, Lord Redesdale, and he absurdly overrated the threat of the Pope as the instrument of a hostile power. But his views were grounded in the faith of the Church of England. He was utterly opposed to the idea that any body of Christians is a church in itself and entitled to full social and political rights. It was in the name of the Church of England, envisaged as a moral force in the nation, that he opposed Roman Catholic claims, framed his education policy and projected reforms to purify the church.

When Pitt was on his way in 1798 to fight the duel that might have ended his life, and was asked about a possible successor, he told Ryder that 'Mr Perceval was the most competent person, and that he appeared the most equal to Mr Fox.' It is a remarkable judgement upon a man who has been dismissed as a political hack or, with memorable unfairness by Sydney Smith, as having 'the head of a country parson and the tongue of an Old Bailey lawyer.' Perceval's qualities did not amount to genius, but they were largely what was needed in the situation created by the demands of war, the weakness of the Whigs and the rigidity of the King on the question of Catholic Emancipation. He was therefore promoted from Solicitor-

General to Attorney-General in 1802, in which office he remained under Pitt after 1803. After Pitt's death he was considered to be the leader of 'Pitt's friends'. A short period in opposition was followed by two years at the Exchequer, from March 1807 until he succeeded Portland in October 1809. Because of Portland's inability to transact any business in the latter months of his administration, Perceval acquired independence and authority. When he became Prime Minister few were surprised and George III was delighted

But the position was deplorable. The reckless behaviour of Canning had removed not only himself but also, for the time being, Castlereagh, from the political scene. Rivalries went so deep that the main question in choosing new ministers was less that of fitness for the job than willingness to work with colleagues. Perceval had also to consider the votes that belonged to leading contenders for office. His first duty was to see that his government was viable in parliamentary divisions.

His Cabinet was hardly impressive. Lord Chancellor Eldon laid twenty to one that the government would not face Parliament. Grey, typically, was torn between admiration for Perceval's courage and indignation that he should dare to form a ministry at such a time. Wynn found a disturbing feature: 'In the whole of the list there is not one man of old property, weight and influence in the country but that idiot Westmoreland.' Auckland held that none of the ministers, except for Perceval, was able enough to devise a strategy to combat the French economic campaign without crippling the country's own economy. Wellesley, Foreign Secretary, was a captious and impatient colleague, making no secret of his ambition to lead. Fortunately his brother was capable of holding his own in Spain, Liverpool proved a capable war minister, Napoleon contributed to his own defeat and Britain's economic strength enabled it to survive the Continental Decrees.

This administration could never be comfortable. That it survived, and with some credit, was due mainly to Perceval. His resilience was exactly what was required. The ministry survived the inquiry into the disastrous Walcheren expedition, helped by Chatham's acceptance of responsibility. Somehow money was found to pay for the Peninsular campaigns. Wellington saw mainly the shortcomings of the Treasury but ministers deserved praise for their efforts to fund the war. These were, in Gladstone's phrase, 'the heroic days of war finance.' In the detailed business of the Exchequer Perceval had owed much to talented subordinates, notably Huskisson and Herries. He still tended to act as he thought his mentor, Pitt, would have done. All the responsibility and much of the work were, however, his. He remained Chancellor of the Exchequer after becoming Prime Minister, despite prolonged efforts to find someone to relieve him of a burdensome post. His five budgets are models of sound finance. Between 1808 and 1812 the supplies needed exceeded those of any comparable period and a greater proportion than ever was raised by taxation. The total of new debt contracted between 1803 and 1807 was £156 million; from 1808 to 1812 it was but £123 million. After Perceval's assassination it rose again steeply. He had prevailed against the bullionists and the defeatism of those who believed that it was impossible to finance continuous operations on the Continent.

Perceval's ministers made capital out of George III's jubilee in 1810. 'The mass of the people', wrote Lord Bulkeley, 'look up to his good moral character and to his age and to a comparison with his sons.' Ministers hoped that some of the old King's popularity would rub off on them. His sons were nothing but an embarrassment. In May 1810, when the Duke of Cumberland's valet was found dead, the verdict was that he had made an attempt on his master's life. The people's verdict was the opposite. The Duke of York had been forced out of the Horse Guards after revelations about the sale of commissions by his mistress. Perceval, who defended him stoutly at that time (1808), insisted upon his reinstatement in 1811. When, in the summer of 1811, George relapsed finally into insanity the question of regency was raised again. Perceval followed the precedents of Pitt and went on with his work, and was confirmed in office. Whig hopes were dashed when the Regent played safe. He feared his father's returning to health; he was also coming to appreciate Perceval. As he survived successive crises his reputation advanced to a point at which 'plucky Perceval' could be described (by J.W. Ward) as 'the most popular man in England'. He worked incessantly and felt the strain, though, said Pitt's friend, Charles Long, he was 'as hard as iron'. Sunday matins at St Margaret's, Westminster, his large brood of children in attendance, nourished the spirit; a tranquil home provided the ideal background for his labours. He would often slip quietly into the nursery to see his children, for 'he was never so happy as when playing in the midst of them'.

In 1812 Wellesley resigned after prolonged intrigues. Talk of coalition was largely a screen for his own ambition. The Regent saw the several incompatible groups, Canning's, Grey's, Grenville's, now Wellesley's, 'rich in debating points but poor in prospects' (Steven Watson), and sensibly stood by Perceval. He was now able to strengthen his administration by bringing back Castlereagh to the Foreign Office and Sidmouth as Lord President: Castlereagh brought talent, Sidmouth votes. In the country these manoeuvres looked insignificant beside outbreaks of popular violence. A trade depression in 1811 had brought unemployment; the Orders in Council were widely blamed, machines and stocking frames were smashed. One of Perceval's last acts was to set up a special commission in Lancashire to deal with the Luddites.

Bellingham had suffered imprisonment in Russia, where he had represented a firm of Liverpool merchants; he may have thought that Perceval was the member for Staffordshire (former ambassador in Russia); he was certainly deranged. Only a loose link connects his murderous act with the distresses of merchants and unemployed weavers. But mobs assembled in London to exult, bonfires were lit and flags waved in Nottingham and Leicester. Some believed that an English revolution was starting. But the country was quiet. The administration survived under Lord Liverpool, no less able and a touch more flexible than Perceval. 'The most reactionary Prime Minister of the century' (Aspinall) had certainly been a stiff defender of the *status quo* in church and constitution. Liverpool, also opposed to Catholic Emancipation, may have been a better man to lead the Tories into the post-war politics of transition. Perceval had proved the right man for his time. That slight figure, that good-tempered spirit, that clear-sighted pursuit of England's essential goals, above all the unselfconscious probity, appealed to independent country members and to declared opponents. He was one of those rare political leaders, one who is entirely trusted. His was a healing ministry at a critical time such as few politicians, certainly none of the Whigs of his day, could have exercised. He died practically penniless, though his family was generously compensated by Parliament. George III said of Perceval that he was 'perhaps the most straightforward man he had ever known'. Wilberforce's tribute may sound uncomfortably to modern ears: 'never had he known any individual die of whose salvation he entertained less doubt.' He touched, nonetheless, on the heart of the matter. The faith was the man.

D. Gray, *Spencer Perceval: The Evangelical Prime Minister, 1762-1812* (1963).

Earl of Liverpool

ROBERT BANKS JENKINSON, 2ND EARL OF LIVERPOOL (1770-1828) was Prime Minister from 1812 to 1827. He stands third to Walpole and the younger Pitt in length of tenure but nowhere near them in reputation. In Disraeli's *Coningsby* he appears as the 'Arch-Mediocrity', his highest attribute 'a meagre diligence'. But Gladstone believed that 'England was never better governed than between the years 1822 and 1830.' His accomplishments were solid rather than brilliant. Yet in a period of threat and novelty he preserved a calm and fortitude that evoke respect. In a fluid political situation he maintained a coherence in government that witnessed to political skill and personal integrity. His ministry contained at different times six future Prime Ministers, Canning, Goderich, Wellington, Peel, Aberdeen and Palmerston, besides the talented Huskisson and Castlereagh. Essentially a manager in outlook and method, Liverpool showed little inclination to lift his eyes above the details or to examine the principles upon which policy rested. From the beginning he showed that mistrust of general ideas which is characteristic of a certain kind of Tory. His was, indeed, the first administration since 1714 to avow the name. It was the last long-lived administration of the old political world.

He was the only son of Charles Jenkinson and Amelia Watts, though his father had two children by a subsequent marriage. One of a line of Oxfordshire baronets who had remained obscure since Arthur Jenkinson, Elizabethan explorer, he was valued by Pitt as an expert in patronage. Without rising in office beyond the Board of Trade he acquired a fortune and an earldom. He meant his son to excel and secured a borough for him. Robert was dutiful and friends noted that he always quoted his father. At Charterhouse and Christ Church he was solemn and consequential; long in the neck and clumsy he cut an awkward figure; good nature and a keen intellect generally saved him from ridicule. An Oxford friend was Canning, the storm petrel of Tory politics throughout Liverpool's political life.

Visiting Paris Jenkinson chanced to be present at the storming of the Bastille. An Englishman's inherited suspicion of things French would harden into opposition to anything that smelt of democracy, of 'mere numbers' against the claims of 'property and intelligence'. While abroad, though still under age, he had been returned for the Lowther borough of Appleby. In 1791 he made his maiden speech, on the Russian question: 'so full', said Pitt, 'of philosophy and science, strong and perspicuous language that it would have done credit to the most practised debater and experienced statesman.' Pitt could recognise an old head on young shoulders. Jenkinson (Lord Hawkesbury, by courtesy title after 1796) rarely rose to this level again but remained a cogent speaker. In 1793 he secured a seat on the India Board. In that year he exchanged Appleby for Rye and freed himself of patronage. He became a colonel in the Kent militia. He took life seriously. Despite his father's opposition he married Lady Louisa Hervey (1795), daughter of the Earl of Bristol. Friends found her dull, but she made him happy.

In 1801, being opposed to Catholic Emancipation, Hawkesbury felt no need to leave office with his chief and with Canning: the issue would remain to rankle and divide. As Foreign Secretary he was responsible for the negotiations which led to the Peace of Amiens but was rightly sceptical about Napoleon's intentions. He did well to insist on holding on to the island of Malta which served as pretext for the French resuming the war. After Addington's fall Pitt offered him the Home Secretaryship. Pitt's opinion was lukewarm: valuable in the House of Lords (where he sat from December 1803, now Baron Hawkesbury), he was not a man 'to whose decisions, singly I would commit a great question of policy'. George III thought otherwise and on Pitt's death he sent for him. Hawkesbury, however, advised him to forget the past and summon Fox. If public spirited, it was also well judged. The Whigs had belatedly accepted the war – let them now try to run it! The field was left to Grenville, Fox and The Talents, but Hawkesbury was given the valuable Wardenship of the Cinque Ports which had been Pitt's. Fox died and The Talents predictably failed. Hawkesbury returned to serve under Portland in an administration which was virtually a committee of four: Castlereagh, Canning, Spencer Perceval and himself. The quarrel between Castlereagh and Canning brought Portland down and ensured that future Tory administrations would be weakened by the absence of one or the other. Defeatist about the war the Whigs were stiff in their political demands: they would come in as a party or not at all. So Perceval grasped the reins: an untried leader at a dark moment when victory seemed far off. Liverpool (he had inherited the Earldom the previous year) took on the crucial post, Secretary for War and the Colonies.

Wellington, embattled in the Peninsula, would have harsh things to say about supply, but to Liverpool he owed unfailing support through all parliamentary storms – and the free hand he needed. When Perceval was assassinated, in May 1812, and Liverpool became Prime Minister, the Peninsular policy had been vindicated and Wellington was on the high road to victory. Napoleon was bound for Moscow and a calamity that would do more than all Wellington's victories to destroy him. But the nation was in the throes of an economic crisis for which war with America and the Orders in Council, the government's retaliation to Napoleon's economic warfare, were held responsible.

The Prince Regent would have preferred a coalition but without Whig co-operation he had to accept Liverpool. The latter wooed the Canningites with the promise that the Catholic question would remain 'open', but without success. He then faced a vote of no confidence in the Commons and resigned. Wellesley and Moira tried in vain to form governments. So in June 1812 Liverpool resumed, second best for all but the Regent and his closest colleagues. No man had come to the top with a wider experience of the great offices. He was transparently honest. He would work in the spirit of his family motto: '*Palma non sine pulvere*'. In practical terms of government he was the indispensable co-ordinator of men and measures. Few could have guessed in 1812 that he would still be thought so ten years on.

To see the war through, to hold a firm course in the depressed post-war economic climate, to encourage and help steer reforming measures – these were to be Liverpool's tasks. He was sustained by the diplomatic skill of Castlereagh and the authority of the victor of Waterloo (brought in as Master of Ordnance in 1819). After 1822, he had Huskisson in the key post of President of the Board of Trade, and Peel, High Tory with a taste for pragmatic reform, following the unimaginative Sidmouth as Home Secretary. Canning had resigned over the Queen's divorce in 1820; in 1822 he became Foreign Secretary following Castlereagh's suicide. So that year has been seen as the dividing line between two phases of the premiership. Yet the

obituarist of the *Annual Register* would stress the importance of continuity in policy: 'The alterations in the Silk Trade, the Navigation
Laws, the Corn Laws, in the whole system, in short, of the duties and
prohibitions, had taken place under Lord Liverpool's authority and
with his approval. His character at the same time was to the public
a sufficient pledge that love of novelty and theory would not be
allowed to run into extravagance ...'

The legislative record was not so barren before 1822, nor so fertile
after it, as to justify a clear distinction between the two periods.
Canning was brought into Cabinet in 1816 (the Board of Control)
and Robinson in 1818 (Board of Trade) respectively. Huskisson
had Liverpool's ear from 1814. He supported the Corn Law of
1815. Canning, like Wilberforce, supported the Six Acts. In 1812
Protestant dissenters had been freed from the relics of penal legislation. In 1814 a generous peace was made with the United States. In
1819 final steps were taken towards resumption of cash payments.
In the same year the Factory Acts gave some protection to children
in cotton mills; in 1820 the first Truck Act was passed. Apart from
the work of Peel at the Home Office after 1822, economic revival
contributed as much as new ministers to the reforms of the 'liberal
period'.

Was the government in the immediate post-war years unneces-
sarily repressive? What of Disraeli's charge that Liverpool was
'peremptory in little questions and great ones he left open'? One
great question was Catholic Emancipation: always divisive, potentially destructive, it had to be left open if Canning and Eldon were
to serve together. Did Disraeli fairly weigh the circumstances of the
time? Population was rising at an unprecedented rate; 400,000 men
were demobilised and left to find work. Trade, with dependent
manufactures, some temporarily boosted by war demand, took time
to recover. The lack of civil police compelled the use of troops in
affairs like that of St Peter's Fields (1819). The turbulence within old
cities like London and Bristol, the congestion and squalor of those
which had expanded beyond traditional parish boundaries and
sanctions, posed a constant threat. Machine breaking expressed the
despair of threatened craftsmen. Flaming ricks and barns advertised
rural misery. The cost of Poor Law relief rose inexorably. Ministers
did not have to invent a terrorist threat. Besides demonstrations and
random riots, like that of Spa Fields (1816), there was cold-blooded
revolutionary plotting. The object of the Cato Street conspiracy

(1819) was to murder the whole Cabinet. Liverpool had misgivings about the action of the magistrates and yeomanry at Peterloo; possibly he should have condemned it as a blunder. But the notorious Six Acts, introduced afterwards to clear up the law about public meetings and prevent a revolutionary outbreak, were more a reasonable precaution than instrument of bigoted repression. No friend to Liverpool, Earl Grey wrote that the 'the leaders of the popular party ... wanted not Reform but Revolution'. No government would opt to have Byron, Shelley and Cobbett among its critics. Their indignation and eloquence have coloured the picture. What Liverpool also heard were clamorous appeals for extraordinary government action, even for the formation of 'armed associations of the well-disposed' – a sure way of fomenting civil war. To his credit Liverpool held calmly to a middle course, between worried magistrates and radicals and agitators. There was a personal cost.

For a successful politician Liverpool was unusually sensitive. He seemed to be genuinely upset by criticism. 'Blinkinson', as Canning called him, was notorious for the twitches and fidgets which betrayed the strains. Periods of depression were more likely to be caused by friction in Cabinet than by public concerns. But colleagues admired, even warmed to him. An opponent's witness is more compelling. Lord Dacre spoke for Queen Caroline in the Lords where Liverpool had the embarrassing task of defending the interest of George IV. To him Liverpool was 'very able and the honestest man that could be dealt with. You may always trust him ... he will not mis-represent you.' Like Baldwin in the abdication crisis of 1936, Liverpool was at his best in such a messy case as this, when issues were complex and public personalities cruelly exposed. His essential respectability was reassuring. He stood above scandal or suspicion of personal gain. Canning realised the extent to which ministry, King and country depended on Liverpool at this time. 'Nothing but plain management, or rather absence of all management will suit the crisis; and happily Liverpool stands in a situation in which his own word will carry him through.' As representatives of the old political order came to terms with the new politics, neither the younger Pitt nor Peel did more than Liverpool to reconcile the rising, soon to be enfranchised, middle classes to the ways of Westminster. The elder Pitt had thought it worth while to parade his honesty as a political virtue; a hundred years later it was taken for granted.

Liverpool 'had no habit of any but official employment'. He could be benign, even unreserved with friends, but when he unbent it was usually with an effort. When he tried to be gay he risked being ridiculous. Princess Lieven made a conquest of him – so she boasted. One evening, 'after a long and solemn dinner, he amused us by the odd fancy of jumping over the back of a big sofa, on which I was seated, and establishing himself on a little footstool in front of me. The great Liverpool hovered and then settled on the ground, looking very comic.' Canning encountered him in Bath in 'a huge pair of jackboots, of the size and colour of fire buckets'. The laughter was rarely malicious and he continued to be respected. There was sufficient thought behind his actions to set him apart from the mere technicians. To read him on the subject of the old representative system is to find a conservatism that was not blind but deep. The House of Commons was 'merely a deliberative assembly. Public opinion ought never to have such weight as to prevent their exercising their deliberative functions.' Of course 'the landed interest is the stamina of the country'. In 1821 he intervened to prevent the representation of the disenfranchised borough of Grampound being given to Leeds, and to give it to the county of Yorkshire instead: to confer upon 'the populous manufacturing towns' the right of election 'would subject the population to a perpetual factious canvass, which would divert more or less the people from their industrious habits and keep alive a permanent spirit of turbulence and disaffection among them ... I do not wish to see more of such boroughs as Westminster, Southwark and Nottingham. I believe them to be more corrupt than any other places when seriously contested ... and the persons who find their way into Parliament from such places are generally those ... who are least likely to be attached to the good order of society.' The principles of representation mattered less to him than the end product.

Liverpool's part in the evolution of economic policy was important from the start: 'When it was asked what should be done to make commerce prosper, the answer was *laissez faire*.' In 1820 he told a free trade deputation that the principle of agricultural protection was wrong: 'Some believe that we have risen because of that system. Others, of whom I am one, believe that we have risen despite that system.' Capitalists should be left 'to find out the way in which their capital could best be employed' and 'on all commercial subjects the fewer laws the better'. To his credit, however, he defended the bill of 1818 to regulate the hours of children in cotton factories: to have free labour there must be free agents; children were not so – and were harmed by excessive labour. Under Liverpool the duties of the First Lord of the Treasury were not nominal. Unlike Perceval he had a Chancellor of the Exchequer but he was still regarded as an assistant. Liverpool guided fiscal policy. After Robinson succeeded Vansittart in 1823 his direction became, if anything, firmer. He also acted as link between fiscal and commercial policies. Huskisson had been an intimate since 1814 and the introduction of free trade measures into Robinson's budgets reflects not only the influence of Huskisson over Robinson, but also Liverpool's personal interest.

In matters of foreign policy Liverpool was fortunate to be served by Castlereagh, then by Canning. Though he supported him loyally he had little sympathy with Castlereagh's European outlook, his close association with Metternich. After 1822 he identified himself closely with Canning's liberalism. The majority of the Cabinet had been in sympathy with Castlereagh. Canning was inevitably regarded with suspicion, though more because of the tone of his pronouncements than for what he did. Liverpool had therefore to come out in open support. He knew that British interests required that Canning should remain Foreign Secretary but that effective government depended upon the 'ultras'. His nerves were frayed by the furious exchanges in Cabinet between Wellington and Canning. Liverpool's success in reconciling the factions; in creating a situation in which positive measures of government could receive general consent, is emphasised by events after his retirement. 'Ours is not, nor ever has been, a controversial cabinet upon any subject,' said Wellington in 1821. That was hardly true after 1822. Yet the crucial policy statement, 'that it is the opinion of the Cabinet that any further step to be taken toward the South American states should be decided without reference to the opinions and wishes of the Continental allied powers' was made with only one dissenting voice. Liverpool tackled the formidable Wellington on the South American issue with courage and tact. After the government decision of December 1824 to recommend that the King recognise the South American republics, Canning acknowledged what he owed to Liverpool. 'Spanish America is free and, if we do not mismanage our affairs sadly, she is English ... You will see how nobly Liverpool fought with me on this occasion.'

It is only rarely that we find measures which were Liverpool's own and reflect his special interests. One such was the grant of a million pounds in 1818 for the building of new churches, another half million being allocated from the repayment of the Austrian loan in 1824. From the same source came £60,000 towards the purchase of pictures from the Angerstein collection for a National Gallery. It is appropriate that Lawrence's portrait of Liverpool should show him holding the charter of the National Gallery. Earnest in a mildly evangelical way, civilised as well as learned, Liverpool may not have acted decisively enough to leave the idea of a great man, with con-temporaries or in the history books. By any standards he was a good man and successful Prime Minister. After the stroke that enforced retirement he lingered, semi-conscious, for nearly two years. He died in December 1828. By then Canning too had died. Robinson, now Lord Goderich, had tried, and failed, to govern. Wellington, Prime Minister, and Peel had already decided that Catholic Emancipation must be granted. Predictably this split the Tories, already weakened by the death of Huskisson and the loss, therefore of Canningite support. Recovery would be slow and painful. But the strength of Toryism has ever been to adapt to circumstances while standing firm on essential principles. Liverpool had done enough to ensure that some of its best features survived, to re-appear in later Conservative governments.

N. Gash, *Lord Liverpool* (1984).

George Canning

GEORGE CANNING (1770-1827) became Prime Minister in April 1827 and died in August. Before that he had been in high office for only seven years, as Foreign Secretary from 1807 to 1809 and from 1822 to 1827. His story reveals less about the office of Prime Minister and the workings of Cabinet government than about a remarkable individual who left an indelible mark on political life. Clues to a career in which he often seemed to be his own worst enemy lie in his Irish family. His father, disinherited heir to a family of Ulster gentry, died when he was one. His mother, Mary Anne Costello, became an actress, then a draper, to support herself and a growing family. Embarrassed, but fond, Canning said that it was to her that he devoted his first years in politics. A financier uncle sent him to Eton, where he shone, before Christ Church, where political ambition went fittingly with scholarship. Lincoln's Inn and a legal practice were but a source of income while waiting for office. In 1800 he married an heiress, Joan Scott, became the Duke of Portland's brother-in-law, and gained financial independence.

Intellectual and ideologue, a romantic individualist in spirit, an actor in style, Canning entered Parliament for the Treasury borough of Newport in 1793. It would be his stolid Oxford friend Jenkinson (later Liverpool) who would come first through the ruck to be Prime Minister. Brilliant, eloquent and witty, Canning was surely destined for the summit. And yet – Liverpool's fifteen years in power? That is unimaginable in Canning. It was not that he chose to swim against the tide. Whig speeches and style had first appealed to the exhibitionist in him. But the French Revolution challenged him and he read Burke. The author of *Reflections* (1790) would be his inspiration as he came to value orderly constitutional development and to detest radical theories. A more fervent patriot never breathed. None was more loud for John Bull than the editor of the *Anti-Jacobin* (1797).

The erratic career, high promise tantalisingly unfulfilled, may be recognised; also the type of politician: prone to intrigue, to live dangerously, bid high, create discomfort by sudden resignation.

In Canning's case personal loyalty counted for much – as notably to Pitt, mentor and idol. And yet his motives were often suspect, his actions seen to be perverse or insincere. He did not think to conceal his ambition. To slower minds it was disconcerting to encounter intellect thus on parade. One can hear the damning verdict: 'too clever by half'.

Canning's friendship with Pitt was based on a true attraction: mind and principles. Here was an admirable model of statesmanship, lofty, austere, patriotic, Roman. Pitt tried to guide Canning to a steady political career. But subordinate offices, Under-Secretary for Foreign Affairs (1796); in the second administration Treasurer of the Navy (1804), were not enough for Canning. Men saw self-promotion and restlessness, as if he could not bear to stand behind others on the political stage. In 1797, with several others, he started the *Anti-Jacobin*. It confirmed the suspicions of those who saw him as a 'light, jesting, paragraph-making man' – unfairly, for the message was serious. Canning believed that Britain should be 'the animating soul' of Europe's resistance and that there should be no negotiation until oppressed nations were delivered. By virtue of superior institutions, rights and liberties enshrined in law, Britain had a special responsibility for opposing revolutionary France. Guard the constitution against Jacobins at home and abroad. That was his message. Britain must be great in order to be happy. In war and peace it would be his master principle.

In 1801 Canning resigned with Pitt over the question of Catholic Emancipation. Devotion to 'the pilot who weathered the storm', opposition to a policy of appeasement, made him attack Addington's government with such venom that his motives were suspect even to those who shared his concern and enjoyed his aphorisms. Pitt would not follow Canning's 'ungovernable ambition' nor harass his successor. When he did resume office the quarrel between Addingtonians and Canningites disrupted his ministry. Pitt dead, Canning held no office in Grenville's 'Ministry of All the Talents', but with the Portland ministry of 1807 he entered the promised land. As Foreign Minister he could act on the principles he had so boldly espoused. The seizure of the Danish fleet in 1807 was a typical Canning stroke. His ardour for total war pleased supporters. But he was always looking a move ahead: now to what would follow the ailing Portland. He would not confine himself to his own department. He criticised Cabinet colleagues, notably Castlereagh, the war minister, responsible for the ill-fated Walcheren expedition. Fraught times, huge responsibilities on a few shoulders, taut nerves – help explain what followed. Hearing that Canning had plotted to oust him Castlereagh challenged Canning, with reasons stretching to three folio sheets. 'I would rather fight than read it,' declared Canning. On 21 September 1809, at 6am, on Putney Heath, at the height of a great war, two of His Majesty's leading ministers fought their duel. Castlereagh lost a button, Canning a piece of his thigh. Both men had to resign. Of the two careers Canning's was also the more damaged.

He rebuffed Perceval's attempts to reunite 'the separated members' of Pitt's party. Foreign Office or nothing – but when it was offered, in 1812, by Liverpool, he turned it down rather than serve under Castlereagh as Leader of the House. Canning was unwise to demand a free hand in policymaking. 'Too fond of writing and too touchy,' commented the Prince Regent. 'Why will not great politicians look at least one year before them?' asked Lansdowne. Two years and the war would be won – and it was Castlereagh who was in place to negotiate.

Canning was in his element at the 1812 contest at Liverpool, as successful candidate for the liberal merchants. With Brougham as opponent, there was a feast of rhetoric and reason. With new men and commercial interests to appeal to, we glimpse the future: a lively debate about national issues, wider representation. But it would take years in the wilderness to bring Whigs to espouse reform. Canning, the minister best able to reach beyond Westminster, would have none of it. Indeed he was the most eloquent defender of the old political order.

In July 1813 Canning formally disbanded his party. By now, it was said, 'they dined fourteen and voted twelve'. Talent, not party interest, would decide his future. Meanwhile he was content to become ambassador to Portugal, at an unprecedented £14,000 a year. Canning thanked Liverpool 'not from politician to politician but with the genuine warmth of old Christ Church feelings'.

In June 1816 Canning went to the Board of Control where, for four and a half years, he brought to the administration of India a stretch of mind, a well-focused work, that highlight the wasted years out of office. But there was another resignation, in December 1820, over the government's plan to deal with Queen Caroline and the Cabinet's plan to implement George IV's wish to divorce her.

He had long been friendly towards her. Now he defended her case in the Commons. Ministers were embarrassed. Canning's prospects were bleak when he accepted the Governor-Generalship of India.

He was about to sail, in August 1822, when Castlereagh killed himself, victim to overwork, possibly a threat of blackmail. Canning went back to the Foreign Office that he regarded as his rightful domain. Liverpool's administration took on a new lease of life. Canning could now mould foreign policy. He distrusted the practice of diplomacy by conference; he had not experienced its value, as at Vienna, in the context of a general settlement. By 1822 collaboration between Britain and the Holy Alliance was breaking down. So Canning's arrival signified less a change of direction than of style. He could interpret British interest in a way that Liverpool merchant and Manchester mill-owner could understand. He would not interfere on behalf of revolution. He did not 'suppose that we alone could regenerate Europe'. But he would not approve military action to impose an absolutist regime. The French invasion of Spain in August 1823 prompted him to start dealing with the American states. In sympathy with the principles of President Monroe and pressed by London merchants, braving the outrage of George IV, Britain recognised the republics of Buenos Aires, Mexico and Colombia as sovereign states. Later Canning mediated to secure the independence of Brazil. He sent a fleet and troops to Lisbon to protect King Pedro against Spanish interference on behalf of the absolutist Miguel. In Parliament he asserted memorably that he 'called the New World into existence to redress the balance of the Old.' Over the issue of Greek independence, following the revolt (1822) against Turkish rule he was first neutral. He would not join in a conference which Czar Alexander could use to promote Russian influence. The Turks recovered ground. Fortunately for Canning the Greeks asked him to mediate. Alexander died and Wellington went to deal with his successor Nicholas. The Treaty of London (July 1827) subsequently brought France into an Anglo-Russian agreement to enforce an armistice on the Turks. Canning was then Prime Minister. When Codrington destroyed Ibrahim's Turkish fleet in Navarino Bay he had been dead for two months.

In the eyes of Europe Canning was the greatest Englishman: prime mover and shaker in the wider world. The King approved his policies when he saw they were popular. Canning reached out boldly to a wider public. He was the first Foreign Minister to explain his policies in platform speeches. But he could not induce trust in his colleagues. When Canning committed himself to a measure of Catholic Emancipation it was as a rational, considered policy, recognising the inevitable. Wellington and Peel would have to eat their words. Meanwhile, with four other Cabinet Ministers, they refused to serve. There were forty-two resignations from government and household. The Tory split was irremediable. Again Canning had disrupted his party. But Wellington should share responsibility. It would be his lot, ironically, to preside over the demise of the confessional state. Huskisson and Robinson stayed and, with Whig forbearance, Canning was able to cobble together a coalition. It was power of a sort, but less than he had enjoyed as Foreign Minister of the world's leading state. He was a tired man. He had always been an exceptionally rapid worker. 'He could not bear to dictate', said one of his secretaries, 'because nobody could keep up with him.' He was known, when incapacitated by gout in his hand, to dictate two despatches at once to different secretaries. He wrote and spoke incessantly. By 1827 he was already dosing himself with laudanum. He had caught a chill at the Duke of York's funeral; he caught another in Lord Lyndhurst's garden in July. Resistance was low. Personal attacks had 'rent that proud heart'. As sure as Castlereagh was killed by overwork so was he; 'just as much as any poor horse that drops dead in the road', wrote Dudley. Like life his power was held on a short lease. The Whigs would soon show their reforming hand. He saw, more clearly than most that there was coming, in his words, 'a great struggle between property and population'. Such a struggle is only to be averted by 'the mildest and most liberal legislation'. Without Canning the Tories could not win – or avoid this struggle. He was buried in the Abbey, next to Pitt. It was his rightful place.

W. Hinde, *George Canning* (1973).

Earl of Ripon

FREDERICK JOHN ROBINSON, VISCOUNT GODERICH, 1ST EARL OF RIPON (1782-1859) was Prime Minister for only five months (1827-8). Unable to master his colleagues, to secure even the semblance of harmony from the reluctant coalition which passed for a Cabinet or, at the end, to keep his nerve, he resigned in despair. Financial ability, a sensitive and philosophic mind, and a pleasant, witty House of Commons manner had carried 'Prosperity' Robinson far, up to that point. He was reluctant to take the Treasury, unexpectedly vacated by Canning's death. He did not believe that he was up to it, and events proved him right. There is greater interest in the factors, economic and intellectual, that affected his rise to the summit than in what he did when he got there.

He was the second son of the second Lord Grantham and of Lady Mary Yorke. At Harrow he was the schoolfellow of two future Prime Ministers, Aberdeen and Palmerston. After his time at St John's College, Cambridge, aristocratic connections eased the path for the promising recruit. After serving for two years as Private Secretary to the Lord Lieutenant of Ireland, his uncle, the third Earl of Hardwicke, he was elected to Parliament for the Irish borough of Carlow, and in the following year, for Ripon, which he represented for twenty years. He was promoted to minor offices in the administrations of Perceval (1809) and Liverpool (1812). He soon resigned from the first (he was Under-Secretary for the Colonies) in sympathy with Castlereagh. He strengthened this alliance when he accompanied Castlereagh to Vienna in 1814. Meanwhile (1813) he had married Lady Sarah Hobart, daughter of the Earl of Buckinghamshire.

It was as Liverpool's Vice-President of the Board of Trade that it fell to him to introduce the 'Corn Law' which prohibited the importation of corn until the home price had reached 80s a quarter, a figure which all but the agricultural interest thought too high. He did so 'with the greatest reluctance', and suffered for it. A mob wrecked his house in Old Burlington Street and destroyed some valuable pictures. His inclination was towards greater freedom of trade. In January 1818 Liverpool enabled him to take steps in this direction as President of the Board of Trade. In May 1820 he told Parliament that 'the restrictive system of commerce in this country was founded in error, and calculated to defeat the object for which it was adopted.'

In January 1823 Robinson was given the chance to go further in the direction of reform when he became Chancellor of the Exchequer, for his successor at the Board of Trade was Huskisson. The two men worked together under Liverpool's direction in the 'economic cabinet' to promote fiscal liberalism. They were assisted by a revival of trade and a climate of opinion increasingly favourable to the axioms and policies of the 'classical economists', Adam Smith the master and David Ricardo the foremost tutor. He was lucky to be able to reduce taxation, but he used his position skilfully, combining the lowering of such taxes as that on windows with the reduction of the debt, and grants for such objects as the purchase of the Angerstein collection for a national gallery, and the erection of buildings for the British Museum. In his Free Trade Budget of 1824 he proposed to use his surplus 'as a means of commencing a system of alterations in the fiscal and commercial regulations of his country.' For the silk trade, for example, this meant the reduction of duties on the raw silk and end of the ban on importation of the manufactured. Stemming from trust in the vitality of British commerce and gambling on its capacity to engender wealth, the policy was brave – and it succeeded.

Robinson had 'the art of enlivening even dry subjects of finance with classical allusions and pleasant humour' (Le Marchant). His style may be studied in his third budget, of 1825. Before reducing a wide range of duties he congratulated the House on the prosperity of the country and invited members to 'contemplate with instructive admiration the harmony of its proportions and the solidity of its basis.' He would not be the last of expansion-minded Chancellors to have had to swallow their budget boasts. Before the end of the year a commercial crisis caused primarily by the over-issue of paper money forced Robinson to prevent the issue of notes under £5. Evidence of mounting distress in 1826 did not, however, deter him from a sanguine assessment of the country's situation in his budget. It was indeed remarkable, as Harriet Martineau pointed out, what different conclusions 'Prosperity Robinson' (Cobbett's name for him) and 'Adversity Hume' could draw from identical statistics.

Robinson wanted Liverpool to promote him to the House of Lords and a less onerous post. When Canning became Prime Minister he was created Viscount Goderich and Secretary of State for War and the Colonies. His failure to uphold the government's position in the Lords against Wellington and the High Tories, relentless in opposition to Canning, should have disqualified him for higher office. But when Canning died George IV chose him to form a Cabinet. A stronger man than 'goody Goderich' might have failed to create the solid front needed to tackle the urgent question of Catholic Emancipation and devise some way of meeting the growing pressure for parliamentary reform. For him it was torment from the start. Even as Chancellor he had expressed his dread of 'the labour and confinement of the situation'. Now he had to direct and found that he couldn't.

He began badly by yielding to the King, as it appeared to his colleagues, over the appointment of High Tory Herries to the exchequer. Herries quarrelled bitterly with Huskisson over the chairmanship of the finance committee. Robinson was surprisingly defeatist. In Cabinet meetings he was ill at ease, his sudden tearful collapses in odd contrast to the bland face he normally presented. It was perhaps fortunate that he never had to face Parliament. On 8 January he resigned – yet seems to have been surprised that he was offered no place by his successor, Wellington.

He supported both the Catholic Emancipation Bill and the Repeal of the Test and Corporation Acts. In 1830, no longer even nominally Tory, he was back on the government bench as Grey's Secretary of War and the Colonies. Old colleagues may have been sceptical about his commitment 'after a sacrifice of many pre-conceived opinions ... and of many long-cherished notions' to parliamentary reform under a Whig Prime Minister. But it probably represented his true position – a mild and guarded liberalism. When his proposals for the abolition of slavery were deemed unacceptable Stanley succeeded him and he became Lord Privy Seal and Earl of Ripon. With Stanley he resigned over the appointment of the Irish Church Commission (May 1834). Ignoring his inconsistent record, valuing his experience Peel made him President of the Board of Trade in 1841. In 1843 he went to the Board of Control. It was fitting that he should move the second reading of the bill for the abolition of the Corn Laws in 1846 – and subsequently resign with Peel.

Ripon died at his house on Putney Heath in January 1859. He was buried at Nocton in Lincolnshire; he had always seized any chance of escaping to his Lincolnshire estate. He managed to give some the impression of wanting the fruits of office while being less enthusiastic about its toils. Yet he is important. Though unwilling at times to stand up for his convictions, as over the Corn Laws, and more administrator than leader, he had been foremost among those politicians, responsive to the commercial spirit of the age, who linked the age of Pitt to that of Peel. That may serve as a more fitting epitaph than the dry observation of Lord Crewe: 'His political convictions were limited to those announced by the diverse governments of which he was a member.'

Duke of Wellington

ARTHUR WELLESLEY, 1ST DUKE OF WELLINGTON (1769-1852) was Prime Minister from 1828 to 1830. He is one of the indisputably great figures in British history, a hero to meet the demands and dreams of the new pride in country and Empire: the idea that being British meant a superior, God-given place in the world, with responsibilities to match. Opinion may differ as to whether he was a greater soldier than Napoleon. It is enough to observe that he was free to savour his fame while Napoleon brooded in Saint Helena: his the indignity of ultimate defeat; Wellington's the lustre and authority of continuous victories. In 1815 he was the first man in Europe. In domestic politics that was a mixed blessing. Like Coriolanus he was at different times the most popular and the most hated man in the land.

He was the fourth son of the first Earl of Mornington and Anne Hill-Trevor, daughter of Lord Dungannon. Theirs was an old Irish family: the name Wellesley had only been added to that of Colley in 1728. A rather solitary boy, he would later be stonily reticent about his boyhood. He left Eton at fifteen, a dim figure after the brilliant career of his elder brother Richard. At the military school of Angers he learned some French and made the acquaintance of local nobles. Friends said it made a man of him; it certainly made him a soldier. At eighteen he was gazetted ensign in the 73rd Highland Regiment. Aide to the Lord Lieutenant, the Duke of Buckingham, he enjoyed Dublin society but found time for serious pursuits. He gambled heavily – but read Locke. Was he impressed by the philosopher's argument that all knowledge is derived from experience? It was with insufficient experience, in 1793, that he wooed Kitty Pakenham, then 17; his offer was rejected by her parents since his prospects were uncertain. Later, and famous, he would honour his pledge.

War called and he advanced by purchase to a lieutenant-colonelcy in the 33rd Foot. In a serious fit he burned his beloved violin; he would be a soldier without distraction. The next twenty-two years, mainly spent in India or in Spain, would bring fame: no single experience of defeat; Indian successes of high importance to Richard, Governor-General, 'the glorious little man', and to the *raj*; stubborn endurance, then a sequence of victories in Spain. Only the name of Nelson could match that of the victor of Assaye and Argaum, Vimiero, Busaco, Torres Vedras, Talavera, Vittoria, the battles of the Pyrenees – and Waterloo. Could such a man have a subordinate political role? How would he fare at the top?

For some his military reputation constituted an instant prejudice. 'A man educated in camps and ignorant of the British constitution', wrote Ellenborough in 1823. 'The duke is a soldier,' wrote Scott in 1826, 'a bad education for a statesman in a free country.' The country was free but conditions were unsettled; for many – his old soldiers among them – precarious and grim. Wellington was indeed authoritarian but he revered the constitution and was far from ignorant of it. His idea of right did not always meet the expectations of colleagues; his idea of loyalty related more to his personal judgement than to his party. But he viewed 'party' as an outsider: at best a coalition of varied interests and views.

On the face of it he was primarily a soldier, so successful that he might be expected to apply military methods in any situation. When he formed his government in 1828 the Cabinet insisted upon his giving up command of the Army. It was feared that he would insist upon martial law. Yet the evidence of his Cabinet career refutes the view that he was simply a disciplinarian who sought military solutions.

From youth he had been a politician as well as a soldier, though his experience was limited to five years, from 1790, as MP for Trim in the Irish Parliament. It was normal for a soldier or sailor to have a parallel political career – and natural for the victor of Waterloo to wish to continue to serve his country. He had always impressed men as being thoughtful and dedicated. 'Why, I have learned what not to do, and that is always something', he declared after serving under the Duke of York. He sailed out to India with a library: military history, but also law, economics and theology. Like Napoleon in this one respect he was hungry for knowledge. Dr Warren examined him before leaving for India: 'A young man', he said, 'whose conversation is the most extraordinary I have ever listened to ... if he lives he must one day be Prime Minister.'

He was a master of the calculated risk. Against the odds and often in danger he took full advantage of the opportunities offered by his brother's aggressive policy. After an inspired guess about a ford, which enabled him to outflank the enemy at Assaye, he declared: 'When one is strongly intent on an object, common sense will usually direct one to the right means.' It was the 'no nonsense' approach he would bring to politics.

After re-acquainting himself with the Irish scene as Chief Secretary (1807) and another dip into Parliament (representing the convenient boroughs of Rye, then Newport) he was sent to Spain, in 1808, to accomplish 'the absolute evacuation of the Peninsula by the troops of France.' After heartening victories he was superseded in command and required to put his name to the Convention of Cintra, providing for the evacuation of Portugal by the French. From public outcry, party venom and a court of inquiry at which he was exonerated, he learned bitter lessons about factious politicians and the fickle mob. But he believed that Portugal could be held. Castlereagh believed in him and sent him back. His staunch character and fine judgement would be a model for Wellington's political career. Meanwhile, in an epic of sustained campaigning, he acquired experience and a philosophy that would always serve him well. His dispatches reveal a clear and powerful mind. He learned to take the long view, to read the mind of his opponent, to weigh odds, to value good professional service, to castigate the amateurish and slipshod. He ever preached the importance of attending to detail, of careful planning. 'Minute and constant attendance to orders' was his constant message. He also revealed a hardiness and self-discipline which earned loyalty from his men and would be his habit for life. He could sound brutally frank, not least about his own troops: were they not 'the scum of the earth enlisted for drink'? If they responded with loyalty and respect is it because they relished the plain speaking and his belief in what they could achieve when well led? The matter-of-fact way in which he spoke of the hazards and horrors of war was his way of coping. He was far from callous. He came off the battlefield of Waterloo in a state of emotional shock. He had been at the centre of battle all day. After receiving reports of casualties which, his doctor reported, made tears splash down, making furrows in the sweat and grime, he sat down to write the Waterloo dispatch: it covered four days of fighting from 15 to 18 June and filled four columns in *The Times*. He had the strength to overcome emotion and to answer the call of duty. It would characterise the 'Iron Duke' of peacetime Britain.

Wellington also brought to politics a considerable diplomatic experience. For three years he served as commander-in-chief of the army of occupation in Paris. It was he who induced Louis XVIII to accept Talleyrand and Fouché as advisors. He opposed resolutely, with Castlereagh's agreement, the dismemberment of France, and reprisals. He also persuaded the House of Baring to advance a loan to the French government which enabled them to discharge their indemnity within three years. The recovery of France, so necessary to the equilibrium of Europe, owed much to his moderation. The statesmen of 1919 would have done well to follow his example.

Back in England in 1818 he became Master of Ordnance under Liverpool with a place in Cabinet. When George IV harassed his ministers by demanding that they support a divorce bill against Queen Caroline, his firmness was invaluable to Liverpool. His generally moderate and practical outlook contributed to the successes of Tory government in the more prosperous conditions of the early 'twenties. It was unfortunate therefore that the unity for which he worked should have been marred by his quarrel with Canning. He had helped put Canning back into the Foreign Office after the death of Castlereagh, but he opposed Canning's most important decision: recognition of the independence of the Spanish colonies. There was a strong personal antipathy too. 'It was not what the duke said', wrote Arbuthnot in 1825, 'but what he looked.' He was sufficiently loyal to Liverpool and to his own ideal of non-partisan government not to join with the 'ultra' peers to undermine Canning's position. But when Canning was chosen to succeed Liverpool as Prime Minister in 1827 he refused to serve under him, and was supported by Peel. Ostensibly the issue was Catholic Emancipation – but the real cause was personal. Uncharacteristically Wellington had allowed himself to act in the spirit of faction. He was the only man at that juncture who could have preserved Tory unity. It was, in Feiling's words, 'the end of a party'.

In January 1828, after Goderich had succeeded Canning as head of a Canningite-Whig alliance of convenience, and it had broken down, the King sent for Wellington. He formed his Cabinet in such a way as to restore the balance of Liverpool's government. Huskisson and three other Canningites were included. They objected when he wished to adjust the new Corn Law to favour home-produced grain. He therefore accepted their resignations, knowing that they could no longer turn to the Whigs and were therefore politically impotent.

By midsummer of 1828, with O'Connell enjoying popular support for his open defiance, he was faced with the choice: Emancipation or civil war in Ireland? He chose Emancipation, and stood firm, with Peel, against an emotional storm which would have overturned a lesser man. Not only at Oxford, where Peel lost his seat, but among responsible Tories such as Winchelsea – with whom Wellington fought a duel! – there was a sense of betrayal. 'It is a bad business', he told Sidmouth, 'but we are aground.' Conducting the measure through the Lords he showed familiarity not only with Ireland but with the concordats of Catholic countries; he resisted the diehards and wrested permission from the King. 'The people of England', he told a friend, 'must be governed by people who are not afraid.' Unfortunately more than firmness was required of a Prime Minister. He must be sensitive to other men's views; he must be prepared to delegate. Wellington tended to regard opposition as disloyalty and he took too much on himself. He need not have lost Huskisson. A subtler politician might have seen that Huskisson's resignation was a bargaining counter over the redistribution of seats. Only an instinctive conservative would have blocked the imaginative scheme for a modified income tax at a time when government needed a diversion from the reform issue. He was a poor public speaker – the worst Carlyle had ever heard. He took too much on himself. He should have listened to his beloved Mrs Arbuthnot: 'It can never be right that the First Lord of the Treasury should be consulted as to who should be colonel of the Life Guards.' We see the strength of Lord Eldon's complaint that the Duke was a man not of reason but of determination. But we see too that Wellington's instinct for what was possible had led him to a momentous step. Catholic Emancipation, following the less controversial Repeal of the Test and Nonconformity Acts, would prove to be a landmark in the evolution of Britain from confessional to secular state.

In 1830 George IV died. After the ensuing general election Wellington failed to adjust his position. Did he misread the message of an election where reform was an issue – but more than half the constituencies were uncontested? He rejected the idea of taking Grey into his Cabinet. But he could only hold off the Whig leader, now openly committed to reform, if he had the solid support of the country gentlemen. Unfortunately they were alienated by his refusal to take steps to deal with the worsening condition of agriculture. The July revolution in France stirred radicals, alarmed others. Along with a trade depression, distress in towns and countryside, and threatening disturbances, went a growing conviction that there must be a government initiative, more than an empty gesture or fiddling measure. Wellington's instinct, however, was to stand firm. Was not Peel's new metropolitan police force capable of dealing with a London mob? Or, if necessary, the military? So he made his greatest blunder. When the new parliament met in the autumn of 1830 he declared unequivocally against reform. No ministry could survive if it did not make some move in that direction. Peel was paralysed by the reaction to his recent 'apostasy'. In November, after losing a vote on the Civil List the duke resigned and Grey came in.

Wellington remained immensely important. The tone and tactics of his opposition affected the nature of the struggle, if not the outcome: many from the start regarded it as inevitable, as eventually did he. 'The duke thinks of nothing but his country,' wrote Ellenborough. He certainly would not seek party advantage where the country's security was at stake. When the Belgian question troubled the government he instructed his political lieutenants not to raise the matter in the Commons. We see, however, a tension between two loyalties: to his country, and to what he believed to be the interests of his class. He had an instinctive understanding of the aristocratic ideal. As he later told Peel: 'it is not so easy to make men feel they are of no consequence in the country, who had heretofore so much weight and still preserve their properties ... and their seats in the House of Lords.' But he could also observe that leading Reformers too were aristocrats, and used reform as a means of preserving their rights and influence.

He was an emotional man, iron only on the surface. In private he could be gloomy, exaggerating problems to the point of hysteria. After the successes of the Reform Party in the election of April 1831 he was apparently saying: 'The revolution has begun and nothing could save us.' Even without his intransigence the peers might have voted against the bill in September 1831; again in May 1832. But his stature and his apparent trust in the essential conservatism of the people helped stiffen the 'ultras'. His position was, of course, equivocal. Many of the 'ultras' saw him as the man who had betrayed them over Catholic Emancipation.

The public face was resolute. In May 1832, when Grey resigned, he conceived it his duty to take office, even to introduce a reform measure himself, to repeat his Emancipation move. 'Go for gold,' called Francis Place, to start a run on the banks. His colleague Peel did more than Place – or the mob who broke his windows at Apsley House on a night when his Duchess lay dead in an upper room – to deter him. So he resigned himself to the Whig reform and saved his King from having to implement his promise to create new peers by persuading enough of the old ones to let the bill become law. It is a flawed human story, not an ignoble one.

After the act Wellington handled the Tory peers with tact, complementing Peel's efforts to instruct the party in the Commons. He was Foreign Minister in Peel's minority administration of 1834. Peel did not return to office until 1841. Meanwhile Wellington found himself on the defensive against a phalanx of peers who had found in Lyndhurst a capable 'ultra' leader. In the circumstances the Duke did well to prevent the peers from using their majority to paralyse Whig government: an example of restraint which the Tory leadership of 1909 would have done well to copy. Wellington affirmed his principle that the peers should not oppose the government on a major question, in 1846, when he persuaded them to pass the Corn Law repeal, though personally he did not approve of it. He held no departmental post in Peel's administration of 1841-6, though he was in the Cabinet. He was wrong to resume command of the Army from his old subordinate Hill in 1842. He obstructed necesssary reforms. Vanity, it might be said, betrayed him. It may have been inevitable that he should have become a national monument. He should have been required to resign. The soldier-statesman who had shown that he could make the hardest of political decisions, would have grumbled – but surely understood. He had always done his duty.

The Iron Duke ennobled the life of his time by what he was, as much as by what he did. Laden with honours and titles, familiar with courts and kings, uniquely trusted and revered, he remained entirely uncorrupted. Disraeli declared at the time of his death that he had left his country a great legacy: the contemplation of his character. It remains true.

E. Longford, *Wellington, Pillar of State* (1972).
N. Gash (ed), *Wellington: Studies in the Military and Political Career of the First Duke of Wellington* (1990).

Earl Grey

CHARLES GREY, 2ND EARL GREY (1764-1845) won popular approval and lasting fame as Prime Minister (1830-4) at the time of the Great Reform Bill. Yet his long political career had been spent, with the exception of one year's office, in opposition. Nor could any leader have been less a man of the people. 'The very type of the *grand seigneur*', handsome, with 'the patrician thoroughbred look' that Byron 'doted on', he had entered on political life at twenty-one as member for his native county of Northumberland. He was enjoying his grand tour and did not bother to return for the formality of election.

He was the first surviving son of General Charles Grey, distinguished soldier, and future Earl, and of Elizabeth Grey, a Northumbrian cousin who brought the Falloden estate into the family. When his childless uncle Henry invited him to take over nearby Howick, it became the centre of his existence. His love of family life in this remote place, sheltered by woods, between Cheviots and North Sea, was to be, sometimes, a frustrating fact of political life. Grey might appear at times to be a reluctant politician but it was his concern for the reform of Parliament, and refusal over discouraging years to be deflected from that single issue, which led to the final, crucial, event.

A childhood experience haunted him for life. His nurse took him to see some Jews hanged for forgery at Tyburn; mounted on a grenadier's shoulders he missed no detail of the spectacle. At nine, he went to Eton, and remained there till he was seventeen. He was happier in the more relaxed life of Trinity's spacious courts though he did not take a degree. Cambridge men noted the arrogance of young Grey, his 'superciliousness' and unfavourable view of Eton. And yet the older, wiser man might seem to have exemplified the virtues of the place, and its system, grounded in intensive study of the classics and aimed, in J.R.M. Butler's words, 'at the training of statesmen, at a time when statesmanship consisted largely in winning and retaining the confidence of an assembly of some six hundred gentlemen.' Grey's maiden speech against Pitt's commercial treaty with France was an exercise in the classical oratory learned at Eton. It impressed Addington: 'In the advantage of figure, voice, elocution and manner, he is not surpassed by any member.' Less creditable was his contribution in the affair of the Prince of Wales's marriage: to ensure he was not excluded from regency, Grey and Sheridan denied the existence of George's marriage with Mrs Fitzherbert. Acting so out of character, was this essentially straight-forward man in danger of being spoiled by the flattering attention of women and of a complacent political clique?

Grey's first political associations were formed before the French Revolution came to turn preferences into principles. 'The fashion was to be in opposition ... all the beauty and wit of London was on that side, and the seduction of Devonshire House prevailed' wrote Lady Holland. Her husband held that 'a certain disposition to reform of Parliament' was 'essential in a good Whig'. But Grey went further than most Whigs could approve when, in 1792, he entered the Society of the Friends of the People. But he was no republican. Electoral reform was conceived by the Whigs, along with 'oeconomical' reform, now mainly accomplished, as a way of weakening the position of the Crown in politics, consolidating that of men of property – and of recovering the chance of office. It was less daring, more self-interested than it appears if read outside the context – an apparently unbreakable coalition of conservative interests, Pittite and neo-Tory – and seen as a disinterested effort to redistribute votes.

But Grey lacked neither principle nor breadth of mind – nor, indeed, courage. He maintained contact with radicals like Edmund Cartwright and Thomas Hardy who represented 'the industrious lower and middle classes of society'. He attended the trial of Hardy for treason, as he told his future wife, Elizabeth Ponsonby, 'in order to learn how to conduct myself when it comes to my turn.' He stood firm in the face of anti-Jacobin hysteria. In 1797, 93 Foxites supported Grey in a reform motion proposing a rate-payer franchise, triennial parliaments and large redistribution of seats. They had made a stand on principle at an inauspicious time. They then seceded from Parliament for three years, enjoying political talk, hunting, dining – and toasting 'our sovereign the people'. They recognised the need to keep their principles intact but also the futility of embodying them in legislation when so large a majority opposed them. When, in 1809,

Brand secured 115 votes for his less drastic reform measure Grey held aloof, although in opposition again and free to act on principle. No statesman has been better suited in temperament and circumstances to play a long game.

A more pressing issue, after 1801 and Pitt's resignation, was Catholic Emancipation: divisive for the Tories but uncomfortable too for the Whigs when the Prince Regent decided to oppose it. The Grenville-Fox 'Ministry of All the Talents' (February 1806 to March 1807) which gave Grey his first taste of public office, at the Admiralty, then, after Fox's death and his taking on the leadership of the party, at the Foreign Office, carried a modest measure of relief. George then insisted on a pledge that the matter be dropped which, he knew, would divide the Whigs. Grey acquiesced. But he lacked the conviction and energy to hold the party together. He had already lost his county seat on the 'No Popery' cry and had to acquire a rotten borough before succeeding in 1807 to his father's earldom and giving up the leadership. Thereafter Westminster saw him but rarely and Ponsonby (his wife's uncle), with Tierney and Whitbread, led an ineffectual opposition to the ministries of Portland, Perceval and Liverpool. They sniped and sometimes scored but appeared to have no coherent strategy. Little help came from the north. Perceval's overtures in 1809 on the death of Portland were rejected by return of post from Howick. In 1811 and 1812 the Regent sought a combination to include 'the old and tried friends of Mr Fox' – but Grey was not tempted. He knew his men, bibulous Sheridan, courtly Yarmouth, vainglorious Wellesley, and held the prince to be 'the worst anchoring ground in Europe'. It was the wrong time and he would be in the wrong place. He probably knew that he was ill-equipped for the grind of wartime administration. He lacked Liverpool's commitment and tenacity. Only the great issue, Reform, and a real chance, would tempt him back.

Grey's value in the Tory years, 1810 to 1830, was simply that he was sufficiently detached to have no need to compromise, sufficiently unambitious to be trusted and respected. So he could preserve a middle position, Foxite as he saw it, between those uninterested in reform and those willing to use any means of achieving it. He hoped that one day the party would be able to offer a comprehensive measure. Meanwhile he appeared generally content, with a beloved wife, fifteen children, his library, horses and beautiful estate. But his correspondence, notably with Princess Lieven, suggests that he had firm ideas, especially about foreign policy; depressed moods suggest that he missed the chance to implement them. He was interested in the Greek struggle for independence and in 1829 suggested the boundary that was eventually adopted. 'I little thought', he wrote to Holland, 'that living here at the bottom of Northumberland I should be marking out the limits of new kingdoms.' At that stage he seemed willing to support Wellington who had carried Catholic Emancipation. But then all changed.

Tory defections and Whig successes at the general election (July 1830) caused by the accession of William IV drew him out. The July Revolution in France roused radical spirits. Tricolour flags appeared in Lancashire. Trade declined. Men were laid off and working men formed unions. The plight of the hand-weavers became desperate. In southern counties ricks blazed and threshing machines were wrecked by starving labourers. Discontents had different causes but together created expectations and corresponding alarms: for some radical reform, for others broken windows – and worse. Henry Hunt called for manhood suffrage, annual parliaments and the secret ballot. Thousands marched for Thomas Attwood's Political Union as the Birmingham banker moved from proposals for currency reform to demands for political action. Tory Peel was inhibited by the fury of the Ultras over Emancipation; he could not 'rat' again. Wellington did not flinch. But he blundered irreparably when he declared his faith in the existing constitution and rejected the very idea of reform. That, and the rapid development of a popular front, convinced Grey that it was necessary and opportune. Ministers lost a vote on the Civil List, Wellington resigned and, on 16 November 1830, Grey was summoned by the King.

'Lord Grey's statesmanlike conviction of the need and advantage of an extensive measure was the prime source of the bill; the wisdom of Russell and the will of Durham embodied this conviction in a bold and simple form' (Butler). He could have added the high repute, tenacity and competence of Althorp, leading in the Commons. Without such a combination of experience and boldness, the jittery and the gradualists could have so emasculated the bill that it would have roused, without satisfying, the country and turned a tense into a revolutionary situation. Grey relished the challenge. In Creevey's diary for the spring of 1831 he is the hero of the day, relaxed and jovial. 'March 26. I wish you could have been with me when I entered the Premier's drawing room last night ... He was standing alone with his back to the fire – the best-dressed, the handsomest, and apparently the happiest man in all his royal master's domains.' Yet his government had other problems beside Reform. The agricultural riots were dealt with by savage sentences. But it was from the towns that authorities had most to fear. Althorp's budget of 1831 ran into difficulties and had to be largely recast: the failure saddled the Whigs with a record, only half-deserved, for economic mismanagement. A cholera outbreak made hideous the winter of 1831-2. Grey's handling of his large and aristocratic Cabinet was easygoing. In the words of Durham, 'Radical Jack', his impatient son-in-law, 'every member of the Cabinet, old or young, able or decrepit, thought himself at liberty to discuss the whole state of Europe.' Grey took a regular interest in foreign affairs – but he concentrated on the issue of reform.

By the terms of the bill of March 1831 many seats were to be transferred from small boroughs – either losing both members or one, 143 by the final act – to the counties and the larger unrepresented towns. Those were the essential proposals and the battleground of intense bargaining, usually over marginal cases, in committee or on the floor of the House. Confusion over population, voting rights and boundaries, the failings of parliamentary draughtsmen, ingenious opposition and a series of close votes, combined to test ministers' resolve. The bill, on second reading, passed by one vote. In April the government was defeated on Gascoyne's motion to retain the present number of members and Grey went to the country. Reformers gained many seats and the slightly revised bill had an easy passage through the Commons. In September, it was defeated in the Lords by 41 votes.

Mobs rampaged in Nottingham, Leicester and Bristol. Grey raised the stakes with a letter to *The Times,* promising 'a not less efficient' bill. He needed the agitators, yet knew that he could scare the moderates if radicals appeared to be in control: a proclamation was issued in November against the organisation of political unions on military lines. Meanwhile diehards were reduced to arguing that the constitution must never be altered by legislation; that the constituencies must be fixed for ever irrespective of social and economic change; that an assault on this one form of property must endanger all. Simply put, the message was: 'take away one part and the whole will collapse.' To Whigs like Macaulay this elevation of the status quo to the sacrosanct was simply absurd, designed to perpetuate 'a narrow oligarchy above – an infuriated multitude below.' Not that the Whigs were insensitive to the advantages of oligarchy. But Brougham saw that they had to secure 'the support of the people as distinct from the populace': that meant a vote for sufficient numbers of the middling sort.

Standing apart from the protracted battle in Parliament, Grey saw the issue clearly. He was saved from most of the fatigues endured by Althorp and his colleagues as they piloted the bill through the Commons. He was particularly successful in dealing with the King. They started from quite different viewpoints but shared the resolve to act correctly, according to 'the sense of my people' (words in the dissolution speech of April 1831) and a preference for stability. Each recognised the honest purpose of the other. Mutual trust was vital when the Reform Bill was reintroduced, followed (January 1832) by a request that the King would create peers as necessary to ensure its passage through the Lords. The bill passed its third reading in the Commons by 355 to 239. In May it was defeated in the Lords by 151 to 116. The King thought excessive the Cabinet's demand that he create 50 to 60 peers – and accepted their resignation. In a spirit more dutiful than hopeful Wellington tried to form a ministry while Francis Place threatened the city by urging a run on the banks: 'Stop the duke and go for gold.' Wellington saw that the game was up and advised the King to recall Grey, with authority to create new peers. The threat worked. On 4 June 1832 only 22 peers were prepared to vote against the Great Reform Bill. It became law.

The organisation of public opinion for political ends was not novel. But it was militant and effective beyond anything seen before. King William was a little afraid of it. Grey was chary of close contact with its leaders. Place did more than any to put Grey back in power. But Grey met him only once, at midnight, when a deputation of London tradesmen came uninvited to Downing Street. His short, perhaps sleepy, replies gave Place the impression that he meant to whittle down the reform proposals and brought about a temporary rupture between the Whigs and their Radical allies. In the end firmness prevailed.

Because Grey had overcome his reluctance to use potentially dangerous allies, he was now raised to a pinnacle of public esteem. He was fêted as a hero. No minister had approached it while still alive since the younger Pitt; nor would until Churchill in 1940-5. Behind the accolades, in each quite different case, was a sense of crisis resolved. Afterwards, for each, there would be reaction, a revision of views. After the passing of the bill Grey enjoyed the election of December 1832 which gave the Whigs a predictably huge majority. The electorate of 1831, 366,000 by the most recent estimate (John Cannon), had been enlarged, with the addition of some categories of lease and copy-holders to the 40-shilling freeholders, to 653,000. It could only be, as critics warned, a first step. But it was a well-judged one. Reformers would not have accepted less; anti-reformers might not have accepted more without bloodshed. 'The principle of my reform', Grey had said, 'is to prevent the necessity for revolution.' To have enacted it by peaceful means was indeed 'a great and beneficent act of statesmanship' (Michael Brock).

1833 saw the great act which abolished slavery in the colonies. Scottish burghs were made open to election. The first Factory Act was passed. In 1834 came the new Poor Law, ruthless and controversial. It could only have been passed in the new climate, and new House, utilitarians being convinced that they had a mandate. Before it passed the Upper House Grey had resigned. In May 1834 Russell had 'upset the coach' by hinting at the disendowment of the Church of Ireland. Stanley, Graham and Richmond promptly resigned and joined Peel. A muddle and division over the renewal of the Irish Coercion Act produced the resignation of Althorp, his faithful lieutenant. Grey had been plagued by cantankerous Durham and the cockily intrusive Russell; illogical Irish and sensitive churchmen were too much for an old man – and he now took his chance, thankfully, of stepping down. Three months later the old Houses of Parliament perished by fire.

Grey retired to pleasant sunset years at Howick where, as Creevey recorded, 'the very servants are of a breed that makes one feel at home'. He described him at the end of his day: 'all day as gay as possible, and not an atom of that gall he was subject to in earlier life ... A curious stranger would discover no out-of-the-way talent in him, no powers of conversation ... A most natural, unaffected, upright man, hospitable and domestic, far surpassing any man one knows in his noble appearance and beautiful simplicity of manners ... Take him all in all, I never saw his fellow; nor can I see any imitation of him on the stocks.'

J. Derry, *Charles Grey, Aristocratic Reformer* (1992).

Viscount Melbourne

WILLIAM LAMB, 2ND VISCOUNT MELBOURNE (1779-1848), was Prime Minister in 1834 and from 1835-41. Born into Whig society, although not a blue-blooded member of it, he was sponsored by the Whig hero Fox when he took his seat in the House of Commons in 1805. He was a handsome young man, with masses of curling hair and dark beetling eyebrows. At Eton, Trinity College, Cambridge and Glasgow University he showed intellectual curiosity but no application; theological interest but a distaste for religious enthusiasm; and a zest for the luxuries of life. His intelligence, wit and mildly eccentric manners were admired by his contemporaries, and the Whigs welcomed a promising recruit.

But the years ahead were dominated by his wife, Caroline, daughter of the Earl of Bessborough and a niece of the Duchess of Devonshire. This vivacious sprite became the most talked-about personality in London society. Her aristocratic upbringing had given free rein to her manic extremes of mood. Early happiness in their marriage was affected by stillborn children, and the son who survived was mentally handicapped. William's apparently cool detachment during her dramatic scenes drove her to 'sadder music and stronger wine', as she set out to catch the shooting star of the Regency scene, Lord Byron. Their romance ended at Lady Heathcote's ball, where she slashed her wrists with a broken glass and a pair of scissors. William was loyal to her even at her wildest – she was seen through a window, on their visit to Paris in 1814, throwing ornaments at him. His family persuaded him into a formal separation from her in 1825, but when she was dying three years later he came back from Ireland to be with her. His dislike of confrontation and his carapace of irony were both cause and result of the prolonged pain of this disastrous marriage.

His political career therefore started slowly. Private problems apart, he had little enthusiasm for the central Whig campaigns for Catholic Emancipation and Parliamentary Reform, and found himself increasingly in sympathy with moderate Tories, especially

Canning. So detached had he become that, when he was opposed in his county seat of Hertfordshire, he could not be bothered to stand, and a fresh seat had to be found for him when he agreed to serve in Canning's Tory Cabinet in 1827, as Chief Secretary for Ireland. After Canning's death he became one of the group of Canningites who left Wellington's High Tory government, and was thus available to the Whigs again when they won the election of 1830.

Their Prime Minister, Grey, made him Home Secretary. It was a well-judged appointment, for it spared Melbourne the onus of advocating reform but gave him the task of keeping order while the bill was going through. His view of Reform was pragmatic. He disliked the changes, but with melancholy eloquence urged the House of Lords, into which he had moved on the death of his father in 1829, to 'yield to the popular vote or be annihilated'. Lord John Russell, mover of the bill, thought him 'very slack' about the measure. But he was not at all slack about keeping order. This was just as well. When the House of Lords threw it out there were more than a thousand outbreaks of violence, culminating in the centre of Bristol being gutted by the rioters. Faced by these, and a threatened run on the banks, magistrates panicked. Melbourne kept calm. He urged them not to hesitate to read the Riot Act, but he refused to hand out weapons to irregular bodies of vigilantes, and he kept in touch with Radical leaders such as Francis Place. His energy was unexpected from one whose image was lethargic, and he showed a streak of decisive toughness when his Special Commissioners followed up the riots with five hundred sentences of transportation.

Even so, he cannot have expected to become Prime Minister. Indeed, when William IV sent for him in 1834, on Grey's resignation, he was said to have 'thought it a damned bore, and he was in many minds what he should do – be minister or not'. A damned bore for a lot of the time it was, too. The Whig aristocrats had no tradition of party discipline, and relied on an alliance with Radicals and Daniel O'Connell's Irish group, sealed by the Lichfield House Compact (1835), for their majority in the House of Commons; while the Tories in the Lords were able to reject, amend or delay their most important measures. In the circumstances, Melbourne was a shrewd choice to lead them. He was a strong enough chairman to cope with such self-important and opinionated men as 'Old Wickedshifts', the Lord Chancellor Brougham; Howick, Grey's principled and prickly son;

and Radical Jack, Lord Durham, immensely rich and explosive. He brought the best out of Lord John Russell, by giving him his head in promoting further measures of reform. He was not much interested in these himself, but for a Prime Minister who said that the whole duty of government was to prevent and punish crime and to preserve contracts, and who advised the young Queen Victoria: 'You'd better try to do no good, then you'll get into no scrapes', his governments were surprisingly active. The Municipal Corporations Act (1835) was a major measure, doing for local elections what the Reform Act had done for national ones, and the Durham Report (1840) paved the way to a long-lasting constitutional settlement in Canada, and was a milestone on the route from Empire to Commonwealth. It has to be admitted, however, that Melbourne was uninterested in Empire, and looked back on his choice of Durham as a blunder.

He was, though, very interested in Ireland. The Catholic majority there had to pay tithes and rates to the Anglican Church of Ireland, whose doors they never entered. Melbourne, sceptically tolerant and fair-minded, had voted for Catholic Emancipation in 1829. Now, with the added spur of the need for O'Connell's party's votes, he supported Russell's efforts to appropriate for Catholic purposes some of the money paid in Irish tithes. But the Lords would have none of it. In the circumstances, Melbourne showed skill in keeping O'Connell as an ally, and Repeal of the Act of Union off the political agenda: he used Irish fear of the Tories as an implied threat. The people who gained from the measures that Russell did manage to pass were the Dissenters, who could now be legally married outside an Anglican church, and for whom a non-sectarian college recently founded was incorporated as University College, London in 1836. The Church of England, however, was scandalised by the Erastian tendencies of Melbourne's governments, and by his dangerous appointments, culminating in the choice of the theologically suspect Hampden as Regius Professor of Divinity at Oxford. The Oxford Movement gathered momentum from the reaction of the orthodox to this.

The Whigs' relations with the monarchy had never been comfortable, and in 1834 William IV had even dismissed them for threatening 'his' Anglican Church with their Irish policy, though he had to accept them back again when the Tories failed to win enough seats at the subsequent election. So, when the young Victoria came to the throne in 1837, Melbourne set out to establish a happier relationship with her. This went further than anyone could have expected. He enjoyed the company of intelligent and forceful women (his mother had been one), and the young Victoria soon showed herself in that light. It was perhaps more surprising that she became so attached to him, a man who had been cited in the courts by two husbands for his relationship with their wives – admittedly on inadequate evidence. But Melbourne had long ceased to be a roué. He soon won her trust with his famous charm, sitting upright in her presence instead of in his usual sprawl and reducing the oaths with which his conversation was habitually peppered. She came to rely on him, expecting him to be at her side for six hours each day at Windsor and leaving his chair empty when he was absent. He was often sceptical – as on education: 'None of the Pagets can read or write and they get on well enough'; on honours: 'What I like about the Order of the Garter is that there is no damned merit about it.' His influence was often for the good, and he inculcated a sense of duty: 'A Queen's life is very laborious ... hardly any leisure.' But he did not train her to be above party, and when, in 1839, having been forced to send for Peel after the Whigs lost a vital division in the House of Commons, she then frustrated him by refusing to dismiss any of her Whig Ladies of the Bedchamber, Melbourne took office again rather than compelling her to behave constitutionally.

It was an unhappy return. There was a recession and a series of bad harvests. Unemployment was made harder to endure by the new Poor Law, with workhouses replacing outdoor relief. The discontented rallied round the People's Charter. Its demands, ranging from manhood suffrage to salaries for MPs, were far from Melbourne's political world. He found it more and more difficult to hold his Cabinet together, especially when Palmerston, his brother-in-law and Foreign Secretary, alarmed the strong pro-French lobby in it by risking war against France in 1840 over her support for Mehemet Ali against the Turks. But it was finance that brought him down in the end. The budget would not balance – the Penny Post, a costly innovation at first, was partly responsible – and the Chancellor of the Exchequer proposed to increase revenue from trade by reducing the duties on foreign sugar, timber and corn. This was an important shift in policy, but Melbourne met the proposals with a characteristic shrug, telling ministers that, in their efforts to raise money, he did not care whether they increased or lowered the duties as long as they all agreed to say the same thing.

Beaten in the Commons and then decisively in the election of 1841, he resigned.

Before Melbourne died, in 1848, he had already become a figure from the past, a Regency man in style and attitude, while the Queen had become a proper Victorian under the influence of her young husband, Albert. The contrast often drawn between Melbourne and Peel, the man of the future, has hidden his most important achievement. This was to ensure that in the post-Reform-Act era the British aristocracy would be found in both parties. He carried the Whigs along with him into an alliance with the Radicals, and thus ensured that the party of reform continued to be led by the landed classes. With Russell subsequently showing his inadequacies as a leader, it may be that no other Whig could have done so.

Lord David Cecil, *Melbourne* (1965).
L.G. Mitchell, *Lord Melbourne* (1997).

Sir Robert Peel

SIR ROBERT PEEL, 2ND BARONET (1788-1850) was Prime Minister from 1834-5, and from 1841-6. The Peel family success story warranted four pages in Samuel Smiles' *Self Help*, and young Robert had the nature and nurture of a budding leader. His father, the first Lancashire 'Cotton King' to sit in Parliament, told his son: 'Bob, you dog, if you are not Prime Minister some day, I'll disinherit you.' Educated amongst the gentry at Harrow, with four other future Prime Ministers, he was awarded a double first at Oxford in Classics and Mathematics. He was well-built and handsome, with striking auburn hair, and when his father organised him into an Irish Borough seat, aged twenty-one, he caught the eye of the Prime Minister, Spencer Perceval, with an impressive maiden speech. By 1812 he had risen to run the government in Ireland (then part of Britain after the Act of Union) as its Chief Secretary. Only the younger Pitt had climbed faster, and it was as Pitt's true heir that his father presented him and the Tories saw him.

Peel enjoyed power: he was in politics to get things done. In Ireland for six years he proved himself a gifted administrator and a staunch Protestant – they called him 'Orange' Peel. He created the Irish Constabulary ('Peelers'), renewed the Insurrection Act when his colleagues wobbled, and was only prevented from fighting a duel with the Catholic leader Daniel O'Connell when the latter was arrested. He enhanced his administrative reputation as Home Secretary between 1822 and 1830. Following years of repression, he set about clearing the undergrowth of archaic criminal laws. His method was to prune and graft, not to plough up and replant. He reduced the thicket of obsolete legislation to a handful of intelligible statutes. He also tackled, cautiously, the problems of enforcing the law. English mistrust of arbitrary government made the introduction of a national police force deeply suspect, but he managed to start the London Metropolitan Police. In their blue uniforms and iron-framed top hats, they were so well run that they became imitated all over the country. The age of the beadle and the spy was over, and the

Bobby on the beat (nicknamed after his creator) had arrived. In order to make the law work more efficiently, he drastically reduced the number of offences for which capital punishment was the sentence, since juries were refusing to condemn petty criminals to the death sentence – his purpose being practical rather than humanitarian.

He appeared to be fulfilling his promise as a Tory leader. He was a robust supporter of the British constitution and the Established Church, and a determined opponent of any stirrings towards democracy. He owned Drayton Manor and a large estate and sat for Oxford University. But all was not as it seemed. Tories were landed, and many of Peel's beliefs were those of the industrial and trading classes from which he sprang, and who were starting to exercise their political muscle. He was, moreover, pragmatic. This got him into trouble when he accepted that Catholics must have the vote in Ireland after it had become apparent that Ireland would otherwise prove ungovernable. He and Wellington, hitherto strong in the Protestant cause, carried the Catholic Emancipation Bill, in 1829, through a shocked and taunting Parliament. To some, his change of heart was 'miserable, contemptible hypocrisy'. 'We were sold,' they cried. Oxford rejected him. To re-establish his Tory credentials he led the opposition to the Whig Parliamentary Reform proposals stridently, speaking sometimes with the 'incoherent red-faced rage' of an often hot-tempered man. But once the bill was carried, he set about adapting his party to the new House of Commons. The mood there, and that of the new electorate, was in fact more attuned to the Lancashire cotton master than to the Whig aristocrat. In the Tamworth Manifesto (1835), Peel showed how well he had grasped this, appealing to 'that great and intelligent class of society ... which is far less interested in the contentions of party than in the maintenance of order and the cause of good government.' This was his *credo*. It was not entirely that of the Tory landowners who filled the back benches of his party: but they followed him grumpily.

Peel fought the election of 1835 as Prime Minister, after William IV, a quirkish monarch, had dismissed his Whig ministers and summoned him from his Italian holiday to form a minority administration. He lost it, but during his four months in office he established the new Conservatism in the eyes of the electorate, and his party's strength in the House of Commons grew from 150 to 290 members. In opposition again, he showed tactical skill, and increasing dominance in debate. He worked hard, his name appearing more frequently than any others on parliamentary committees, and his style of speaking, coolly rational rather than oratorical, commanded respect. Former Canningites like Stanley and Graham returned to the fold and he promoted Gladstone and Herbert, able young men of his own ilk. Meanwhile the Conservative Party, as it was becoming known, was developing an effective organisation, the work of Bonham, a professional organiser, and centred on the Carlton Club. In 1839 Melbourne resigned, and the Whigs were expected to go out. Their departure was delayed by the young Queen, who greatly preferred the elderly charms of Melbourne to the stiff formality of Peel and refused to change any of the Whig Ladies of her Bedchamber. Peel properly refused to take office without some gesture of royal confidence, and had to wait until the election of 1841. This returned him to power with a solid majority. By then he was seen as the natural Prime Minister, and the Conservatives as the party of the future, transformed in a decade from the helpless opponents of the national will.

He took office in difficult circumstances, at the start of the 'Hungry Forties', with bad harvests, trade depressed, industry stagnant and the Chartists turning violent. Peel had grown up during the French Revolution, and believed that the right way to prevent revolution in Britain was to create prosperity. This was the purpose which underlay his approach to premiership. So, while supporting the Mines Bill on humanitarian grounds, he opposed Ashley's Ten Hour Bill because he feared that a reduction in working hours would damage Britain's competitiveness. His fiscal achievements were remarkable. The Whigs had left a government deficit of £7.5 million, but in his great budget of 1842 Peel was able to repeal export duties on all British manufactures, and to reduce those on imported raw materials to 5% or less and those on foreign manufactured goods to 20% or less. He paid for this by reintroducing income tax, for three years at first. This was a sensational move, for it had previously been levied only in wartime: yet such was the respect already felt for him that one Whig MP commented: 'One felt all the time he was speaking, "Thank God Peel is Minister."' The medicine worked. Trade expanded, and the budget went into surplus. In 1845, encouraged, he abolished import duties on 430 of the remaining 813 articles still on the tariff book, and drastically reduced the contentious sugar duties. Britain was poised to take full advantage of its head start over the rest of the world in the techniques of industrial production.

He also confirmed his reputation as a financial strategist by carrying the Bank Charter Act (1844). Throughout his political life, Peel stuck closely to two fundamental theories. In commerce he was a free-trader, in finance a bullionist. 'What is a pound?' he had asked at the start of a major speech, and answered that it was nothing if not backed by gold. 'Peel's Act' (1819), so known because he chaired the committee which shaped it, had put Britain back onto the gold standard. The Bank Charter Act reinforced this by gradually giving the Bank of England the monopoly of issuing notes, and separating its issue and banking departments, laying down that the gold reserves supporting note issue could not be used in its banking operations. Sound money would create the right conditions for industrial expansion, and sustain the value of the wages of the poor. Many economists now regard his policy as dangerously deflationary, and he did indeed have a rigid and theoretical cast of mind in money matters: but to contemporaries it gave confidence, and had much to do with the admiration for Peel across the country.

'He sums up the whole Cabinet in his person.' Peel was one of the most dominant Prime Ministers of the nineteenth century, matched only by his disciple, Gladstone. He introduced the 1842 and 1845 budgets himself, rather than leaving them to his Chancellor of the Exchequer. When he lost the bill repealing the duties on sugar, he went back to the House of Commons and successfully demanded that they reverse their decision. Because he thought his peace-loving Foreign Secretary, Aberdeen, underestimated the danger of a French invasion (a frequent mid-nineteenth-century scare) he launched a million-pound naval rearmament programme which nearly drove Aberdeen to resignation. Over policy towards Ireland his experience gave him special authority. He destroyed the Repeal Association there, in the middle of its campaign to repeal the Act of Union, by having his old enemy O'Connell arrested (1843), a bold and what proved a well-timed decision which ended the Liberator's career as an effective leader. He then set out to 'wean from the cause of Repeal the great body of intelligent and wealthy Roman Catholics' by opening up opportunities for higher education in Ireland for them, with new non-denominational colleges to be grouped into a new university (a scheme eventually scotched by the Vatican, which felt threatened by them), and by trebling the grant to Maynooth, the training

College for Catholic priests, to raise their social level and incline them to moderate policies. The Maynooth Bill he did eventually carry (1845). But the uproar against this use of government money revealed the depth of anti-Catholic feeling still running through the country, and led to the first major revolt on the Conservative back benches, as well as the resignation of Gladstone, a High Anglican.

His sense of authority grew with his successes: but so did the gulf between him and his back-benchers. Reserved in public, his shyness and thin skin made him cold and unapproachable except to gifted younger men: O'Connell saw his smile as the 'gleam on the silver plate on a coffin'. And there loomed all through his years of government the problem of the Corn Laws, kept in the foreground of politics by the Anti Corn Law League. How could a free trader like Peel accept duties on foreign corn, which pushed up the price of bread, and which did not even benefit the farm labourers, who suffered like everyone else from the high cost of food? Always sensitive to any threat to the stability of society, he felt the dangers of the growing isolation of a landed class defending its privileges. He hoped to reduce the duties gradually, and in 1842 introduced a sliding scale, which lowered them as the price of corn rose. But the League hammered away at a gradually opening door, and in 1845 Peel turned to his neighbour on the front bench at the end of a speech by Cobden: 'You answer this, for I cannot.'

There is evidence that his decision to go for total Repeal of the Corn Laws had been taken as early as 1843, but the timing of his move sprang directly from the failure of the Irish potato crop, and imminent famine there. He was driven by a moral imperative, and it came from the heart when he exclaimed in the House of Commons, 'Good God! Are you to sit in Cabinet and consider how much diarrhoea and bloody flux and dysentery a people can take before it becomes necessary for you to provide them with food?' Foreign corn would have to be let into Ireland free of duty. That being so, could the duties in England be maintained? Peel felt not. As leader of the landed party, he thought it more appropriate that the Whigs should take office to repeal them, but when Russell failed to form a government, he did not hesitate to put his own beliefs before those of his followers. 'I claim for myself the right to give my sovereign ... that advice which I believe the interests of the country require.' After Maynooth and the reduction of sugar duties, and with memories of Catholic Emancipation, Conservative back-benchers were on the brink of revolt. They found an unlikely leader in the ringleted Jew, Disraeli, who savaged the Prime Minister in a series of brilliant speeches. His theme was clear. 'The Right Honourable gentleman has caught the Whigs bathing and has walked off with their clothes.' 'Let men stand by the principle by which they rise.' 'A Conservative government is an organised hypocrisy.' Peel carried the bill repealing the Corn Laws with Whig support, but two thirds of the Conservatives present voted against it and, on the day it passed the Lords, they combined with the Whigs to defeat the government over the Irish Coercion Bill. Peel resigned, never to regain power.

Modern Conservatives have seen Peel as the founder of their party. In fact, he broke what he had started to build, splitting its leaders from their followers. Nearly all his ablest ministers left it with him, and after he himself had refused to form a new party, these 'Peelites' drifted gradually over to join the Whigs and Radicals in what became the new Liberal Party, with one of them, Gladstone, as its leader. It was therefore in the Liberal Party that his influence lasted. The Conservatives were left with only one former minister, Stanley, as their leader in the Lords, and had perforce to accept Disraeli in the Commons. It was nearly thirty years before a Conservative government with a parliamentary majority came to power. Peel himself did not live long into the period of political instability which followed his resignation. His early death was caused by a fall from his horse at the gates of Hyde Park, which stumbled over him after it had thrown him.

There followed his national apotheosis. In his person as well as his policies he had caught the mood of early Victorian Britain, earnest, progressive, with a high moral tone. 'The British People being subject to fogs and possessing a powerful Middle Class require grave statesmen,' observed Disraeli. He was a devoted family man whose wife Julia was as private a person as he. His broad interests were those of his time: he had a fine collection of pictures, centred on contemporary portraits, which he left to the nation, was a trustee of the British Museum, and was keenly interested in the applied sciences, especially when they related to agricultural improvements. He was an enthusiast for the new railways, and George Stephenson was one of his heroes. He had much in common with the Prince Consort, who soon persuaded the Queen, at first alienated by his formal behaviour, that he was a great man. As with Victoria, so with the Victorians. They identified with his convictions and hailed his courage as a leader. Statues of him went up all over the country, and the leading national newspaper proclaimed him 'the greatest statesman of his time'.

N. Gash, *Mr Secretary Peel: The Life of Sir Robert Peel to 1830* and *Sir Robert Peel: The Life of Sir Robert Peel After 1830* (2 vols, 1961 and 1972).

Lord John Russell

LORD JOHN RUSSELL, IST EARL RUSSELL (1792-1878), Prime Minister 1846-52 and 1865, was born into a famous Whig family as the third son of the sixth Duke of Bedford, and his devotion to the Whig principles which had been handed down through the eighteenth century from the Glorious Revolution of 1688 inspired the whole of his long political career. He was not regarded, then or since, as a successful Prime Minister, but he was the central figure in the development of those principles into Victorian Liberalism, which emerged as a dominant political force under Gladstone.

An MP aged twenty-one, Russell made his way quickly to the forefront of politics through his energy, his ability and his championship of a cause. He was one of the few young stars in a party which had been long in opposition. His mind was exploratory, quick and restless, and he was to command the respect of intellectuals such as Mill and Jowett, as befitted the grandfather of Bertrand Russell. The cause was Parliamentary Reform, long championed by the Whigs. He helped to draft the First Reform Bill, and his name was made when Grey asked him to introduce it in the House of Commons in 1831. He was at the heart of the struggle to get it passed, he and Althorp being described respectively as the vinegar and the oil in its committee stages. Although he earned the reputation of a dangerous Radical when he excited the Birmingham Political Union, telling them that it was 'impossible that the whisper of a faction should prevail against the voice of a nation', he was promoted to the Cabinet, and Melbourne made him Leader of the House of Commons in 1834. Throughout Melbourne's ministries (1835-41), his was the driving force. 'No man', wrote Gladstone, 'ever led the House of Commons with a more many-sided activity or more indomitable pluck.' He became Melbourne's natural successor as leader of the Whigs in 1841, and Prime Minister in 1846. His ministry lasted for nearly six years, but he then found himself superseded as the dominant Whig personality by Palmerston, and although active all the time in the middle of a confused political scene, did not return to the top until Palmerston died in 1865.

He was not a natural leader and did not command respect. This had something to do with his appearance, for although he had a very large head (a gift for cartoonists), he was only five feet four-and-three-quarter inches tall. He shared a distaste for social occasions with his wife, and was dogged by poverty, for his brother, the seventh Duke, was mean with family resources: the Queen eventually had to provide him with a house appropriate to his position as Prime Minister, Pembroke Lodge in Petersham. He had a bad memory for faces. He was so unbusinesslike that he would put a letter in the wrong envelope, leave out enclosures, mislay papers and forget to give official boxes to the messenger. He was cocksure and impulsive, and did not think through his policies before presenting them. When in 1851 he complained in frustration at the lack of initiative shown by his Cabinet, one of them retorted; 'Good heavens, I am sure you are always bringing forward something new about everything.' 'He has not a shadow of authority,' was the Queen's verdict; Sydney Smith found it 'impossible to sleep soundly while Lord John has command of the watch.'

Circumstances too, which had helped him to get to the leadership, now made his time there difficult. The Whigs on their own did not have a parliamentary majority. Between 1846 and 1867 a shift in political alignment was going on, from the old Whigs and Tories to the new Liberals and Conservatives. Peel split the Tory Party when he repealed the Corn Laws and his landowning back-benchers rejected him. His fellow ministers nearly all followed him into the political no man's land, and these Peelites, small in number but dominant in ability, were at the centre of manoeuvres to attract them back into a party structure. Most of them ended with the Whig/Liberals; but not under Russell, for he had personally alienated them. Though a respected tactician, he made an uncharacteristic mistake over a burning religious topic of the day. In 1850 Pope Pius IX introduced a formal Roman Catholic structure to England, with an Archbishop of Westminster (Wiseman) and twelve sees under him. Protestants were already on the boil after the explosive excitement within the Church of England caused by the Oxford Movement and Newman's conversion to Rome. Russell was a Broad Churchman who had repealed the Test and Corporation Acts which had barred religious minorities from universities and public office, and he had supported the admission of Jews to Parliament. But the Whig Protestant tradition now led him to write to the Bishop of Durham denouncing the threat of 'the mummeries of superstition', and to pass the Ecclesiastical Titles Act, banning the use of Roman Catholic titles in England. The Peelites, tolerant or High Church, thereafter turned their backs on him, and were more ready to accept the lead of Palmerston, even though he was well to the right of Russell on every other issue.

Russell was Prime Minister when the Chartist movement reached its climax in 1848 and the Irish endured their worst years of famine. His handling of Chartism was much to his credit. He had already managed the Chartist risings of 1839 with an effective blend of firmness and moderation, appointing Sir Charles Napier, a good soldier but a Chartist sympathiser, to command the troops. He now refused to be rushed into suspending habeas corpus and kept his nerve as their mass petition was peacefully presented by a delegation. For Ireland, at a time when free trade dogma made large-scale relief unthinkable, he pressed for more help than English public opinion was ready to accept. Over Irish issues his heart was in the right place. 'The Statute Book is full of Insurrection Acts,' he said, 'but ... I can find no Act admitting the Irish Catholics to be treated as the free subjects of a free country.' But his efforts to help them were ineffectual. The House of Lords blocked the use of Anglican tithe money, paid by a nine-tenths Catholic population, for purposes outside the Anglican Church of Ireland, and they rejected all his moves for land reforms. It was left to Gladstone to carry the measures which Russell had often unsuccessfully introduced through thirty years. His record in educational reform was honourable. He realised that a wider franchise required a better educated population, and inspired the Education Act of 1839 which laid the base for the future development of state education by setting up a Privy Council to appoint inspectors. Almost his last intervention in politics was to suggest to Gladstone that there should be a Minister of Education in the Cabinet. His Public Health Act pioneered state intervention, setting up local health boards to impose proper sewers and drains. By repealing the Navigation Acts, he had made an important contribution to the Free Trade Movement. But when, after dismissing Palmerston for going his own way in the Foreign Office once too often, he was defeated by a combination of Peelites and Tory Protectionists, he left an overall impression of vacillation and

17   Stanley Baldwin, 1st Earl Baldwin of Bewdley
(Photo: Bassano)

18   J. Ramsay MacDonald
(Artist: Sir John Lavery)

19   Neville Chamberlain
(Photo: Bassano)

20 Sir Winston Churchill, KG
(Photo: Yousuf Karsh)

21   Clement Attlee, 1st Earl Attlee
(Photo: Howard Coster)

22   Harold Macmillan, 1st Earl of Stockton
(Photo: Pamela Chandler)

23   James Harold Wilson, Baron Wilson of Rievaulx
(Photo: Rex Coleman for Baron Studios)

24   Margaret Hilda Thatcher, Baroness Thatcher of Kesteven
(Photo: Gemma Levine)

incompetence, especially over finance. In 1848 the budget he intro-duced himself had had to be withdrawn after ten days, as the sums did not add up.

To achieve a government which could command a majority, the Queen invited Aberdeen, a Peelite and a favourite of hers, to form a coalition ministry. Russell, still the Whig leader, joined it, but behaved like a prima donna in it, constantly threatening resignation and finally timing it in a conspicuously disloyal way, when the government faced a hostile motion from the Radical, Roebuck, for its handling of the Crimean War. So, when Aberdeen fell, it was Palmerston who led the next Whig government. Russell became his Foreign Secretary in his second ministry (1859-65), and the two, astonishingly, worked closely together: indeed the Queen called them 'those two dreadful old men'. They were not conspicuously successful. They did help the cause of Italian nationalism by allow-ing Garibaldi to cross the Straits of Messina from Sicily. But it was partly Russell's dilatoriness that allowed the Confederate *Alabama* to sail from Liverpool during the American Civil War and wreak havoc among Unionist shipping, for which Gladstone later had to pay handsomely; and their efforts to stop the Germans expelling the Danes from Schleswig failed humiliatingly. However, when Palmerston eventually died, Russell became Prime Minister once more. By then the Peelites had settled down with the Whigs to create the new Liberal Party, and Russell, now an Earl, had Gladstone to lead the House of Commons. He looked to round off his career with a fresh Reform Act. But he was to have one last frustration, when he and Gladstone failed to carry all their party with them: a group led by a powerful orator, Robert Lowe, rebelled, and Russell, defeated, resigned, and had to watch the Conservatives achieve a more radical Reform Act.

Many of the reforms which Russell had suggested, in Ireland, education and the Army, were carried through by the Liberal Party, which emerged from the election after the 1867 Reform Act with a cohesive majority, and a strong leader, Gladstone. His ideas were forward-looking, but in a period of political instability he lacked the personal qualities to get them onto the Statute Book, and was overshadowed by Peel and Palmerston. He was 'little Johnny Russell' to the end.

Paul Scherer, *Lord John Russell* (1999).

Earl of Derby

EDWARD STANLEY, 14TH EARL OF DERBY (1799-1869), Prime
Minister 1852, 1858-9 and 1866-8, was every inch an aristocrat: handsome, casual, a 'lively, rattling sportsman' who was Steward of the
Jockey Club and could be seen at Newmarket joking in the crowd
round the bookies. He ran his large estates effectively, and in
Lancashire, where most of them were to be found, he played the part
of *grand seigneur* so effectively that his family's fame has been secure
there ever since. His donation to the Relief Fund for the cotton
workers made unemployed by the American Civil War, which he
chaired, was the largest single gift ever made up till then to a charity.
His political standpoint was aristocratic too. He championed the
landowners: 'men who for generation after generation have been the
centre each of his respective locality ... who conduct the business of
their counties', and was also a robust supporter of the Established
Church. His often light-hearted style made some regard him as
cavalier and casual. 'What fun we shall have now that you have
come,' he said when his old adversary Russell joined him in the
House of Lords. But it was a sense of obligation which kept him in
politics through long periods of painful illness.

The young Stanley had one outstanding gift among many. His
voice, his looks and his intellectual wit made him the most highly
regarded orator of his generation in an age when oratory was the
making of political giants. Daniel Webster, visiting the Commons
from America in 1839, wrote that Stanley had made the best speech
he had ever heard. He was 'the Rupert of debate'. Melbourne
thought he would be the next Prime Minister after himself through
'the mere force of superior will and eloquence ... a young eagle above
them all.' He was indeed to be Prime Minister, three times. But
there was a wicked fairy present at his birth, for he never led a government with a majority in the House of Commons.

With aristocratic confidence he changed party three times –
leaving the Whigs to serve as a Tory under Canning, moving back to
them when Wellington became Tory Prime Minister in 1828, but

resigning from the Whig Cabinet when Russell proposed to use Irish Church lands for lay purposes (1834). He appeared settled as Colonial Secretary in Peel's Tory government from 1841, where his most lasting achievement was to arrange for the island of Hong Kong, a new British acquisition, to become a free port, thus laying the foundation for its future wealth. But one more resignation lay ahead, the most significant of his career. When Peel decided to abandon his agricultural supporters and repeal the Corn Laws in 1846, Stanley was the only important minister to leave the Cabinet. It was a bitter break, for his old political friends, former Canningites such as Graham and Aberdeen, all followed Peel. When an alliance of Whigs and Protectionists drove Peel from office, a period of political uncertainty followed. Stanley put loyalty to the landed classes first, and soon found himself at the head of the Protectionists, strong in numbers but without any other recognisable leader. For the rest of his life this group was the largest in the Commons, but never in a majority. Derby, as he became when his father died in 1851, enabled it to continue as the Conservative Party, but he failed to win back his old Peelite friends, who nearly all ended up with the Whigs to form the nucleus of the future Liberal Party. He also failed to build up any party organisation, or gain a foothold in the new Penny Press. Disunity amongst the Whigs, the Peelites, the Radicals and the rogue elephant Palmerston, enabled him to form three governments, but the inexperience of the first was such that it was nicknamed the 'Who? Who?' ministry, after the deaf Duke of Wellington's enquiries as the names were read out to him, and only the third lasted for more than a year.

Derby was still an instinctive traditionalist. His foreign policy was old-fashioned, looking to the great powers to keep the peace after the nationalist rebellions of 1848: his support for Austria against Italian liberals won the favour of the Queen. But at home he showed concern for the plight of the poor, inspired by genuine sympathy as well as anxiety about social instability. His most important contribution to British politics was to preserve the continuity of the Conservative Party; his second was to enable Disraeli to become its leader. Though the Protectionists had cheered Disraeli on when he led the attack on Peel, most of them mistrusted and disliked him. Derby, from the House of Lords, backed him as Conservative leader in the Commons against plots to replace him, even when the rival was his own son, and stayed on, gout-ridden, until the majority of his colleagues realised that an alternative successor would be absurd. He also proved a surprisingly zestful backer of Disraeli's plans for Parliamentary Reform. He had been impressed by the responsible behaviour of the unemployed Lancashire cotton workers, and thought that the right extension of the franchise, with a careful redistribution of constituencies, might help the Conservatives to the overall majority which eluded them in the existing electorate. So when in 1866 Whig rebels defeated their own government's Reform Bill and he became Prime Minister for the third time, he urged Disraeli to frame a bill which Gladstone, the new Liberal leader, could not oppose without being inconsistent. They went for household suffrage in the boroughs, but only for those who paid their own rates and had a two-year residential qualification. This was 'a leap in the dark', and it became a bigger leap when the Liberals carried amendments simplifying and further broadening the proposed franchise. But Derby was all out to 'dish the Whigs'. His influence and Disraeli's oratory held their party together, and the bill succeeded where several earlier attempts had failed. 'I have the greatest confidence in my fellow countrymen', he said, 'and I entertain a strong hope that the extended franchise ... will be the means of placing the institutions of this country on a firmer basis.'

It certainly left the Conservative Party on a firmer basis. For over eighty of the next one hundred and thirty years the country was run by Conservative governments or coalitions with a Conservative preponderance. But Derby was not there to lead it. The gout which had persistently attacked him finally overwhelmed him, and in 1868, the year after the bill was passed as the Second Reform Act, he handed over to Disraeli the leadership which that more famous Tory Prime Minister could never have had without his patronage.

There is no twentieth-century biography. The best political study is: W.D. Jones, *Lord Derby and Victorian Conservatism* (1956).

Earl of Aberdeen

GEORGE HAMILTON GORDON, 4TH EARL OF ABERDEEN (1784-1860) was Prime Minister from 1853 until 1855. He might have been happier as a Scottish laird, living at Haddo, the beautiful Aberdeenshire Adam home of his family. But fate pulled him onto the political stage. Both his parents died early and he was brought up by two guardians, Dundas and Pitt, the most powerful politicians in Scotland and England, and educated at Harrow, Cambridge and on an unusually enterprising Grand Tour, which took him as far as Smyrna, involved a protracted stay in Athens and gave him a scholarly interest in archaeology: he later became President of the Society of Antiquaries.

His private life was sad. His first marriage was a love match, to Catherine Hamilton, but she died seven years later: he never took their wedding ring from his finger. They had four children: a son who lived for half an hour, and three daughters who were all dead before they were twenty. His second wife died in 1833, as did their daughter a year later. Small wonder that this shy man became an austere widower: 'Old Brown Bread', disrespectful children called him, for his skin was dark and pock-marked. But colleagues soon discovered the kindness and gentleness beneath.

His political career developed slowly, and was focused on foreign affairs. He started his public life as a diplomat, sent by Castlereagh as special envoy to the Emperor of Austria while the Allies closed in on Napoleon in 1813. These were formative times for him. He saw on the battlefield of Leipzig 'wounded men, unable to crawl, crying for water', and learnt to hate war. He also shared a hay loft with Metternich and remained staunchly pro-Austrian thereafter. After the war he spoke regularly as a Tory in the House of Lords. He became the Tories' expert in foreign affairs, Wellington's Foreign Secretary in 1829 and Peel's in 1841, and in his own government his influence in shaping foreign policy was dominant. The principle underlying his policy was to keep the peace in Europe by working in concert with the Great Powers.

He deplored the rasping tone and nationalist gunboat diplomacy of Palmerston during the Whig hegemony of the 1830s, and when the Tories came back he set out to show what a pacific policy could achieve. He successfully sorted out the disputes with the United States over its borders with Canada, and soothed the French after they had felt outmanoeuvred and isolated by Palmerston: Guizot, Louis Philippe's chief minister, liked Aberdeen, and his portrait is still to be seen in Haddo House, where the phrase *'entente cordiale'* was first coined. Although the French broke the compromise the two of them had achieved over Louis Philippe's plan to marry his son to the Queen of Spain and unite the French and Spanish thrones, Aberdeen's reputation for conciliation, caution and gravitas was high on the Continent and at court, especially after the revolutions of 1848 had shaken so many thrones.

He did not see himself as a future Prime Minister. Indeed, when Peel fell he considered leaving politics and retiring to Haddo. But deep dislike of Palmerston's aggressive policies pulled him back, and on the changed political stage he was to play an unexpectedly big part. The Repeal of the Corn Laws left the Tory Party divided between its back-benchers who remained Protectionists and its front-benchers who followed their leader out of office. Aberdeen was firmly behind Peel: a conservative abroad, he shared Peel's reforming instincts at home. His standing amongst his Peelite contemporaries was such that, when Peel died in 1850, they asked him to lead them. They were a gifted group, but by 1852 there were only thirty of them in the Commons. However, neither the Whigs nor the Tory Protectionists could command a majority on their own, and a fusion of Whigs and Peelites seemed the most promising route to stability. The Whigs had become disenchanted with their leader Russell, and Aberdeen emerged as the man most likely to unite the various elements which ought to be collected in what some were already describing as a Liberal government. He had the seniority to enable Russell to serve under him; he was aristocratic enough to appeal to the Whigs; he was a favourite at court. When Derby's brief Tory administration was defeated, he was able to collect the most talented Cabinet in Victoria's reign: even Palmerston joined it, as Home Secretary. Many looked forward to a great reforming government and the emergence of a new party. Aberdeen saw himself as its midwife, to hand over to Russell once Peelites, Whigs and Radicals had learnt to work together.

He failed: and like Eden a hundred years later his downfall came from the foreign policy which had been the making of his reputation. At home his government promised much. Gladstone's Free Trade Budget in 1852 slashed customs duties, and held out the prospect of abolishing income tax by 1860 on the strength of a higher return from ever-increasing trade: the pure milk of Peel's gospel. Russell prepared a Parliamentary Reform Bill. Plans were laid for environmental, penal and legal reforms, and the Northcote Trevelyan Report was commissioned, which was to lead to a professional civil service. But almost all these projects were aborted by the outbreak of the Crimean War.

The Crimean War destroyed Aberdeen's government and left his own reputation in tatters. Between the settlements of Vienna in 1815 and Versailles in 1919 the Great Powers hovered and snarled round the edge of the weakening Ottoman Empire in the Balkans, while its Christian subjects looked for their help to throw off the Turkish yoke. One of the many crises arose in 1852 over the rights of rival Christian groups in the Holy Places in Jerusalem and between their patrons, France and Russia. For the diplomatic mistakes which led to its escalation into war, Aberdeen took a large share of the blame. He had misled Tsar Nicholas I at an earlier meeting into believing that Britain would co-operate with Russia in the event of a break-up of the Ottoman Empire. In his anxiety for peace he continued to send confusing signals as Russia started to bully the Sultan. Having no party behind him in Parliament, and no personal prestige in the country, he was unable to carry his Cabinet with him in a policy of conciliatory negotiations: Palmerston's aggressive noises off were more to the liking of a bellicose nation. So he prevaricated. When he did send a fleet to the Straits, it arrived too late to stop the Russian advance, but it encouraged the Turks to declare war on Russia. The Russian fleet soon sank a Turkish squadron at Sinope (1853), and after that the attitude of France and British public opinion made war inevitable.

Aberdeen was no wartime leader. He was unlucky that the new telegraph gave the war a fresh immediacy back home, as television from Vietnam was later to do in the USA. Nor was it his fault that the Army was still led by the men of Waterloo, officered by amateurs, with commissariat and medical arrangements entirely inadequate for a distant campaign and a Russian winter. But it was all too clear that his heart was not in it. 'I make peace my first object and my first vow,' he told the House of Lords. He clung to power, hoping to finish the struggle into which he had led the country. But two Russells did for him. W.H. Russell's reports to *The Times* from the front and the hospital at Scutari shocked his readers, while Lord John Russell resigned from the Cabinet on the eve of a debate on the radical Roebuck's demand for an enquiry into the conduct of the war. The government lost that debate by 157 votes, and Aberdeen resigned.

His reputation has never quite recovered. He had no biographer until the end of the century, and the hostile diaries of his contemporaries have dominated the historiography of the period. To balance them, it should be remembered that Aberdeen was looked up to with near veneration by Gladstone and other Peelites, and also by the Queen and Albert, for his integrity. The Greek inscription below his bust in Westminster Abbey translates: 'Most Just'.

M.E. Chamberlain, *Lord Aberdeen: A Political Biography* (1983).
L. Iremonger, *Lord Aberdeen* (1978).

Viscount Palmerston

HENRY TEMPLE, 3RD VISCOUNT PALMERSTON (1784-1865), Prime Minister 1855-8 and 1859-65, has a controversial reputation among historians. To some he was a robust conservative, to others a liberal Whig. All, however, agree that he lived life to the full with exceptional stamina. Becoming an MP (and junior minister) in 1807, he remained in the House of Commons, with one six-month gap, until his death fifty-eight years later, and was in government for nearly fifty of them, longer than any other statesman in British history. From his father, an Irish peer, he inherited 10,000 acres around Sligo, some Welsh slate quarries and a handsome country house, Broadlands in Hampshire, with land worth £2,000 a year in rents – together with large debts which he never paid off. His conservative instincts may have been acquired young: his father, with young Henry in tow, left Paris four days before the mob stormed the Tuileries in 1789. But as an undergraduate in Edinburgh he imbibed Free Trade doctrines, shared with Peel, who had been four years his junior at Harrow.

His career was built on solid hard work. For nineteen years from 1809 he was a pertinacious Secretary at War, a junior man alongside the Commander-in-Chief. He stayed there by choice and dealt efficiently with what came onto his desk. He defended flogging and duelling, cut the estimates, and drove his staff hard. In the heroic events of the last years of the Napoleonic Wars his role was humdrum. His social life, however, was not. 'I suppose we may be glad of it', wrote the young Lady Lyttelton when told of his appointment to the War Office, 'as it may divert his lordship from flirting.' It did not. In Almack's, a mixed club in St James's, for which you had to be approved by the seven patronesses, Palmerston – 'Lord Cupid' – was reputed to have enjoyed the favours of three of these as his mistresses. One of them, Lady Cowper, became the love of his life, and they eventually married after her husband's death, when Palmerston was fifty-five. Meanwhile he went his merry way as a bachelor, and got into serious trouble with the Queen when he tried to seduce a Lady in Waiting in Windsor Castle. The public came to admire his aplomb, and chuckled when, aged seventy-eight and Prime Minister, he was cited as co-respondent by O'Kane, an Irish MP. 'We know she's Kane, but is he Abel?' He rode hard, too, galloping so fast from Broadlands to his stables that he had to ride round the yard several times before he could dismount.

Palmerston left the Tories after Canning died, and in 1830 Grey appointed him Foreign Secretary in his Whig government, sensing that a former Tory would reassure Russia, Austria and Prussia, all suspicious of the Whigs. He was still seen as a second-ranker, and no one anticipated that he would be Foreign Secretary for fifteen of the next twenty-one years, and become a hero to the British public, and a villain to nearly all the rulers of Europe, including his own sovereign. But so it proved to be. Palmerston's popularity in the country was built on his foreign policy. He was an unabashed nationalist with a loud bark, and shrewd judgment about when to bite. 'We have no eternal allies and we have no perpetual enemies. Our interests are eternal and perpetual, and those interests it is our duty to follow': thus he responded to critics who accused him of being temporarily pro-Russian. As Foreign Secretary of a constitutional monarchy and an industrial trading nation he was normally to be found supporting other constitutional monarchies and promoting English trade. He had grown up in the age of Napoleon, so the threats posed by French aggression were never far from his mind, and he looked to the arrangements of the Congress of Vienna (1815) to preserve the peace in which trade might flourish. His use of the Navy was forthright, and when diplomacy was concerned with areas within range of the British fleet he was normally successful: in the new kingdom of Belgium, where Leopold, widower of George IV's daughter and uncle to the future Prince Consort, became King instead of the French King's son; in Portugal, where he supported the constitutional Queen against reactionary challenges, and when she then abolished the constitution, persuaded her to restore it.

Events in the Near East could also be influenced by sea power. In 1839 Mehemet Ali, the powerful Pasha of Egypt, looked like overwhelming his nominal overlord, the Sultan. The French were backing Mehemet and the Russians, hoping to exploit the Sultan's collapse, but Palmerston got together with Austria, Prussia and Russia to impose a settlement. With the Navy capturing Beirut and Acre, Mehemet's son was forced to retreat to Egypt, and by the Straits Convention (1841) the Dardanelles were closed to foreign warships. France was isolated, Russia contained and the Mediterranean a safer place for British trade. It was a triumph achieved by proactive diplomacy. All this appealed to public opinion at home. His response to the revolutions which swept through Europe in 1848 was also in tune with popular feeling. He disliked autocrats, and Metternich saw him as the *agent provocateur* of rebellion. But he did not want them to be replaced by republicans. In his Italian policy, all his attitudes emerged clearly: denunciation of the *ancien regime* of King 'Bomba' of Naples, support for the Kings of Sardinia in their efforts to push the Austrian Empire out of Venetia and Lombardy, suspicion of the republican Garibaldi, concern about French influence and papal power. The British electorate saw and approved.

The Queen did not. The rakish Palmerston was out of place in the new court after Albert's arrival. His blunt despatches and his 'rollicking air' (Disraeli's description) had an undiplomatic flavour, and his rudeness was notorious: the Belgian minister complained that he had read the whole of Richardson's *Clarissa* while waiting in Palmerston's anteroom. He liked to fly solo, sending important despatches without showing them to the Queen, sometimes not even consulting the Cabinet. All this infuriated his colleagues, but especially Victoria and Albert, to whom he was 'Lord Pumicestone'. His brinkmanship alarmed them. They were offended by his open contempt for 'petty German princelings' – Albert was one – and his hostility towards Louis Philippe, 'the dear King' of France. They wanted him dismissed. An opportunity arose in 1850. Don Pacifico, a shifty Portuguese merchant who was a British citizen by virtue of his birth in Gibraltar, claimed compensation from the Greek government after his house was ransacked by a mob. Palmerston sent a fleet to the Piraeus, where it seized a Greek ship and instituted a blockade until payment was made. He had gone too far. France and Russia, joint protectors of Greece with Britain, objected to his unilateral action, and he misled the House of Commons. His enemies pounced, but he won a surprise victory in one of the most famous parliamentary debates of the century, after a speech in which he claimed that any British subject should expect the same protection of 'the watchful eye and the strong arm of England' that a Roman had commanded when he claimed: *'Civis Romanus sum.'* Next year the Prime Minister, Russell, did find an opportunity to be rid of him, when, again without consultation, he congratulated Louis Napoleon on his coup d'etat against the Second Republic. But it took him only two months to achieve his 'tit-for-tat with Johnny Russell' and set up a Radical-Conservative alliance which brought down the government. By the end of 1852 he was back in office, this time as Home Secretary in Aberdeen's coalition ministry. This was the ministry which bungled the diplomacy leading to, and the management of, the Crimean War. But public opinion did not hold him responsible (though the suggestion that the war should be fought in the Crimea had been his), and it was this opinion, with a *Punch* cartoon of little Pam the pugilist rolling up his sleeves, that forced the Queen to invite him to succeed Aberdeen as Prime Minister in 1855. He was her fifth choice, seventy years old, and described by Disraeli as 'at best only ginger beer and not champagne, and now an old painted pantaloon'. But Disraeli misjudged him. With one fifteen-month interlude, he was to be Prime Minister for the remaining ten years of his life.

The political scene at Westminster after Peel split the Tory Party, when he repealed the Corn Laws in 1846, was confused. The Tories were still the largest party, but nearly all their leaders had left it with him to become Peelites, gifted, but political floaters. The Whigs, aristocratic, needed Radical support, but the Radicals themselves were divided between Manchester free-traders and vociferous nationalists. On this stage, with Peel gone, Palmerston became the dominant actor. He had no personal power base in Parliament, although he enjoyed the support of Roebuck and the patriotic Radicals, whose motion on the misconduct of the war had brought down the Aberdeen government. He was a Whig, and his Free Trade beliefs made it impossible for him to rejoin the Tories, but he was a maverick; the leader of the traditional Whigs was Russell. His emergence as Prime Minister was due to his longevity in government, the shortcomings of Russell and Aberdeen, and his own popularity in the country. This he cultivated carefully. He gave information to favoured newspapers and wrote unsigned articles himself. After a successful public debate on the hustings at Tiverton with a Chartist leader in 1847, he took to making speeches round the country, wooing Manchester as 'the cradle and nursery of genius', and addressing large audiences in Leeds, Sheffield, Bradford and Glasgow. Once in power, he made it his business to appeal to the skilled workers, whom he wanted to encourage to rise through the social hierarchy to become responsible voting citizens – his preferred route towards democracy, for he resolutely opposed Reform Bills which would enfranchise the poor. He hoped to reduce the gap between Dissent, often the religion of the artisans, and the Church, and consistently appointed Low Churchmen to bishoprics (he features in Trollope as the head of the incoming ministry who made Dr Proudie Bishop of Barchester). He appealed to popular patriotism with oratorical flourishes. His defence budget was the largest in peacetime England in the nineteenth century. Tennyson caught the mood, as so often, in his poem about the new Volunteers: 'Better a rotten borough or two, than a rotten fleet and a city in flames.' In 1856, the *Arrow*, a ship manned by Chinese but registered as British, was boarded by Chinese coastguards. Palmerston ordered the Navy to bombard Canton. A vote of censure was passed against him in the Commons, but he won the subsequent election on the theme: 'an insolent barbarian wielding authority in Canton has violated the British flag.'

Recent historians have modified the picture of the conservative Palmerston, and seen him as the most modern politician of his day. His handling of the Indian Mutiny showed him at his shrewdest: he won applause for its suppression but also the admiration of the Governor-General, 'Clemency' Canning, for abating the subsequent mood of revenge. He was well tuned to the middle-class mid-Victorian electorate. He tried to introduce life peerages in order to enable more industrialists and businessmen to become peers (his motive was to strengthen the House of Lords). As Home Secretary he piloted through significant reforms: the ending of transportation, the creation of reform schools for juvenile prisoners, a Clean Air Act for London; and as Prime Minister an act creating a Divorce Court, from which modern divorce law has developed.

He also became the leader of the first Liberal government. In 1858 he had lost office, blamed for uncharacteristically kowtowing to Napoleon III after the discovery that Orsini, the Emperor's would-be assassin, had made his bombs in England. When he regained power in 1861, he gathered round him Whigs, Peelites and Radicals in a grouping which held together as the Liberal Party. With the Whigs still holding up the banner of Parliamentary Reform, the Peelites proclaiming the importance of free trade and setting a high moral tone, and the Radicals demanding efficient government, this was a potent combination. Palmerston, in many ways its unlikely leader, gave it stability, and the impatient were ready to wait for the old man to die.

There was much to cause them impatience. After injecting new energy into the conduct of the Crimean War, he presided over a fallow period in Parliament. He kept Parliamentary Reform firmly off the agenda. He made no attempt to change the structure of the Army, inadequate though it had proved. In Ireland he saw 'tenants' right as landlords' wrong', and resisted change to the Land Laws, though he was a considerate landlord himself. During the American Civil War his sympathies were with the Southern gentry. He wrote rasping letters to Lincoln's minister in London and allowed the *Alabama*, a Confederate ship built in Birkenhead, to set sail into the Atlantic, where she inflicted heavy damage on Federal shipping. He was not concerned to balance the budgets, and his relations with Gladstone, his ex-Peelite Chancellor of the Exchequer, were uncomfortable. But his last years were golden ones. They coincided with a period of economic prosperity, and the most optimistic mood of the Victorian era. Age had mellowed Lord Pumicestone: even the Queen accepted him. He had always been easy among MPs in the Smoking Room, and Lady Palmerston gave sparkling parties. He was losing his diplomatic skill, underestimating the emerging Prussia and blustering to no avail when Bismarck pushed the Danes out of Schleswig-Holstein. He slept more often in Cabinet meetings, and met an enquiry about his programme with: 'Oh, there is really nothing to be done ... we cannot go on legislating for ever.' But his physical energy remained worthy of the Palmerston legend: the man who used to swim in the Thames before breakfast rode to the Harrow School Speech Day from Piccadilly in 1864 in under an hour. In 1865 he summoned the strength to campaign in Tiverton for his last election. He won it with an increased majority, but died soon afterwards, having enjoyed mutton chops and port for breakfast a week earlier; a Regency buck to the last.

J. Ridley, *Lord Palmerston* (1970).
J. Chambers, *Palmerston: The People's Darling* (2004).

Benjamin Disraeli

BENJAMIN DISRAELI, EARL OF BEACONSFIELD (1804-81) was
Prime Minister in 1868 and from 1874 until 1880. 'Well now, tell me
what you want to be?' said Melbourne to Disraeli when they met for
the first time. 'I want to be Prime Minister,' answered the ringleted
young socialite and budding author. Thirty-four years later, he was
able to reply to the congratulations of his friends: 'Yes, I have
climbed to the top of the greasy pole.' It was a triumph without
parallel, of daring, ability and persistence over apparently insuper-
able handicaps.

He was the first Prime Minister to start as a complete outsider,
without land, inherited wealth or an education at a famous school or
university. He was also the only one to enter politics from a literary
background, and he remained a novelist all his life, writing most of
his last novel, *Endymion*, during his last government. His father, Isaac
D'Israeli, highly regarded as an anthologist after publishing *The
Curiosities of Literature*, provided him with an entrée into the literary
world, and had him baptised as a Christian. But no one meeting
Benjamin could be in doubt about his origins. His name, his black
curls, dark eyes and pale complexion marked him as 'Young Disraeli
the Jew'. His Jewish ancestry was a source of pride to him. By
fantasising about it he felt himself the equal of the British aristocracy, amongst whom he was to spend his political life. Having a sharp
wit and high spirits, he set out to storm, rather than infiltrate, the
citadel of society, and in the process earned a reputation which
dogged him until late in life. He first became notorious as a dandy.
He dressed to shock, walking down Regent Street in military light
blue trousers and black stockings with red stripes. He made
damaging friends like Alfred d'Orsay, dragonfly of the raffish set, and
dangerous enemies like the publisher John Murray, subject of a lively
caricature in his novel *Vivian Gray* (1826), a *succès de scandale*. Society
thought him sexually dangerous, and his mistress, Henrietta Sykes,
had a disreputable past. He also accumulated alarming debts, having
to disappear abroad occasionally to escape his creditors. Determined

to find a seat in the House of Commons, he stood first as a Radical and then as a Tory. At the fifth attempt he won one at Maidstone in 1837, but promptly added to his reputation for sharp practice by marrying Mary Anne Wyndham, the wealthy widow of his fellow member there who had died soon after the election. His maiden speech became famous in the annals of Hansard, described by Greville as 'beginning with florid assurance, speedily degenerating into ludicrous absurdity, and at last being put down with inextinguishable shouts of laughter.' But his voice rose above them: 'The time will come when you will hear me.'

During the next ten years he made sure that they did. He created an informal opposition group within the Conservative Party, wrote three famous novels, and then led the Tory squires in a rebellion which overthrew Peel and transformed the political scene. When Peel became Prime Minister in 1841, Disraeli brashly asked him for a post in his government and was refused. Mortified, he found three others who shared his romantic Toryism, including Lord John Manners, son of the Duke of Rutland. As 'Young England', the four sat together in the House and attacked the 'millocracy' with which Peel, son of a Lancashire cotton magnate, was filling his front bench. Disraeli developed their ideas in three novels. *Coningsby* (1844), the political book of the trilogy, reinterpreted English history. Charles I was the King who laid down his life for the Church and the poor, the Whigs were a clique who hijacked the constitution for their own class, and Peel was just a pseudo-Tory who had attempted 'to construct a party without principles'. In *Sybil* (1845), the social novel, he described the England of the day as 'two nations between whom there is no intercourse and no sympathy ... the Rich and the Poor'. *Tancred* (1847), the most personal of the three, with race and religion as its themes, claimed a place of honour in the history of the world for the Hebrew people and urged the 'mitred nullities' of the Church of England to proclaim again 'the mysteries of Sinai and Calvary'. Together, these novels presented his political credo, that civilisation was based on a hierarchic society, protected by traditional institutions and inspired by religious instincts: men were made 'to adore and to obey'.

In 1844, he found the cause which transformed his career. Peel had come to feel that the Corn Laws, imposing duties on imported corn, were damaging the economy of the country by keeping the price of bread and the level of wages artificially high. He so dominated the

House of Commons that, with almost the whole Cabinet on his side, he believed that he could carry through their repeal himself, even though he led a party of country gentry representing the agricultural interest. The Tory squires might sullenly have let him do so, too, had not Disraeli emerged as their spokesman. He roused them with a series of sparkling speeches. His theme was betrayal. 'It was a great thing to hear the Right Honourable Gentleman say, "I would rather be the leader of the gentlemen of England than possess the confidence of sovereigns." That was a grand thing. We don't hear much of the gentlemen of England now.' Free trade in corn was a Whig policy, but 'The Right Honourable gentleman caught the Whigs bathing and walked away with their clothes. He has left them in the full enjoyment of their Liberal position, and is himself the strict Conservative of their garments.' The louder the applause and laughter, the more measured and impassive the speaker became. It was studied oratory of the highest order, and it had Peel hanging his head. When Disraeli described this Conservative government as 'an organised hypocrisy', Lord George Bentinck emerged from its back benches to form a new Protectionist Party. Though the Repeal was carried with Whig help, a Protectionist/Whig alliance brought Peel down a week later (June 1846).

The Tory Party was to be split for a generation. Almost all Peel's Cabinet followed him out of office, leaving a gap into which Disraeli moved, so that he became its leader in the House of Commons. But the extraordinary upheaval which gave him prominence also kept him from power. None of those loyal to Peel would sit in a Cabinet with him. For twenty years, therefore, a majority in the House of Commons could only be established by an alliance of Whigs and Peelites, and the three short Conservative governments (1852, 1858-9, 1866-8), with the Earl of Derby as Prime Minister and Disraeli leading the Commons, were all minority ones. Disraeli was a master of the arts of opposition, and gradually won the confidence of the aristocratic Derby. Without it he would never have become Prime Minister himself, for Tories mistrusted him as much as they were later to distrust Churchill before he reached Downing Street. Although the ringlets and gaudy clothes had gone, and he had started to play the part of a country gentleman, buying Hughenden Manor (with money borrowed from the Duke of Portland), his early reputation remained, one dark curl brushed carefully and proudly across his forehead, and his policies were those of a manoeuverer. He

soon abandoned agricultural protection, and his budget as
Chancellor of the Exchequer in 1852 was a bundle of ingenious expedients. The Parliamentary Reform Bill which he introduced in 1859
was planned for party gain, and the Second Reform Act which he
and Derby carried in 1867 stole as many of the Whigs' clothes as Peel
had done. Indeed, it went further than the one Gladstone had failed
to get passed, nearly doubling the electorate by giving the vote to all
householders in the boroughs, but also protecting the electoral
strength of the landed interest by removing boroughs from the
counties. There was discontent on the right wing, dangerously
articulated by Lord Salisbury, but Disraeli's parliamentary leadership
gave the party its only prospect of power. Derby realised this and,
when he resigned in 1868, he rebuffed those who backed his own son
as his heir. Tenacity, courage and skill had made Disraeli Prime
Minister, but his was still a minority government, and a heavy defeat
at the polls in 1868 meant six more years of opposition. Against the
flood of the reforms of Gladstone's first ministry, he showed all his
old gifts in opposition. The more exuberant Gladstone's oratory became, the more impassively he sat. By 1872 he was ready to emerge.
At the Crystal Palace he compared the weary Liberal ministers to 'a
range of exhausted volcanoes. Not a flame flickers on a single pallid
crest. But the situation is still dangerous. There are occasional
earthquakes, and ever and anon the dark rumblings of the sea.'
When the election came in 1874, the freshly geared Conservative
Party machinery pulled in the votes of the poorer householders: the
vested interests threatened by Gladstone's reforms swung away from
the Liberals, and their majority of a hundred was converted into a
Conservative majority of 105. This, at last, was power.

For Disraeli it came late. The spirit still burned strongly behind
the mask, and, with the wife to whom he had been devoted now
dead, he fell in love with the fifty-four-year-old Lady Bradford, and
poured out his feelings in letters to her and her sister, sometimes
twice a day; he even rode to hounds with her. But he was seventy,
gouty and asthmatic, and in 1876 he left the Commons, scene of
many triumphs, and accepted a move to the House of Lords as Earl
of Beaconsfield. 'I am dead – dead, but in the Elysian Fields.' His
government lasted for six years, but its importance lies as much in
his style, and the myths he left behind, as in its achievements.
Achievements there were: significant social reforms, urgently needed
in post-Industrial-Revolution Britain. They included trade union

measures which legalised peaceful picketing; an Artisan Dwelling
Act which started slum clearance; Public Health, Factory, Education
and Merchant Shipping Acts; and a Sale of Food and Drugs Act
which lasted for fifty years. Many of these did not involve compul-
sion. It was Disraeli's belief that 'in England you must trust to persuasion and example if you wish to effect any considerable change in
the manners and customs of the people.' He never had a strong grasp
of detail, and left legislation, for which he had an instinctive distaste,
to capable ministers, such as 'Mr Secretary Cross, who I always forget to call Sir Richard'. He reserved his main energies for a dramatic
foreign policy, for he wanted the British people to be proud to take
their place in the great events of the world. He brought off a
spectacular coup in 1875 when he trumped a French syndicate's bid
and bought the Khedive of Egypt's Suez Canal shares with money
borrowed from the Rothschilds. He stood up to the Russians, sending a fleet to the Straits when they took advantage of Christian
revolts against the Turks to march through the Balkans towards
Constantinople, and playing a lead part at the Congress at Berlin
which Bismarck called to resolve the crisis in 1878. When negotiations stalled there, Disraeli ordered a special train to take him home
early. The move worked and agreements were signed, leaving Turkey
in Europe and the British with Cyprus, the Russians limiting their
gains to the Caucasus. Disraeli won the admiration of Bismarck –
'der alte Jude, das ist der Mann' – and returned to present 'Peace with
Honour' to an enthusiastic London, where the music halls had just
coined the word 'jingoism'. But Disraeli's lifelong sympathy for the
Turks ran across currents of nationalism, the potency of which he
never grasped, and the survival of Turkey in Europe left a power
vacuum in the Balkans which was to lead to the First World War.
Further afield, the record was stained by frontier disasters and the
massacre of British troops and civilians, by Afghans at Kabul (1878)
and by Zulus at Isandhlwana (1879), while public reaction to the
Royal Titles Act (1876), by which the Queen became Empress of
India, was hostile.

Perhaps the most significant feature of Disraeli's government was
a change outside his control. The long and deep agricultural depression which began towards the end of it, caused by cheap grain from
the American prairies and exacerbated by three bad harvests, was to
destroy the hegemony of the great aristocratic landowners. 'The
office of the leader of the Conservative party ... is to uphold the

aristocratic settlement of this country,' Disraeli had written in 1846. But with the urban workers dependent upon cheap food, the reintroduction of agricultural protection was deemed politically impossible. It was a cruel irony that the man who had made his political career by defending the Corn Laws, and whose credo was profoundly aristocratic, should have presided over the start of the downfall of the economic and social structure on which the hierarchy he believed in was based. The electorate certainly sensed that something was wrong. With Gladstone emerging from retirement to lead them against the evils of 'Beaconsfieldism', the Liberals swept back into power in 1880. Within a year, Disraeli was dead.

But from the Elysian Fields his became a name to conjure with, as the founder of the modern Conservative Party. The Primrose League, which organised Conservative working-class support and was named after the flowers which the Queen had laid on his grave, kept his memory bright. This was a party which stood for Queen and Empire, and for One Nation. There was truth, if selective truth, in the image of Disraeli which his followers projected. He had indeed transformed the unpopular 'Widow of Windsor' into a Queen Empress whose Diamond Jubilee was to be the apogee of the British Empire, wooing and winning her as his Faerie in his most elaborate literary style. Although he had never used the phrase 'One Nation', and had absolutely no democratic instincts, he had written *Sybil*, had passed a Reform Act and had switched the political agenda from Liberal constitutional to Conservative social reform. His vision of a society bound together in common loyalty to the throne, the Church and the landed aristocracy was a chimera. But the breadth and haziness of his ideas made them available for adaptable interpretation – and he was a potent mythmaker himself. He invented a romantic role for the Tory Party in the past and gave it a sense of purpose for the future. He understood the importance of image and style in leadership. His duels with Gladstone across the floor of the House of Commons excited a widespread public at a time when 'the great council of the nation assembled at Westminster' was the unchallenged focus of British political life. He enlivened his own times, and the pages of history, with his oratory, his courage and success against the odds, and his sheer enjoyment of life in politics.

R. Blake, *Disraeli* (1969).
P. Smith, *Disraeli: A Brief Life* (1996).

William Ewart Gladstone

WILLIAM EWART GLADSTONE (1809-98) was four times Prime Minister (1868-74, 1880-5, 1886 and 1892-4). He was the most enduring Victorian statesman, sitting in the House of Commons for sixty-three years, and a minister for over thirty of them. His intellectual energy and his physical stamina became legendary. In office he wrote 25,000 letters a year; out of office he completed a three-volume study, *Homer and the Homeric Age,* and composed over two hundred sermons for the family prayers at his home, Hawarden. In 1884, aged nearly seventy-five, he climbed Ben Macdhui (4,300ft) from Balmoral, a twenty-five-mile walk, in seven hours forty minutes. In Parliament he was a dominant figure; in the country he became *the* dominant figure. To some he was a hero, to others a dangerous lunatic. Few were neutral about the man who took politics out of the narrow bounds of Westminster and the great country houses, and brought them into the arena of the people.

He was the son of a successful Liverpool merchant and rentier who had used his wealth, made largely from West Indian trading in sugar, tobacco and cotton, to buy land and political standing. Eton and Christ Church, Oxford, completed William's naturalisation amongst the aristocratic elite, and, seen after a speech at the Oxford Union attacking the Reform Bill as the 'rising hope of the stern, unbending Tories', he became MP for a pocket borough, Newark, in 1832. As a serious churchman, who based his religion on the sacraments as well as prayer, he regarded the Whig government's interference with Church doctrines as dangerous and corrupt. But under the influence of his hero, Peel, he started a long move leftwards across the political spectrum. When the Conservative Party split after the Repeal of the Corn Laws he became a Peelite, joined Palmerston's Whig government in 1859, and emerged as leader of the new Liberal Party, from which he eventually drove the old Whigs. His progress from the High Tory to 'the people's William' carried him down the broad stream of Victorian history, and he was to promote and encapsulate many of the central Victorian achievements and values.

He was already an experienced statesman when he became Prime Minister in 1868, having served under Peel as President of the Board of Trade and under Aberdeen, Palmerston and Russell as Chancellor of the Exchequer. His first government, formed after the Second Reform Bill had enfranchised about a million new voters, was his most creative. He disestablished the Church of Ireland and passed an Irish Land Act. Forster's Education Act, Cardwell's Army reforms and Selwyn's Judicature Act laid the foundations of compulsory state education, a modern Army and a new structure of central law courts. The civil service was opened to entry by competitive examination, and religious tests for university appointments were abolished. Income tax came down to four pence, with revenue still rising. After defeat at the polls in 1874 ('swept from office on a torrent of gin and beer', after the unpopular Licensing Act, was his verdict; others felt that he had done too much too quickly), he resigned the party leadership. But, as Aberdeen had already observed, he was 'terrible on the rebound'. He emerged to denounce Disraeli's pro-Turkish policy, in a series of pamphlets on the Bulgarian atrocities and a speaking tour of Midlothian. The Liberals duly won the election of 1880 and the Queen, who disliked him as much as she liked Disraeli, had to accept him again as Prime Minister.

His second ministry (1880-5) was much less successful. He suffered prolonged embarrassment over Charles Bradlaugh, whose refusal as an atheist to take the oath required of incoming MPs pulled Gladstone in contradictory directions between his Christianity and his Liberalism. He did manage to protect Irish tenant farmers more effectively with another Land Act, giving them the three 'F's, Fixity of tenure, Fair rents and Free sale, but his efforts to end coercion and work with the Irish leader Parnell were ended by the brutal murder in Phoenix Park of the newly arrived Chief Secretary Lord Frederick Cavendish. He steered the Third Reform Bill through Parliament. But events abroad harassed him increasingly. Defeat by the Boers at Majuba was followed by British withdrawal from the Transvaal, and the invasion of Egypt in 1882 led three years later to the spectacular catastrophe of Gordon's death at Khartoum.

After the Liberals lost the election of 1885, Gladstone introduced a new dimension into British politics by proposing Home Rule as the solution to Ireland's problems. This gave him the backing of the Irish nationalists, and a fresh government based on a Liberal/Irish alliance, but it split the Liberal Party. The old Whigs broke away. Some were big landowners in Ireland, and many were bewildered and mistrustful of their increasingly egocentric leader. So Gladstone could not carry the First Home Rule Bill (1886) even through the House of Commons, and his third ministry lasted only five months. But he did not give up, and had one more electoral victory. For this he had had to accept from his Radical supporters the Newcastle Programme (a hodgepodge of triennial parliaments, district and parish councils, employers' responsibility for workers' accidents and compulsory land-purchase powers for the state). But he himself focused on his Second Home Rule Bill. He carried it through the House of Commons, bearing the brunt of marathon debates himself, aged eighty-three. 'I have never seen Mr Gladstone so dramatic, so prolific of all the resources of an actor's art,' wrote an observer. When the bill was decisively thrown out by the House of Lords, he had to be dissuaded by his Cabinet from calling a Peers versus People election, before resigning for the last time.

What sort of a man was this political colossus? In his diary on his birthday in 1868, the first he celebrated as Prime Minister, Gladstone wrote: 'The Almighty seems to sustain and spare me for some purpose of His own, deeply unworthy though I know myself to be. Glory be to His name.' He lived his life in the belief that he would be called to account for it by his Maker. There lies the key to his political career. Towards the Church his attitude underwent a transformation. In 1838 he published *The State in its Relations to the Church*, in which he asserted that membership of the Church of England should be a fundamental qualification for holding any office in the national community. But its failure to achieve the spiritual regeneration of the nation perplexed him. He came to feel that Christian salvation did not belong to one particular church or even belief in one particular creed, but rather in the freedom to search for it in one's own way. Though he himself was a steadfast Anglican worshipper, the erstwhile High Anglican ended as the disestablisher of the Church of Ireland (1869), the abolisher of religious tests for university appointments (1871) and the ally of Nonconformists.

His sense of personal responsibility before God influenced his approach to finance: Roy Jenkins described him as God's Vicar in the Treasury. Finance became his special expertise. His double first in Classics and Mathematics at Oxford had not included any aspects of economics, but he learnt about them under Peel, who made him

President of the Board of Trade in 1843. Thenceforward he became, after Peel, the driving force towards free trade, which he saw as the engine of prosperity for the poor, and of peace for the world. As Aberdeen's Chancellor of the Exchequer in 1853 he presented the first of his great budgets (twelve in all), which steadily reduced tariffs on raw materials and industrial goods, and underlay the expansion of trade on which later Victorian wealth was based. Although, to pay for the short-term loss to the Treasury which this involved, Gladstone had to keep income tax, he planned to reduce and eventually abolish it. Low taxation gave each person control over his own resources, and was right on moral as well as economic grounds. Economy in the management of public money was the duty of a minister. 'No Chancellor is worth his salt who is not ready to ... save candle ends and cheese parings in the cause of his country.' When he finally resigned in 1894 it was over the naval estimates, which he thought excessive. Gladstone was instinctively suspicious of central government expenditure, though keen to develop local government. But it was a corollary of low taxation that rich men should give away much of their wealth: thus 'the surplus property of the few will become a treasury for the common good.' Near the end of his life he became embittered by the irresponsible attitude of the great landowners.

The importance of personal responsibility governed his changing attitude towards Parliamentary Reform. The opponent of the First Reform Bill became the leader who in 1865 aimed to extend the franchise to artisans; who in 1884, through the Third Reform Act, did extend the vote to all householders in the counties and who was talking in terms of triennial parliaments and 'one man one vote' by the end of his life. He favoured open voting and only agreed to the introduction of secret voting in The Ballot Act (1872) after he had been persuaded that the occupations of many new voters made them vulnerable to pressure. But it was not merely through legislation that Gladstone changed the political life of the nation. In 1865, rejected as their MP by Oxford University, who expected to be represented by a proper Tory, he moved to South Lancashire. His opening address of the campaign, given appropriately at the Free Trade Hall in Manchester, began: 'At last, my friends, I am come amongst you ... and I am come unmuzzled.' Thenceforward he delivered long, dramatic political speeches to large crowds in great halls all round the country, most famously in Scotland, where his Midlothian campaign involved thirty speeches in fifteen days, and sent waves which brought him back to power a year later. Audiences were huge, 8,000 at Galashiels Station, 20,000 in the Waverley Market, 14,000 for the three speeches in Glasgow that he delivered in one day. His physical presence was formidable, eyes glittering, voice ringing out. He never talked down to audiences, but raised them to his level of indignation or exaltation. So, to a crowd of Scots, 'The sanctity of life in the hill villages of Afghanistan, in the winter snows, is as inviolable in the eyes of Almighty God as can be your own.' And for every one who heard him, hundreds more read his speeches in the columns of the press. Gladstone was the first great national orator, and only Lloyd George and Churchill have matched him since.

It was a sense of national responsibility before God which informed Gladstone's foreign policy, and his Irish policy too. This sometimes made him popular. British people shared his revulsion against what he saw going on in the King of Naples' prisons, and his sympathy for the young nations of Europe emerging from the stifling rule of old empires, epitomised by the Italian Risorgimento. Later, in his Midlothian campaign (1879), they were stirred by the fervour of his denunciation of the atrocities of Disraeli's Turkish allies in the Balkans, who, he hoped, 'shall clear out, one and all, bag and bagage, from the provinces they have desolated and profaned'. More often, however, his high-mindedness aroused jingoistic opposition. Few were happy when in 1872 he asserted the rule of international law by paying large compensation to the United States for the damage inflicted on their shipping by the *Alabama*, a Confederate ship which Russell and Palmerston had allowed to sail from Liverpool. Fewer still applauded the Convention of Pretoria, handing the Transvaal back to the Boers. When he did send a British Army into Egypt in 1882, to protect British interests against the nationalist uprising of Arabi Pasha, he justified it by the need to 'convert the interior state of Egypt from anarchy and conflict to peace and order.' But his ambivalence towards the undertaking proved fatal when in 1885 Gordon, sent to withdraw garrisons from the Sudan, stayed put in Khartoum. Gladstone, most unwilling of imperialists, refused to authorise a relief force until too late, and had to face an explosion of public revulsion. The G.O.M. (Grand Old Man), became the M.O.G. (Murderer of Gordon).

Hearing that he was to be asked to form a government in 1868, he proclaimed, 'My mission is to pacify Ireland.' He saw Protestant rule in Ireland as 'some tall tree of noxious growth ... poisoning the atmosphere of the land so far as its shadow can extend. It is still there, gentlemen, but ... the axe has been laid to the root of the tree.' When it falls, 'the conscience of England and Scotland will repose ... upon the thought that something has been done towards the discharge of national duty.' What other British statesman, at any other period, could have spoken to his electors thus? The power of his leadership did rouse and keep a surprisingly large body of support for his efforts; but the Land Acts and Home Rule antagonised the landed classes, and after a quarter of a century the conscience of the nation grew noticeably weaker. When the Second Home Rule Bill was thrown out by the Lords in 1893, not a dog barked from Land's End to John o'Groats.

As his features gazed from the walls and shelves of more and more cottages throughout her realm, the Queen's dislike of Gladstone turned to revulsion. Her seclusion at Windsor after Albert's death, and the Prince of Wales's idle and disreputable lifestyle, had made the monarchy unpopular. In 1870 Gladstone tackled the 'Royalty Question' by urging her to perform her public duties in London and by suggesting that the Prince of Wales should become Lord Lieutenant of Ireland. He also showed himself sceptical about her ill health. She never forgave him. Disestablishment of her Church, the alarming extension of the franchise, his demagogic speeches and the disgrace of Khartoum all fed the flames. 'Such conduct', she wrote of the Midlothian campaign, 'is unheard of, and the only excuse is – that he is not quite sane.' She kept her contact with him to a minimum, and did not consult him about his successor when he finally resigned. Being a convinced monarchist, who put the institution on a pedestal, he was deeply wounded. But much of the blame must lie with him, for the naïve and insensitive way in which he pursued his aim.

As he aged, Gladstone also became estranged from the great landowners, amongst whom he had earlier been accustomed to move. He felt they used their wealth irresponsibly: they believed that his policies were threatening the foundations of society. Their near-loathing for him reached its peak during his last ministry. When he was knocked down in the park at Hawarden by a wild heifer, which had to be shot, a wreath was sent with a card attached, 'To the memory of the patriotic cow which sacrificed its life in an attempt to save Ireland from Home Rule.' His public parading of his conscience aroused their distaste. Disraeli protested that he would not mind Mr Gladstone having the ace of trumps up his sleeve if he did not always claim that God had put it there. The contrast in the style of these two added piquancy to politics through the fourteen years in which they faced each other as party leaders. To Gladstone, Dizzy was a play actor, whose only principle was to win power: the truth was not in him, and his creation of Victoria, his 'Faery Queen', as Empress of India was romantic nonsense with a jingoist flavour.

The most complex aspect of Gladstone's personality was his work in rescuing prostitutes. For many years he would walk the streets at night on his own, and encourage them to come home, where he and his wife would give them food and shelter, and try to help them to change their way of life. This brought scandal upon him, and could have been politically damaging. He became attracted by more than one of them, and his diaries are filled with expressions of remorse (and symbols indicating days when he scourged himself, a custom not uncommon at the time amongst High Churchmen). But though he 'trod the path of danger' – a diary entry – he told his son that he was never 'guilty of infidelity to the marriage bed', and to a lady who passed on gossip from an MP who had seen him talking to a prostitute he replied: 'It may be true that the gentleman saw me in such conversation, but the object was not what he assumed, or, as I am afraid, hoped.' He went boldly on, and only agreed to give the work up in 1886.

His family life was close and happy. He married Catherine Glynne in 1839 and she survived him. Their eight children enjoyed a sometimes riotous life at Hawarden, often in the company of their Lyttleton cousins, with whom they spoke a special language, Glynnese. From his library he could be enticed to join the family brouhaha. Mrs Gladstone was intelligent and lively, and ready to tease him: 'Oh, William dear, if you weren't such a great man you would be a terrible bore.' She was too disorganised to be an effective political hostess, and much of their entertaining was done at breakfast. At the end of their lives, when Gladstone had become a legend, Hawarden became a place of pilgrimage: 26,000 people went there for a flower show in 1896. He was by then out of sympathy with the trends towards state interference and imperialism personified in his erstwhile Radical ally Joseph Chamberlain. But when he died – on Ascension Day 1898 – he was honoured as his country's greatest citizen, with the Prince of Wales and the Duke of York, two future kings, among his pallbearers. Almost everyone in public life, as well as the crowds at his meetings around the country, had come under the spell of his eloquence, 'his falcon's eye, with strange imperious flash' (Morley). The impact of his personality, the passion of his convictions, his superhuman stamina and the enduring strength of his sense of duty, made him the giant of his time.

H.C.G. Mathew, *Gladstone* (2 vols, 1986 and 1995).
R. Jenkins, *Gladstone* (1995).

Marquess of Salisbury

Robert Gascoyne-Cecil, 3rd Marquess of Salisbury (1830-1903), Prime Minister 1885-6, 1886-92 and 1895-1902, was the last to run the government from the House of Lords. With two ancestors who were the ablest chief ministers to serve Elizabeth I and James I, his was a name to conjure with, and he proved to be the first Cecil to match them. He was aristocratic in his detachment as well as his birth. He spent as much time as he could in his home, the great Elizabethan mansion, Hatfield House. There he could pursue his interests, botany, physics and photography as well as theology. Hatfield was the first English country house to be lit by electricity, and guests had to be careful not to trip over the telephone cords which curled loose on the floors. When Gladstone received the summons to Downing Street, he was wielding an axe at the base of an oak; when his came, Salisbury was experimenting with a piece of wiring.

At Hatfield, too, he could play the host without having to endure the social round of London dinner parties, for he was uncomfortably shy. Overgrown, short-sighted and scholarly, he was bullied at Eton, and would later cross the road to avoid meeting an Etonian contemporary. He disliked the smoking rooms of politics and did not listen to a single debate in the House of Commons after he moved to the Lords in 1868. He relied on his buoyant and sociable wife to pull him out of his study or his laboratory, and from his occasional deep depression. Their marriage was close and his home happy, with eight children, but it made him still more detached from what went on outside it. He was a religious man, whose faith was described by his daughter as 'a personal surrender in love and trust to the living Christ', and he viewed this world in the perspective of the life to come. Later he developed aristocratic eccentricities. He had always been unusual to look at, the gangling youth developing into a very tall and heavy man with bowed shoulders and a large beard. He dressed so badly that he was once refused permission to enter the Casino at Monte Carlo. He rode a tricycle for exercise. Peering myopically, he failed to recognise a member of his Cabinet at the breakfast table, and was said to have held a long conversation with a 'delightful sporting peer' under the impression that he was Lord Roberts, recently returned from commanding the Army in the Boer War.

Salisbury was an intellectual conservative. Estranged from his father, he had to write to earn a living. His political articles, published in the 1860s mostly for the Tory *Quarterly Review*, were often starkly reactionary. He feared the advance of democracy, where 'passion is the rule', and 'the rich pay taxes and the poor make the laws.' Therein lay the danger 'in the bestowal on any class of a voting power disproportionate to their stake in the country.' He saw the politics of his time as, at root, 'a struggle between those who have, to keep what they have got, and those who have not, to get it.' For him it became a struggle on four fronts, ecclesiastical, constitutional, fiscal and imperial. He believed the Church of England to be an essential part of the established order of his country, so he opposed the admission of Jews into the House of Commons and the abolition of Church rates, supported the maintenance of religious tests for entry into Oxford and Cambridge, and bitterly fought the disestablishment of the Church of Ireland. As a defender of the constitution he saw Disraeli as a leader who betrayed his own side, and who, by his devious personality, alone prevented a coalition between Tories and moderate Whigs in the defence of property. Salisbury did not like Disraeli. 'Mr Disraeli is the grain of dirt that clogs the whole machine,' he wrote, and although he agreed to serve in a Tory Cabinet under Derby he resigned when it produced the Second Reform Bill. Later Disraeli was justly to describe Salisbury as 'a great master of gibes and flouts and jeers'.

That this erstwhile rebel should become Prime Minister was unlikely; that he should head three ministries for a total of nearly fourteen years defied augury. He was seen as formidably able, but a right-wing maverick. Good fortune played a part in his rise to power and in his success in using it. Disraeli's magnanimity in inviting him back to his new government in 1874 as Secretary for India, and promoting him to be Foreign Secretary in 1878, gave him his opening. When Disraeli died and was succeeded by a duumvirate, Sir Stafford Northcote in the Commons and Salisbury in the Lords, Northcote proved an uninspiring leader, overawed by Gladstone. He was mauled by the young tigers on his back benches who dubbed him 'The Goat', and Salisbury emerged as the strong man of the party. Gladstone's conversion to Home Rule for Ireland in 1886 then split the Liberal Party and led the more conservative Whigs to create a Liberal Unionist Party, on which Salisbury was able to rely for his majorities. The landed classes were at last coming together on the Conservative side, while Disraeli, through his assertive foreign policy, had broadened its support by making it the focus for the growing popular belief in a Great and Greater Britain. After his big victory over Gladstone in 1886, his one dangerous rival, Lord Randolph Churchill, destroyed himself by an ill-timed and ill-tempered resignation, before succumbing to a mortal illness. Fate certainly dealt a good hand to the most electorally successful of all Conservative Prime Ministers.

But he also played it with skill: indeed, he enjoyed the political game. He had the most important conservative instinct of all, of realising when reform must be accepted and how to get the best out of it. So the opponent of the 1867 Reform Bill was the realist who sealed his authority over his party by the skill with which he turned Gladstone's 1885 Reform Bill to advantage. He linked its wider franchise to a massive increase in single-member constituencies, which favoured Conservatives in the suburbs and also stopped the Liberals from sharing two-member seats between Whigs and Radicals. He followed closely the activities of his energetic Chief Agent, 'Skipper' Middleton, in the constituencies, and his able Chief Whip, Akers-Douglas, in the Commons, and was ready to help them with a generous (though properly monitored) use of Honours. Despite his initially sardonic comments, he became a Grand Master of the Primrose League, which promoted a vision of Disraelian conservatism through tea parties and fêtes, and brought women onto the political scene. He showed astute patience in his handling of Churchill, and in the gradual forging of links with the Liberal Unionists.

Salisbury first revealed his ability to run a department as Secretary of State for India. Shaken by the horrors of a famine in Orissa in 1866, and concerned about possible native risings, he strengthened the powers of the Secretary over the Viceroy, and used them to promote prosperity in India, with lower taxes and cheaper credit. He was delighted to succeed the cautious and pacific Derby as Foreign Secretary in 1878. 'I like the Foreign Office,' he wrote. Indeed, he liked it so much that he was his own Foreign Secretary for all but two of his years as Prime Minister, and ran the government from the Foreign Office building. He had the instincts of a diplomat: 'there is always a pass through the mountains.' Because the British Empire reached its apogee while he was Prime Minister, with more of the map painted red than at any other time and Victoria's Diamond Jubilee (1897) an imperial celebration, it is tempting to see Salisbury as a jingoist. Nothing could be further from the truth. The preservation of peace was at the heart of his foreign policy. He understood, earlier than most, the limitations imposed by economic constraints, and shunned policies which risked increases in taxation, falling as these did mainly on the landowners to whose interest he was dedicated. So he avoided commitments to allies which could be fulfilled only at a damaging cost, and tried to work through consensus, the 'Concert of Europe'. He was also especially sensitive to events in those parts of the world where British trading interests were involved: China, for example, which was becoming the chief market for Lancashire cotton, and where he obtained a ninety-nine-year lease on the mainland opposite the British colony of Hong Kong.

Competitive nations made Europe and the wider world restless and dangerous. Their jostling often focused on the Balkans and on Africa. The decline of the Turkish Empire was creating a vacuum in the Balkans. Faced with the choice of reviving and reforming the Turks or dismembering their Empire into small nations under the influence of Russia and Austria-Hungary, Disraeli from the first, and Salisbury eventually, backed the Turks. Salisbury's firm despatches brought the Russians to the negotiating table, and the Congress of Berlin (1878) sent Russian armies back from the outskirts of Constantinople and produced a settlement guaranteed by the Great Powers. Britain annexed Cyprus, as a base from which to support Turkey and protect the route to India. But, as Prime Minister, Salisbury came to despair of the Turks. 'We have backed the wrong horse,' he confessed, and the power vacuum remained, to be the immediate cause of the First World War. In Africa his successes lasted longer. As that continent was opened up by explorers and missionaries, his diplomacy was at its most effective in arranging for the spoils of the scramble for territory there to be divided peacefully between the European nations involved. France, Germany, Belgium, Italy and Portugal all sought their share. Salisbury's chief concern was to keep them away from the basin of the Nile, for Britain had been drawn into Egypt through her interest in the Suez Canal and the route to India. Three treaties in 1890 settled most of the problems. It required an ultimatum to get Portugal to drop her claims to a belt through the centre of Africa along the Zambesi, to link her colonies in Angola and Mozambique. Germany limited her interest in East Africa to Tanganyika (now Tanzania), in exchange for Heligoland, a British-owned island off her North Sea coast. The French got large areas, mostly desert, in North West Africa. In 1898 they sent an expedition across to the Nile headwaters. Rumours of it had prompted Salisbury to reconquer the Sudan, which the British had abandoned when Gordon was killed at Khartoum. Kitchener's victory there, at Omdurman, brought him face to face with the French at Fashoda. War threatened, but Salisbury remained impassive, the realities of power showed, and the French, foiled, sailed down the Nile amidst British congratulations on the courage of their expedition. Courtesy, not bravado, was Salisbury's way. As for British expansion, much of it was achieved by the East Africa and South Africa Companies, to which he gave charters but no money.

One cannot but sense the 'melancholy long withdrawing roar' of Salisbury's ministries. He was a masterly political manager, who faced down the dangerous Randolph Churchill, fostered the alliance with the Liberal Unionists until he persuaded them into his last ministry, and diverted the Radical among them, Joe Chamberlain, into becoming Secretary for the Colonies. There was some important legislation, alongside slum clearance and housing improvements in which he had a long-standing interest. County Councils were set up by the Local Government Act (1888), and free education was established by the abolition of school fees (1891). But these were pre-emptive measures, to avert the risk of more drastic change. In Ireland he and his nephew Balfour lowered the temperature with firm government and Purchase Acts, which enabled tenants to buy their land: but these spelt doom in the long run for the landlords. A realist, he would not rescue his fellow landowners by restoring protection for agriculture or repealing the death duties introduced by the Liberals in 1894. He knew that he was living with two trends against which he could do little: the growing power of new voters at home, and of Germany abroad. His religious faith enabled him to accept his world with equanimity. 'The events of our day ... are but infinitesimal atoms in the great whole' of God's creation.

Towards the end he grew tired. 'That strange, powerful, brilliant, obstructive deadweight at the top' was how Curzon saw him. He had always run his Cabinets on a loose rein: now, although finding places in his last ministry for four members of his own family ('the Hotel Cecil' it was dubbed), he left much of the making of policy to Chamberlain. He did not, for instance, know about the Jameson Raid: but when the Kaiser sent a public telegram congratulating Kruger on defeating it, Salisbury took charge, sending ships to Delagoa Bay, but damping down press reaction. The Boer War, which he might have prevented had he been more consistently active, overshadowed the closing years of his life with its griefs, its threats, and an increase in direct taxation which fell heavily on the landed gentry. He saw it through stoically, calm as ever in a crisis, and, when the worst was over, prolonged Conservative rule by staging the 'Khaki Election' and handing over an apparently secure position to Balfour in 1902. But, shrewd and sceptical, he realised that he had only slowed down the progress of democracy: that he had given ground in his struggle to defend property. Perhaps because he lived at the end of an era, with beliefs and policies which looked more to the past than the future, he does not now rank alongside Peel, Disraeli or Thatcher as a Conservative Party hero. But his standing in it then, as in the country and in Europe, was massive.

A. Roberts, *Salisbury, Victorian Titan* (1999).

Earl of Rosebery

ARCHIBALD PRIMROSE, 5TH EARL OF ROSEBERY (1847-1929) was
Prime Minister for only sixteen months (1894-5). Taking over from
Gladstone was never going to be easy, and there were warning
signs aplenty that his would not be a smooth ride. Most of the
Whig aristocrats had left the Liberal Party over Home Rule.
Traditional Nonconformists and reforming Radicals, who now made
up its bulk, were not natural bedfellows, and they had recently lost
two gifted leaders in Chamberlain (defected) and Dilke (disgraced).
Only a man with Machiavellian political skills could have reunited
the old Liberal Party: only an inspiring Radical leader could have
mapped out a place for the new one. Rosebery was neither. Yet many
saw him as Gladstone's natural heir. He had a power base in
Scotland, where he owned two fine houses on the Firth of Forth,
Dalmeny and Barnbougle. Gladstone's Midlothian campaign was
run from Dalmeny, and Rosebery himself was capable of rousing the
enthusiasm of crowds from a platform. His considerable wealth
became exceptional when he married Hannah Rothschild. He had
political experience, as the first Chairman of the London County
Council in 1889, and in three of Gladstone's Cabinets, with special
responsibility for Scotland from 1881 to 1885, and then as Lord Privy
Seal and twice Foreign Secretary, 1886 and 1892 to 1894. Gladstone's
alternative successor, Sir William Harcourt, large, able and in the
House of Commons, was hot tempered and quarrelsome, and none
of his Cabinet colleagues would serve under him. It had to be
Rosebery.

His was a complex character. Great men fascinated him, and he
wrote about such as Cromwell, Frederick the Great and Chatham, as
well as a popular life of the younger Pitt. But he hated politicking:
'He would not stoop, he did not conquer,' was Winston Churchill's
verdict. He was moody, switching from lively charm to silent
arrogance; rude even to his devoted Hannah, whose early death in
1890 left him devastated and drove him into solitude or the company
of younger men. He was temperamentally incapable of being part of

a team, let alone running a Cabinet; indeed, it was sometimes hard for his ministers to find him, as he flitted from one of his houses to another. Nonconformists mistrusted him, as the owner of a string of racehorses – their outcry grew stronger when he won the Derby twice – and as a leader who could not resist the flippant *mot* on serious subjects: the Queen advised him to be 'less jocular' in his speeches. As Foreign Secretary he had waved the big stick at the Khedive of Egypt and had rescued the East Africa Company from financial difficulties by annexing Uganda: a very un-Gladstonian imperialist.

The relationship between him and Harcourt dominated his ministry. It was conducted on paper, for they seldom met. Their main quarrels, expressed violently by Harcourt and with disdain by Rosebery, were over foreign policy and Harcourt's radical budget. Rosebery took office only on condition that he could have unfettered choice of Foreign Secretary, and picked a fellow peer, the Earl of Kimberley. Harcourt made his condition that, as Leader in the Commons, he would always be informed before any important foreign initiatives were taken; but much diplomacy was confidential, not least over the spheres of European influence in Africa. To protect the British position in the Sudan from the French, Rosebery negotiated a treaty with King Leopold of Belgium, leasing him former Egyptian land to the south and east. He also started negotiations with France about the future position in Egypt itself. On neither of these was Harcourt informed. When he discovered them, he stirred up such wrath among the Radicals at home, and in rival countries abroad, that they had to be abandoned. Radicals were further angered by their government using gunboats against Nicaragua when our Vice-Consul there was expelled; and by the Foreign Secretary, Grey, claiming the whole Nile basin as a sphere of British influence and warning the French off. Rosebery, indeed, prized continuity in foreign policy, which Radicals deplored. Meanwhile, Harcourt had produced a draft budget which included graduated death duties, a radical innovation. Rosebery was concerned that the Liberals would lose the rest of the Whig landowners, and that the two parties would thenceforward be completely divided by class. When he sent a memorandum to that effect, Harcourt wrote to a fellow minister 'there is nothing to do with rubbish of this sort except to treat it with the contempt it deserves.'

Rosebery damaged himself by his cavalier treatment of delicate subjects. In his first speech in the Lords as Prime Minister, he agreed that England 'as the predominant member of the Three Kingdoms' would have to be convinced of the merits of Irish Home Rule before it could be passed. This open statement of what to him was obvious outraged the Irish MPs, on whom his majority depended – which should have been obvious to him too. Six months later he turned to the reform of the House of Lords, describing it, in its existing state, as 'a great national danger'. The Queen was very angry and so were his colleagues, whom he had not consulted; so his campaign never got off the ground. His frustration led to insomnia, and in the last months of his ministry he was only sleeping for two hours a night. Liberal Party funds ran low, the Queen was hostile, by-elections were lost, and his majority depended on the support of so many disparate groups that he could not even win agreement for a statue of Oliver Cromwell to be erected outside Parliament. When the government was defeated on a snap and easily reversible vote in the Commons, the Cabinet decided with relief to resign. Later Rosebery wrote, 'There are two supreme pleasures in life ... The ideal is when a man receives the seals of office from his Sovereign. The real pleasure comes when he hands them back.'

Although he resigned the leadership of the Liberal Party in 1896, he did not immediately retire, hoping to pursue his aims of national efficiency and an influential British Empire independently. Many intelligent contemporaries and younger men found him fascinating, with his well-stored mind, his gift for words and his wide interests, and several persuaded him to become President of the new Liberal League, a vehicle for Liberal Imperialism. But his Gladstonian beliefs in free trade and low taxation made it impossible for him to make common cause with that other ardent imperialist, Chamberlain, whose campaign for Empire was based on protection. He had always required to be invited more than once to undertake a new task, and his followers now found him intolerably remote. He enjoyed the company of the racing world and the early morning matches on Epsom Downs, and he was a magpie collector, with a library containing, among much else, a first edition of the King James Bible, a copy of Shakespeare's First Folio, and the manuscripts of Dr Johnson's last prayer and Disraeli's early novel, *Vivian Gray*. But active politics became anathema, and he slipped away into loneliness, a recluse long before his death.

L. McKinstry, *Rosebery: Statesman in Turmoil* (2005).
R.R. James, *Rosebery* (1964).

Earl of Balfour

ARTHUR JAMES, EARL OF BALFOUR (1848-1930), was Prime Minister from 1902 until 1905. It was the unhappiest period of his public life. Any sketch of him which focuses on it, as this must, cannot do justice to him as a person or a politician. He was a gifted and privileged young man, who rose languidly to high political office. His privileges sprang from his family: land, wealth and a large house in Lothian from the Balfours; aristocratic connection and political patronage from his mother, sister of Lord Salisbury, who was to become Prime Minister. His gifts put him at the centre of 'The Souls', a high-minded, high-spirited group of friends from country-house backgrounds, whose interests were intellectual and artistic. Curzon dubbed him their 'High Priest'. He was enough of a philosopher to write *A Defence of Philosophic Doubt* (1878) and *Foundations of Belief* (1895). He was musical, once sponsoring a concert of his favourite composer, Handel, in the Albert Hall; artistic, hiring Burne-Jones to decorate the drawing-room of his London house; and a keen tennis player and eventually obsessive golfer. He was tall, willowy and strikingly handsome. In his early days he was full of fun, but after the loss of May Lyttelton, who died of typhoid when he was wooing her and in whose coffin he placed his mother's emerald ring, he hid his emotions behind a cool exterior, and never married. Two of his sisters married leading academics, the philosopher Henry Sidgwick and the scientist Lord Rayleigh, Eleanor Sidgwick becoming Principal of Newnham College, Cambridge. No subsequent Prime Minister has grown up in such a talented circle.

He became MP for Hertford in 1874 (Hatfield, his uncle's house, was nearby), and made his mark from 1880 in an informal group nicknamed the Fourth Party, who sat together on the front bench below the gangway (Balfour claimed to have gone there as a comfortable way of stretching his long legs), and harried not only Gladstone but also their own leader, Stafford Northcote, whom they christened The Goat and so damaged his reputation that the Queen invited Salisbury rather than him to form the next Conservative administration. Balfour was given junior office in that, and then, in 1887, made Chief Secretary for Ireland.

The cry was 'nepotism'. But Salisbury saw toughness through his nephew's elegant veneer, and proved right. Ireland was in a dangerous mood. Only six years before, a Chief Secretary had been assassinated in Dublin, and now, after the dashing of hopes for Home Rule and in an agricultural recession, a National League was co-ordinating a rent strike by tenants. Balfour outlawed the League, and ordered the police to use force. Liberal MPs who came over to support rallies were arrested, and political prisoners had their heads shaved like criminals. Balfour rode furious attacks at Westminster with sharp dialectical skill. 'Miss Fanny' became 'Bloody Balfour'. Luck was with him, as economic conditions improved, and Irish leaders split after the disgrace of their leader, Parnell. With order restored, he set about killing Home Rule by kindness; land-purchase loans for tenants, new railways, subsidies for local industries and advice on agricultural techniques (he persuaded the Queen to provide a stallion to improve Irish breeding). After the storms of the previous twenty years, Ireland settled into a period of comparative calm, and Balfour's name was made. There was no shock, not even surprise, when in 1891 Salisbury made him First Lord of the Treasury and the government's leader in the House of Commons. He became heir apparent and succeeded his uncle in 1902.

Thereafter Balfour failed in most of what he attempted. He wanted to protect property, but saw his own wealth and that of his class whittled away as agricultural recession bit deeper. He fought against Home Rule for Ireland, but succeeded only in delaying it for long enough to ensure that when it happened there would be a separated Ulster, with all the hatred that has ensued ever since. He wanted to balance power in Europe by joining the French in a defensive alliance against the growing strength of Germany: there followed the catastrophe of the First World War. After it he hoped to avoid humiliating Germany and to preserve the Dual Monarchy of Austria-Hungary, but as Lloyd George's Foreign Secretary he went along with the Treaty of Versailles, which did neither and left the fragmented and embittered Europe that he had feared. He tried to hold his party together when it was split over the issue of Tariff Reform, but his efforts to do so led it to a defeat unequalled until 1997, and he lost two further elections. His most lasting legacy has been the Balfour Declaration, an initiative based on his instinctive sympathy for sophisticated Jews with their intellectual and artistic interests, and for the plight of poorer Jews harried and emigrating from Eastern Europe. The home which he proposed for them in Palestine clashed with promises made to Arabs. From it the state of Israel has emerged, but also a Middle Eastern problem which may yet prove cataclysmic.

As a leader he was indecisive and often appeared indolent. He was a sharp debater but no good on a platform: his appeal 'was to the salon and the senate rather than to the street'. It therefore tells us much about the admiration which his contemporaries, friends and foes alike, had for his keen mind, social ease and range of interests that he held office for much of the rest of his life after his resignation from the leadership of the Unionist Party in 1911, ending as Lord President of the Council for Baldwin's Conservative government from 1925 until 1929 (when he was over eighty and palpably unfit). Churchill described him as passing from one Cabinet to another 'like a powerful, graceful cat walking delicately and unsoiled across a rather muddy street'.

A comparison between his government (1902-05) and that of John Major at the opposite end of the century is revealing. Each succeeded a strong Prime Minister, Salisbury and Thatcher respectively, at a time when his party had been long in power. Each had to face an issue which became increasingly dominant, which split his party down the middle, and which his supporters regarded as fundamental: for Major a currency change, the Euro, and for Balfour a fiscal change, Tariff Reform. Each tried to hold his party together by urging delay and by producing a compromise formula. Each ended in electoral catastrophe. Balfour did have one important achievement, his Education Act of 1902, which transferred responsibility for schools to County and County Borough Councils, and protected Church schools by decreeing that they, as well as the old Board schools, should be supported by the local rates. A long-burning issue was thus settled. But in 1903 a new one emerged, on which his own party was divided while his opponents were united. Free trade had underpinned Victorian prosperity since the days of Peel and Gladstone, bringing with it cheap food as well as industrial expansion. To most in politics it was sacrosanct. In April, the Chancellor of the Exchequer, Ritchie, produced a Free Trade Budget, repealing the corn duties which had been imposed during the Boer War. But the most powerful member of the government, Joseph Chamberlain, had a vision of a British Empire bound together within a tariff wall, and a month later he made an explosive speech proclaiming a policy of Imperial Preference, which involved import duties on food coming from non-imperial countries. He then resigned, to free himself for a grand oratorical stump round the country. Balfour tried to play down the issue as nonchalantly as only he knew how; accepted or enforced the resignations of extremist ministers; and devised a compromise, Retaliatory Duties to be imposed on goods from countries which were putting duties on British exports. But this was so subtly refined that nobody but him could understand it. From the autumn of 1903 he gave the impression of a Prime Minister under siege. His Conservative Unionist Party, suffering a series of by-election defeats, became depressed, divided and embittered, and Balfour was so frustrated at the lack of loyalty its members showed towards him that he and his government resigned. At the subsequent general election only 157 Unionists were returned in a House of 670.

Unlike Major, Balfour did not resign as party leader. But his clever debating style was out of place in the new, more democratic, House of Commons: 'Away with this foolery,' cried Campbell-Bannerman, the new Prime Minister. Though emasculated in the Commons, the Unionists still had a huge majority of peers, and used this so frequently to block Liberal government measures that the House of Lords was described by Lloyd George as Mr Balfour's Poodle. However, when the peers, encouraged by Balfour, rejected Lloyd George's budget of 1909, they provoked the government to introduce the Parliament Bill, which restricted the powers of the House of Lords to a two-year delaying veto. The Unionists fought it through two general elections in 1910. At the climax of the struggle, the new King George V agreed to create enough Liberal peers to force the bill through if it was defeated. Against Balfour's advice, some diehard Tory peers, the (last) Ditchers, still voted against it and, though they were unsuccessful, he was so disenchanted by this latest disloyalty that he gave up the leadership.

He was happier as a non-party elder statesman, but not much more successful. As First Lord of the Admiralty from 1915 he rejected proposals for a convoy system to combat the U-boat menace, and managed, through an over-scrupulous publication of early reports of losses, to make the Battle of Jutland look like a defeat, although what was a tactical draw turned out to be a strategic success. His old enemy, Lloyd George, made him Foreign Secretary in his Coalition Cabinet. As such, he showed his talent for behind-the-scenes diplomacy by winning the confidence of President Woodrow Wilson on a visit to the USA; but at the Peace Conference at Versailles he played second fiddle to Lloyd George. As a person he continued to command a certain awe, and set the tone for Tories of a sceptical cast of mind – 'nothing matters very much and very few things matter at all' – but he had been a disappointing statesman and an unhappy Prime Minister.

M. Egremont, *Balfour* (1980).

Sir Henry Campbell-Bannerman

SIR HENRY CAMPBELL-BANNERMAN (1836-1908) was Prime
Minister from 1905 until a few days before his death, the first man
formally to hold that title. It fell to him to lead the Liberal Party
to its greatest electoral triumph, and to preside over a government
with an overall majority of 132 (356 if its normal allies, the Irish
Nationalists and the Labour Party, were included). That he found
himself in this position was due to a collection of circumstances
which nobody expected. Nor did anyone anticipate the widespread
respect he earned there. He has subsequently been described as the
leader who more than any other made possible the decade of Liberal
dominance.

His father was a wholesale draper in Glasgow and his mother the
daughter of a Manchester manufacturer: he was the first Prime
Minister to have direct business experience. He went to Glasgow
University when he was only fourteen, but he was no academic, and
ended with a third in Classics from Trinity, Cambridge. In a Tory
family, it was surprising that Henry Campbell (the Bannerman was
added to ensure a substantial inheritance) should become Liberal
Member for Stirling Burghs, a seat which he won in 1868 and held
until his death. But he had a strong breadth of sympathy for his fellows of all classes, which led him as Prime Minister to speak and vote
for reforms of trade union law and workers' compensation more
radical than the legal experts in his own party recommended. It also
led him to travel in Europe every year with his wife, with whom he
often spoke French. Yet in his habits he remained conservative. He
and Charlotte, childless, settled into a comfortable routine in their
large London and Perthshire houses, entertaining handsomely but
seldom going out into society. He had a pawky humour – of a disloyal
colleague he said, 'Haldane prefers the back stairs, but it does not
matter, for the clatter can be heard all over the house.' Heavily built,
with an easy, direct, unhurried approach, he inspired confidence
among his friends, and won the devotion of all who worked for him.
But no one saw him as a leader. In the House of Commons he was a

poor speaker, sticking short-sightedly to a bundle of notes which he held as a fan. Beatrice Webb, the Fabian Socialist, thought him 'quite stupid ... suited to a position of wealthy squire or sleeping partner in an inherited business.' He was easy-going, and did not always master his briefs.

After a spell in the War Office, where the Army liked him, and a year as Chief Secretary for Ireland in 1884, where he defused Irish tensions with Scottish jokes, his hope was to become Speaker of the House of Commons, but this steady minister could not be spared from the Liberal Cabinet. The circumstances in which he became Liberal leader over brighter stars were exceptional. Dominant politicians like Chamberlain and Whig aristocrats like Hartington left the party over Home Rule for Ireland. When Gladstone retired, his two most gifted heirs, Rosebery and Harcourt, fought each other to the death. The rising Asquith could not yet afford to give up his practice at the Bar. With the party already divided between the Imperialists and the Little Englanders, C.B., as he was known, was thought to be a safe pair of hands and a shrewd conciliator. So it was that in 1899 he was unanimously chosen to lead the Liberals in the House of Commons.

There were some rough seas to steer through before the party emerged intact to win the election of 1906. In them, C.B. showed what a strong and honest man he was. The Boer War put strains on the unity of the Liberals. C.B. found flag-wagging Imperialism deeply distasteful – 'Rule Britannia screeching'. For a time he compromised, making a distinction between the soldiers, who had to be backed, and the jingoist politicians, Chamberlain and Milner, who had started an avoidable war. But when descriptions of British treatment of Boer families in concentration camps reached him, he denounced from a warm heart those 'methods of barbarism'. It was a phrase which stung. He was a cad, a coward and a murderer. The press rounded on him, the King wanted to send for him, and the Liberal League was formed, which operated as a separate imperialist group within the party, with Rosebery as President and Asquith and Grey two of its Vice-Presidents. But he stayed calm and kept the loyalty of the rank-and-file Liberals through electoral defeat in the 'Khaki Election' of 1900, admired for his courage and his unparaded conscience. The war dragged on and became less popular, and the Unionists entered a period of self-inflicted decline, split by Chamberlain's campaign for tariff reform and imperial preference.

Balfour's Education Act infuriated the Nonconformists by putting the cost of Church schools onto their rates, and the introduction of Chinese coolies into South African mines scandalised a broad swathe of the electorate. Liberals of all sections united over these issues, and by 1905 C.B. was ready to lead his party, against a bickering and discredited Unionist government, into the promised land. There was one last hiccup when the leading 'Lib Imps', Asquith, Grey and Haldane, staying for golf and fishing in Scotland while he was at Marienbad, made the Relugas compact to force him to take a peerage while Asquith led the House of Commons. Their collective refusal to join a ministry would have been fatal to it. C.B. did not hurry back – it was not his way – but as soon as he reached London he took the initiative, offering Asquith his choice of job and consulting him about the others. The 'compact' collapsed and C.B. formed one of the strongest governments of the twentieth century, containing Liberals of all shades, from Asquith to Lloyd George. It was a remarkable achievement.

C.B. was a Gladstonian Liberal, who knew the direction in which he wanted the country to go. Many of his hopes have a modern flavour – Home Rule for Scotland as well as Ireland, free trade, disestablished churches, a small efficient Army, improvements to the environment for children 'starved of air and space and sunshine'. He wanted to reform the House of Lords (its powers, not its composition). His desire to encourage small holdings of land, against the tide of change then, was to find an echo in the property-owning democracy policies of later governments. But by 1905 he was an old man in poor health, and his wife was dying. The main achievements of the Liberal government came after him. His own influence was felt in the pact he made with Labour at the 1906 election, which left the way clear for Labour victories in 51 seats; and, most directly, in the settlement of South Africa. Here he overrode the caution of many in his own Cabinet, and carried through a constitution with complete self-government for the two Boer States of Transvaal and the Orange River Colony. When he chose to exert himself he proved a decisive leader. But cardiac asthma wore him down, and in his last months he left the work of government to others. He resigned in April 1908, and died three weeks later. In this sensible Scot, Asquith saw a man who 'even on the verge of old age could see visions and dream dreams'.

J. Wilson, *CB: A Life of Sir Henry Campbell-Bannerman* (1973).

Herbert Henry Asquith

HERBERT HENRY ASQUITH, 1ST EARL OF OXFORD AND ASQUITH, (1852-1928) was the last Liberal Prime Minister (1908-16). There was no red carpet for him: his father, in the Yorkshire wool trade, died early, leaving little money. Intellectual ability and hard work saw him through to the top. From the City of London School, where an uncle paid for him, he won a classical scholarship to Balliol, was awarded a first in Greats, and became President of the Oxford Union. 'Asquith will get on,' said Jowett, Master of Balliol. 'He is so direct.' But, lacking connections, he had seven lean years in the Law before, devilling for the Junior Council to the Treasury, the quality of his work caught the attention of Gladstone. Three years later, in 1886, there was a last-minute vacancy for a Liberal candidate in East Fife. Asquith, already married and with children to support, risked his growing legal practice for the unpaid position of an MP.

The speed of his rise thereafter owed much to circumstance. There was a shortage of experience in the Liberal Party after its split over Home Rule. In opposition for six years, Asquith emerged as a formidable speaker, both in the House of Commons and on platforms round the country. At a time when solid argument was listened to, and gimmickry suspect, he rose above his rivals through clear logic and powerful conviction. He brought his Rolls-Royce mind to bear with steady force upon an issue, driving home his points with the concentration of a sledgehammer. His reputation as a lawyer grew too, and he was able to earn a good living, though he was never in the top flight of fashionable barristers.

The Liberals came back to power in 1892, and Gladstone made Asquith Home Secretary, 'a just and ... signal tribute to your character, abilities and eloquence.' For the next twelve years the Liberals were an unhappy and divided party, in government and in opposition alike, with personal quarrels between Rosebery and Harcourt and policy splits over Home Rule and the Boer War. But Asquith's reputation grew steadily. As Home Secretary he was the one success, under Gladstone and Rosebery, in two unhappy Cabinets; an exceptionally capable administrator and a strong man, tough on striking miners and Irish terrorists alike. He joined the upper reaches of society through his second marriage. His first wife, quiet daughter of a Manchester doctor, died young, and he married Margot Tennant, fashionable daughter of a Scottish Liberal baronet. She became an expensive wife, but her husband's formidable ally as a renowned political hostess. He became a Vice-President of the imperialist Liberal League, and might have become party leader as early as 1898, but could not then afford to give up his practice at the Bar. Under the elderly Campbell-Bannerman he was recognised as the heir apparent. His rise was timely. Liberals reunited against an Education Act which made nonconformists pay for Church schools, and in defence of free trade. Joseph Chamberlain's crusade for Imperial Protection split the government, and Asquith followed him round the country refuting his arguments. In 1906 the Liberals won a majority of 132 over all other parties combined. Asquith became Chancellor of the Exchequer, and, when Campbell-Bannerman retired, Prime Minister.

For the six years before the First World War he ably led a government of gifted ministers. He relished a task for which his skills and his temperament alike made him especially suited. Unlike a Thatcher or a Blair, he ran his government through a Cabinet of responsible ministers, collecting opinions and taking decisions there. Policy initiatives came from younger Radicals, Lloyd George and Churchill, or his old patron Haldane. His command over them seemed almost effortless: they respected his ability, his muscular intelligence and his gravitas. The lean Home Secretary of 1892 had put on weight and let his hair grow; 'dignified benevolent shagginess'. He could despatch business with speed, but his exceptional quality was calm. This was just as well, for those were stormy years. There were many angry strikes: cotton workers, seamen, dockers, railwaymen and miners all came out, and troops were used, notoriously, if reluctantly, against the Welsh miners at Ton-y-pandy by the Home Secretary, Churchill. The suffragettes campaigned spectacularly for 'Votes for Women': the Rokeby Venus was slashed and Emily Davidson was killed when she threw herself under the King's horse in the Derby. They especially targeted Asquith, who was against them. There were recurring and increasing rolls of thunder in Europe from the bombastic Kaiser, as he built up the German fleet and looked for imperial expansion. The Irish expected the

Liberals to deliver the Home Rule which Gladstone had failed to achieve for them. The House of Lords, with a Unionist majority even larger than that of the Liberals in the House of Commons, set out to frustrate that, and most of the other reforms planned by the government. Through all this Asquith steered shrewdly, with 'genial tact and judicious compromises'. He appointed a Royal Commission to look into the causes of industrial discontent, but was prepared to use all the forces of the Crown to keep order. He kept the Admiralty and the Treasury together as the naval race with the Germans developed; the building of Dreadnought battleships went ahead but not at full speed. And he patiently endured the mutilation by the Lords of legislation on education, plural voting and liquor licensing, waiting for them to overreach themselves. His sense of timing was sure.

Lloyd George's budget of 1909, as Asquith foresaw, brought matters to a head. A non-contributory Old Age Pensions Act and the Dreadnoughts had to be paid for. The budget included steep rises in death duties and income tax, and the introduction of taxes on land, as well as a new super-tax on larger incomes. The Lords threw it out. By doing so they broke a long-standing convention that they should accept money bills. Asquith, earlier preaching 'wait and see' (but steadily supporting Lloyd George against doubters in the Cabinet), now moved in, accusing the Lords of usurping the rights of the elected House of Commons. He asked the King for a general election. Through the prolonged constitutional crisis that followed, he moved cautiously but inexorably towards his goal, to end the power of the Lords to block the will of the Commons. To do this, he had to keep two kings on side (George V succeeded Edward VII in 1910, in the middle of the crisis), since only if the King agreed to create enough Liberal peers to swamp the Unionist majority in the Lords might their lordships give way. And he had to persuade his Irish allies, on whose votes in the Commons his majority depended after 1910, to wait in patience. He resisted compromises and survived two elections. The Parliament Act of 1911 enshrined all that he had worked for, with the Lords' veto on legislation limited to virtually two years (none for money bills). It was a profound constitutional change, achieved without violence or damage to the monarchy, in the middle of a hot political climate (and a glaringly hot summer).

This was Asquith's own success, perhaps the high point of his career. Now he had to face the Irish problem. With the Parliament

Act passed, the Liberals were free to bring to a triumphant conclusion Gladstone's long fought battle for Home Rule. But was it to be
for the whole of Ireland? Or was Protestant Ulster to be excluded?
Unionist opinion was hardening. Defeated in Parliament, they
were spoiling for a fight outside. This time 'wait and see' proved a
dangerous policy; although, with his Irish allies pressing Asquith
from one side, and conservative forces in England (including the
King, the powerful absentee Irish landlords and parts of the Army)
from the other, it was a natural one. Between 1912 and 1914, as the
Home Rule Bill was twice passed by the House of Commons and
rejected by the Lords, Asquith allowed private armies to develop on
both sides, which brought Ireland to the brink of civil war. 80,000
Ulster Volunteers drilled and Sir Edward Carson, a speaker of
incendiary power, took the salute. Bonar Law, the Unionist leader,
declared that Ulster should go to any limit to preserve its independence from Dublin. Dublin Volunteers were formed to meet this
threat. One reason for Asquith's hesitation had been concern about
the loyalty of Army officers with Ulster connections. In March 1914
took place the so-called 'Curragh mutiny', when most of the officers
of the 3rd Cavalry Brigade took advantage of an unwise offer to allow
them to resign rather than fight in Ulster. Volunteers on both sides
started gun-running. Now, dangerously late, Asquith moved in. He
took over as War Secretary and searched actively for compromise.
Discussion centred on whether Ulster's exclusion should be permanent or for a limited period, and on how many counties should be
involved, but even a Buckingham Palace Conference summoned by
the King failed to reach agreement. There remains a question mark
over what would have happened next, for ten days later Britain was
at war with Germany. The Home Rule Bill became an act, but
was suspended, and the Ulster problem, disastrously for Ireland's
future, was left unsolved.

Asquith had been Prime Minister for six and a half years when
Europe went to war. He left the conduct of foreign policy to his
Foreign Secretary, Grey, a fellow Liberal Imperialist. They both
supported the Anglo-French entente which had ended the British
policy of 'glorious isolation', and Asquith had gone along, uneasily,
with the military talks between Britain and France which had started
in 1906. When Austria-Hungary and Germany lined up on one side
and France and Russia on the other, he was slow to accept that
Britain needed to be involved. But he was never a pacifist, and

during the last days of peace his priority was to take his country into the war without large-scale resignations by the many pacifists in his Cabinet. In this he was successful, thanks to the German invasion of Belgium, which shocked them. Britain went to war under a Liberal government.

Asquith was not a natural wartime leader, in style, temperament or method, especially after an already long spell as Prime Minister. His bland ease, reassuring in peacetime, did not catch the spirit of war, and the tempo of his life did not greatly change. He continued to play bridge after dinner, to read widely and extensively, and to write long letters every day to Venetia Stanley, a friend much younger than himself who made his heart beat faster. He drank a lot: Haig commented (in his diary) after an evening together in France: 'his legs were unsteady, but his head was quite clear.' In the House of Commons others saw the unsteady legs and coined a new word, 'squiffy'. But none of this mattered (for he was never accused of not being master of his brief, and the speed with which he efficiently despatched business remained impressive) as much as his old habit of governing through Cabinet and by compromise. Britain had to learn what total war meant, and Asquith was not the man to teach it. At the onset of the war he worked for two months through a full Cabinet which kept no minutes. He then set up a War Council, which met only once a week. As an instinctive delegator he trusted his experts to run the war. When they disagreed, as over the Dardanelles in 1915, he found a halfway house, agreeing to the expedition but hoping to let the Navy force the Straits by itself. When that failed he sent troops and reinforcements too slowly. He was loyal for too long to Sir John French, commanding the British Army in France. Like most Liberals, he disliked conscription. He resisted broadening his government until the failure of the Dardanelles campaign forced coalition on him, and was never at ease with the Unionists: the coalition War Council meetings under his Chairmanship were described by their Secretary as 'dreadful'. By the autumn of 1916 he was tired and depressed. Venetia Stanley had married one of his junior colleagues, and his eldest son had been killed on the Somme.

In a democratic Britain, Asquith would not have survived for so long as Prime Minister. But government went on inside a closed circle in Edwardian times, and, whatever the fulminations of the press – 'Northcliffe and his obscure crew', Asquith called them –

it took a political conspiracy to oust him. When Kitchener was sensationally drowned on his way to Russia (June 1916) he was succeeded in the War Office by Lloyd George, who had transformed the munitions industry and had the drive which Asquith lacked. There followed a campaign by Max Aitken, the future Lord Beaverbrook, to forge an unnatural alliance between this erstwhile and slippery Radical and Bonar Law, dour Unionist leader, to push the Prime Minister up to a position of only nominal power, or oust him altogether. Asquith was not ready to go quietly: indeed, such was his sense of authority after so many years that he underestimated, as Mrs Thatcher was to do later, the threat to his position. But when Aitken persuaded Law to side with Lloyd George, and Law persuaded the Unionists to go with him, Asquith found himself without a majority, and in December 1916 he resigned. It was a fateful political manoeuvre. In the short run it enabled a new government to survive yet more bad news, and pursue the war through to victory. In the long run it destroyed Lloyd George and split the Liberal Party to near-extinction.

For Asquith there was to be no return. He led the Opposition with characteristic caution, until it seemed that Lloyd George had been caught lying about the size of the army in France by General Maurice. In the Commons debate which followed, Lloyd George produced a different set of statistics, proving that he had not, as accused, starved the Western Front of troops. The truth lay with Maurice, though it may be that Lloyd George had not seen the amended figures, as they were found in one of his boxes four years later. But by the end of the debate Lloyd George had branded Asquith a malicious conspirator with Maurice. So his hopes of playing a part in the peace conference were dashed. In the general election which was rushed through at the end of the war, every member who had voted against the government in that debate had to fight a Unionist opponent, while other Liberals were given what Asquith described as a 'coupon', and were not opposed by a Coalition candidate. Only 26 Asquith Liberals were returned, and Asquith lost his own seat.

He made one triumphant rally when he won a by-election at Paisley in 1920. When he took his seat crowds followed him from his home in Cavendish Square to Westminster. For him it was a revival. But there was to be no real revival for the Liberal Party, to which he had devoted his political life. Attempts to reunite with Lloyd George were short-lived, and while Liberals were divided, Labour emerged to claim the loyalty of the industrial working classes. When Asquith, honoured with an Earldom and the Garter, resigned the Liberal leadership in 1926, there had already been a Labour government, and the political map had changed.

S. Koss, *Asquith* (1976).
M. & E. Brock (ed), H.H. *Asquith: Letters to Venetia Stanley.* (1982).

David Lloyd George

DAVID LLOYD GEORGE, 1ST EARL LLOYD-GEORGE (1863-1945), Prime Minister from 1916 until 1922, was one of the two great wartime Premiers of the last century. There were many similarities between him and Churchill, and some important differences. Both worked uneasily in party politics and preferred coalitions or National Governments. Both were mistrusted, and reached the highest office solely because they were the best natural war leaders at Westminster. As such, both were amateur strategists who alarmed and infuriated their generals. Both became heroes to their people, but lived through their period of fame to be rejected by the electorate. Of their differences the most striking was their social background: Lloyd George the son of a Welsh teacher who stormed the citadel of the English establishment, and Churchill born in its heart. As war leader, Churchill had much the stronger position, since the experience of the First World War made obvious the need for the overall authority of the Prime Minister in the Second. In peace, while they both lost their moorings in the safe harbour of party, Churchill was the more successful in regaining his: Lloyd George never did. Churchill's oratory, carried over the radio into almost every home, has left him the giant of the century. But, until then, Lloyd George's wartime reputation had been second to none, and the range and importance of his peacetime achievements was far the greater. He helped inaugurate the Welfare State, he broke the power of the House of Lords, he brokered an Irish peace where others, from Gladstone on, had failed, and after his fall he became the first leading politician to adopt Keynes's solutions to unemployment.

Brought up in rural North Wales, and helped by an uncle to become a solicitor, he became Liberal MP for Caernarvon Boroughs in 1890, and held the seat until 1945: there, at any rate, his political base was secure. He made his name championing Welsh causes, and he always went to the Eisteddfod, latterly cutting a spectacular figure with his flowing cape and white mane. He earned notoriety as a pacifist in the Boer War (he had to be smuggled through a hostile mob in Birmingham disguised as a policeman), but won the admiration of Liberals for his advocacy of free trade. Campbell-Bannerman made him President of the Board of Trade, and there he showed that he was no mere Celtic firebrand orator, but an administrator and negotiator of masterful energy. He pushed through five major Acts in a period when the Lords were being obstructive, and he prevented a national railway strike by getting the employers to accept nation-wide collective bargaining and a conciliation board. By the time he became Chancellor of the Exchequer in 1908 he was recognised, with Churchill (his junior), as the Radical dynamo of the government.

As Chancellor, Lloyd George created the basis of the Welfare State. Never a socialist, he was nonetheless a champion of the 'have-nots', and he used power to help them. Old-age pensions started in 1908 (pensioners collected their 'Lloyd Georges' once a week), and the National Insurance Act of 1911 introduced a comprehensive system of health insurance for all on low wages, with contributions from employers and employed; and unemployment insurance for certain trades (in 1921 he was to make this, too, comprehensive). He met loud opposition from trade unionists who resented the contributions, from Friendly Societies losing business, and from duchesses and their housemaids who campaigned against having to lick stamps. It all had to be paid for, too, at the same time as Dreadnoughts were being built: hence a budget, in 1909, which became famous to some, infamous to others. As well as new taxes, including a super-tax on the rich, he introduced a revolutionary concept, the taxation of increments in the value of land. These had been a prop for aristocrats who, suffering in the long agricultural depression, sold land for property development or extracted minerals. So wrathful were they that the House of Lords threw out the budget. There followed a long constitutional battle, with two general elections, 'Peers versus People', ending in the Parliament Act which reduced the legislative veto of the Lords to a two-year suspension. Inevitably, Lloyd George became villain or hero, the Welsh Wizard who, describing the peers as 'the first of the litter', 'chosen at random from among the unemployed', brought their future before 'the great assize of the people'.

How did this Radical pacifist become wartime leader of a coalition dominated by conservative Unionists? There is mystery in his move away from pacifism, especially into a war in alliance with

Czarist Russia: 'I am filled with horror at the prospect,' he wrote to his wife. But his intensely active personality prevented him from standing back and watching the Germans move into France. Once committed, he entered the struggle with the enthusiasm of a man released from doubt. Recruiting speeches raised his reputation in the country, as did his efficient handling of wartime finance at Westminster. Far more than any other minister, he saw what was needed to reorganise government for war. Labour relations had been desperately bad in Edwardian England. Lloyd George now persuaded the unions to suspend strikes and to admit unskilled workers into skilled jobs. In 1915 Asquith asked him to head the new ministry of Munitions, and find a way to end the shortage of shells which had become critical for Army and government alike. His success finally confirmed his prestige in the country and across the whole political spectrum (except, paradoxically, among some Liberals, who found his style distasteful and his methods authoritarian). He circumvented Parliament with Orders in Council; he treated his ministry as a business organisation, with managers from outside the Civil Service; he brought large numbers of women into factories. It was on the base of his achievements that Britain was able to sustain the Western Front until 1918.

In the Cabinet Lloyd George chafed against Asquith's increasing indecision and the stalemate and slaughter among the trenches in France, and with Unionists he pressed conscription on his tired leader. When Kitchener was drowned in June 1916, he became Secretary at War. That summer the Army was slaughtered on the battlefield of the Somme, the Navy under Jellicoe fought indecisively off Jutland, and German submarines sank record numbers of British ships. In the autumn, Russian offensives ground to a halt and the Germans overran Rumania, rich in grain and oil. 'We are going to lose this war,' Lloyd George said to the Secretary of the War Commission on 9 November. There had to be a change of government.

The way in which this happened left Lloyd George with a reputation for trickery and disloyalty. The Canadian press baron Max Aitken, the future Lord Beaverbrook, persuaded his friend Bonar Law, leader of the Unionists, to overcome his suspicions of the Welsh Radical. Together Lloyd George and Law got Asquith to agree to remain Prime Minister but not in the War Committee of three. Next day, moved by a contemptuous press article wrongly believed to have been inspired by Lloyd George, he changed his mind. They resigned. Asquith, unable to command a majority without the Unionists, resigned too. When the King asked Bonar Law to form a government, he bowed off the stage and left it to Lloyd George.

Asquith saw this as backstairs plotting, but to the country at large Lloyd George was the man for the times. He streamlined the government of the country. The main Cabinet was normally bypassed. There was a War Cabinet of five, and individual problems were tackled by Cabinet Committees (more than a hundred of them by the end). All this was organised by a Cabinet Secretariat, which for the first time provided formal agendas for meetings, and kept minutes. As in his Ministry of Munitions, Lloyd George introduced businessmen into government. He also set up his own private secretariat, dubbed the 'Garden Suburb' from its start in huts in his Downing Street garden. He himself, a man of the people as only Gladstone among his predecessors had become, was constantly in the public eye with visits and speeches: a quasi-Presidential figure in the style later adopted by Churchill, Thatcher and Blair.

If the impact of these sweeping changes in government on the conduct of the war was surprisingly small, this was due to the relationship between the armed forces and the civilians, quite different in the First and Second World Wars. Over the Navy Lloyd George managed to assert his authority, forcing an unwilling Admiralty to adopt the convoy system in the Atlantic and easing Jellicoe out. But he never controlled the generals. The C.I.G.S., Sir William Robertson, wanted to prevent ministers from having any say in the conduct of the war: 'I've 'eard different' was his standard reply to their criticisms. Lloyd George's relations with Haig were especially bad, mercurial Welshman versus dour Scot. Unlike Churchill later, Lloyd George could not dismiss generals at will; Haig, married to a lady-in-waiting, was a special favourite of the King's. So, characteristically, he manoeuvred. He failed to prevent a last, terrible, blood and mud bath across the trenches at Passchendaele, but he did stop Robertson and Haig from depleting the successful armies in the Middle East for reinforcements on the Western Front. Eventually he achieved a Supreme Anglo-French War Council, with control over central reserves. When Robertson refused to work under it, he was supported by Haig, the King and many in the Cabinet, but Lloyd George took them on, and won. Robertson resigned, though Haig accepted defeat and stayed on. But it was too late for Lloyd George to influence the conduct of the war, for within two months the Germans launched their last big offensives in France (March 1918), and Allied strategy became reactive. His leadership was focused on what he did best, raising the morale of the people. With his musical voice, his lightning wit and his rich resources of biblical and literary quotation, he was an uplifting platform orator, drawing inspiration from the audiences in front of him, not least from factory workers. This was what gave him his popular appeal, on which his political power was based. When the war suddenly ended, a general election was long overdue, and in December Lloyd George won it over-whelmingly.

His Coalition Government (1918-22) has had a bad press, yet Lloyd George had considerable successes. At home, in an exhausted country crippled by debt and with industries in urgent need of modernisation, he broke the Triple Alliance of the miners, the dock-ers and the railwaymen in 1921, by detaching the miners with the promise from the mine owners of a national wages pool: a General Strike was averted. He broadened unemployment insurance, and started subsidised house-building. Abroad, he, Clemenceau and Woodrow Wilson were the shapers of the Treaty of Versailles. The former pacifist and Little Englander now extended the Empire, and took on mandates in Mesopotamia which proved the foundation of British power – and problems – in the Middle East. In Europe he wanted to promote economic recovery, and tried, but failed, to per-suade France to reduce her demands on the stricken Germany in return for a British guarantee of her eastern frontier. He promoted and dominated a series of international conferences, but French opposition again frustrated his plan to get a de facto recognition of Communist Russia, and to develop commerce with the new central European states. So Germany was still required to pay war repara-tions beyond her means, and the bitterness which Lloyd George feared was never far away. Closer to home, there was violence in Ireland, as Irish republicans claimed the Home Rule which they had been promised. Lloyd George at first backed the Black and Tans in trying to suppress the Fenians: 'We have murder by the throat.' But from 1921 he used all his agility, patience and timing to negotiate a settlement which left an Irish Free State inside the Commonwealth, with the six counties in the north 'temporarily' separated and remaining part of Great Britain. He thus went further than any pre-vious British Prime Minister towards solving the Irish Problem.

But from the peaks of 1918, Lloyd George fell so far in 1922 that he never recovered. He dazzled, but was never trusted. Negotiation was his special skill, and as he went along he left many who felt disappointed and deceived, for nimble negotiators often conjure away disagreement with false hopes. There were personal reasons. Society gossips had long fed on his reputation for sexual and financial laxity: dubbed 'the Goat', he had also had to defend himself against accusations of illicit share-dealing in the Marconi scandal of 1912. There was not much truth in all this. He never bought the Marconi shares about which ministers had inside knowledge, and by the time he became Prime Minister his roving eye had settled for good on one woman, his devoted Secretary Frances Stevenson, although the happy home of his early years had gradually become more distant, his wife staying in Criccieth and his eldest son being one of his harshest critics. But there was more truth in the attacks on the use he made of the Honours List. Lloyd George had hoped to link formally the Unionists and the Coalition Liberals. When this failed, he was without party funds with which to fight elections, so he set out to build up his own political fund. In this he was astonishingly successful, to the tune of more than £3 million. But this was partly achieved through the sale of honours, on a larger scale than previous Prime Ministers, and without the cloak of respectability which a traditional party gave to the process. Giving money to the Lloyd George fund to earn a peerage was less reputable than giving to the Liberal Party, and corrupt intermediaries such as Maundy Gregory made the taint worse.

Critically, he had no political base. Most Liberals had followed Asquith into opposition in 1916, and their split from Lloyd George became complete in 1918 after the Maurice Debate. General Maurice had written to the press accusing Lloyd George of lying about the strength of the army in France. Asquith took this up, but the Prime Minister refuted him, using statistics which disproved Maurice's allegations. (It has since emerged that he used, perhaps unintentionally, figures which included non-combatants.) In the election which followed, all Liberals who backed the government in that debate were unopposed by Unionists, but those who backed Asquith were not given this 'coupon', and only 26 of them won seats. In the victorious Coalition, Unionists greatly outnumbered the 'Coaly Libs', and they were not at ease under Lloyd George. He had 'surrendered to terrorism' in Ireland and flirted with Communist

Russia. As he pirouetted round European Conferences, they growled in their clubs. Matters came to a head when Lloyd George encouraged Greece to occupy the western seaboard of Turkey, and felt committed to helping the Greeks when the Turks drove them back. He could find no allies as Mustapha Kemal's army advanced on the British troops at Chanak; only a deep revulsion against further war in an exhausted Britain. The Unionists, meeting at the Carlton Club, refused to fight the next election in a coalition. Lloyd George, shorn of his majority, resigned.

He was only fifty-nine, and the most formidable leader in Britain. But at Westminster coalitions and quasi-presidential government were rejected. To Baldwin, new leader of the Conservatives, Lloyd George was anathema, the 'Big Beast'. The rising Labour Party and the trade unions saw him as a foe after he broke the Triple Alliance, and he had little time for Ramsay MacDonald: 'Just a fussy Baldwin, nothing more.' Liberal reunion proved short-lived: old wounds were deep, and Lloyd George would not release money from his fund for no-hope candidates. From the wings he preached Keynesian economics, with a programme of public works to reduce unemployment, and a strong central government. He sympathised with the constructive side of fascism, and saw Hitler as 'a born leader of men', though he also urged rearmament. Living for politics, he ended as an outsider. He remained true to his ideals of social justice, popular democracy and international harmony, but his roots were not firm enough to enable him to work effectively for them. Unlike Churchill there was, for many, 'something of the night' about him to the end.

K.O. Morgan, *Lloyd George* (1974).
B.B. Gilbert, *David Lloyd George: A Political Life* (2 vols, 1987 and 1992).
M. Pugh, *Lloyd George* (1988).

Bonar Law

ANDREW BONAR LAW (1858-1923) was Prime Minister for less than seven months, from October 1922 until May 1923, but he had been a powerful figure at the centre of British politics for eleven years before that. Son of a sombre Presbyterian minister from Ulster, he started life in Canada but moved to Scotland, where, under the auspices of his cousins, he was made a partner in William Jacks, iron merchants. He acquired financial independence through two legacies, and domestic happiness with a spontaneous and lovable wife, Annie, and six children. He had early shown his interest in politics by making his mark in the Glasgow Parliamentary Debating Society, and in 1900 he unexpectedly won a Glasgow seat for the Conservatives when the Liberal vote was split. Balfour made him Parliamentary Secretary to the Board of Trade. He shone in opposition after the rout of the Conservatives in 1906, as an effective speaker in the House of Commons who showed a mastery of detail without notes, thanks to a remarkable memory. His political ambitions were sharpened by his friendship with a sparkling young Canadian, Max Aitken, the future Lord Beaverbrook, and when Balfour resigned in 1911 Aitken encouraged him to put his name forward as his successor. He was an outsider, but the two leading candidates, Austen Chamberlain and Walter Long, disliked each other so much that they both stood down rather than let the other win, and Law found himself leader of the Conservative Party.

No one like him had ever led it before. The contrast with Balfour was particularly sharp. His mind was practical, not philosophical, and his interests centred on games, not culture: music and the arts bored him, and tennis, golf, bridge and especially chess were his relaxations from politics. He was a teetotaller who disliked dinner parties and gossip, and his reserve could sometimes slip into depression. In 1909 his wife died, a blow from which he never fully recovered. Politics filled the gap.

Conservatives found Law a refreshingly direct leader after the subtleties of Balfour. He had arrived at Westminster when

Imperialism was rampant and, although never a jingoist, his political career was devoted to the maintenance and strengthening of the bonds of the Empire. Two great issues hung over the domestic scene, Tariff Reform and Irish Home Rule, and Law approached them both as an imperialist. When Joseph Chamberlain launched his campaign for Tariff Reform, his aim was to create a tariff wall round the countries in the Empire, Imperial Preference. Law was a forceful supporter of this policy, even of taxes on non-imperial food imports. Although he saw such duties as a way of paying for welfare reforms without increasing direct taxation, what mattered most to him was the link they would provide between countries in the Empire. But Free Trade had been the sacred cow of British politics since the Repeal of the Corn Laws, and in the end he held back from forcing food taxes onto his party. The defeat of his successor, Baldwin, when he went to the country on a Protection platform in 1923, showed the wisdom of his caution.

Over Irish Home Rule Britain came as near to civil war as it had been since the seventeenth century. The Liberal government, with the House of Lords only able to delay legislation for two years after the Parliament Act (1911), was determined to deliver the prize of Home Rule to its Irish National Party Catholic allies. Bonar Law fought them on behalf of the Empire and of Protestant Ulster. He made the battle a rallying point for his depressed and divided party, and was prepared to use unconstitutional weapons to force a dissolution of Parliament before the Home Rule Bill could be passed. In 1912 he attended a march-past of 100,000 Ulster Volunteers in Belfast, and told them that they would save the Empire by their example. Later that year he pledged Unionist Party support for Ulster if they resisted Home Rule by force. On several occasions he publicly doubted whether the Army would be ready to fight against Ulstermen, and in 1914 he helped to create the climate in which Army officers stationed in Ireland resigned their commissions rather than risk advancing into Ulster (the so-called Curragh Mutiny). But even in his most strongly held beliefs there was a crucial vein of caution in Law. He abandoned wholesale opposition to Home Rule, and negotiated for Ulster to have the right to opt out. He was not, however, ready to concede a limited period for this, 'a sentence of death with a stay of execution', nor to exclude from it Ulster's traditionally Catholic counties, on which Irish Nationalists insisted; and the negotiations had reached an impasse when the

First World War broke out. The eventual Irish Treaty of 1921, which gave Ulster the right to withdraw unconditionally and remain part of the United Kingdom, was passed with his support. It had been shaped by him.

Asquith unwillingly brought the Unionists into a wartime coalition in 1915. Their impatience with him as leader grew to a bursting point, but it took Max Aitken to engineer their alliance with Lloyd George, which ousted him. Law turned down the offer to form a government himself, and for the next six years supported Lloyd George faithfully and effectively. For the rest of the war they met daily in Law's room, thick with pipe smoke: Lloyd George the dynamic leader, Law the shrewd critic. It was a strong partnership: Stanley Baldwin thought it 'the most perfect partnership in political history.' As Chancellor of the Exchequer, Law refinanced national borrowing with low-interest, long-term War Loans and National War Bonds. Later as Lord Privy Seal he took charge of the government while Lloyd George was at Versailles negotiating the peace. He led the House of Commons with authority, and kept Conservatives loyal to a Prime Minister whom most of them disliked and distrusted. This was more difficult after the general election of 1918 had returned an overwhelming Coalition majority, most of whom were Conservatives. It was tough going, and in 1921 Bonar Law, warned by his doctors about his high blood pressure, resigned.

His importance to the Coalition soon became obvious, for Austen Chamberlain, his successor as Conservative leader, did not command the same respect in the party. Things went badly for Lloyd George. The Provisional Irish government failed to square up to its extremists, and one of those shot Field Marshal Sir Henry Wilson on his London front doorstep. There were scandals over the sale of honours, and Labour gains at by-elections. Crucially, Lloyd George's pro-Greek interventions in the Near East threatened to land the country in a war against Turkey, at a time when it was in no mood to face more fighting and in a cause distasteful to traditionally pro-Turkish Tories. Law had recovered, and now warned his old partner 'we cannot act alone as policeman of the world.' In October 1922 the Coalition Cabinet agreed to go for a quick general election, and to forestall trouble Chamberlain called a meeting of Conservative MPs at the Carlton Club. With most of their leaders in the Coalition, Conservatives desperately appealed to Law to return, to save them from being tied to Lloyd George for five more years. Uncertain of his health and typically cautious, he did some electoral soundings. When these proved satisfactory, he came to the Carlton Club to support the motion that the Conservatives should leave the Coalition. Lloyd George resigned that afternoon, and Bonar Law became Prime Minister.

Asquith dubbed him 'the unknown Prime Minister'; he had to be pushed to the top. But he was widely trusted for his direct truthfulness and liked for his modesty. His premiership was a brief coda to his political life, lasting for seven months. Cancer of the throat struck him soon after it began, with spells of voicelessness and much pain, stoically concealed. He was sceptical about government intervention to reduce unemployment, although he did put a vigorous minister, Neville Chamberlain, to work on housing. Curzon, his Foreign Secretary, failed to persuade the French to reduce their claims for reparations from Germany (or to pay back what they owed Britain), while Baldwin, his Chancellor, struck a bad deal over debt repayment with the USA, which Law accepted only when the rest of his Cabinet backed it. He resigned in May 1923 and died in October. But far more important than this meagre record had been the Conservative triumph at the 1922 election which he called when he became leader, a majority of 77 over all other parties, and their first victory since 1900. It destroyed Lloyd George's dream of a Centre Party, decimated the divided Liberals and opened a new two-party era of Conservatives and Labour.

R. Blake, *The Unknown Prime Minister* (1955).
R.J.O. Adams, *Bonar Law* (1999).

Stanley Baldwin

Stanley Baldwin, 1st Earl Baldwin of Bewdley (1867-1947), Prime Minister 1923-4, 1925-9 and 1935-7, dominated the British political scene for most of the inter-war years and created the largest Conservative majorities of the twentieth century. But within three years of his retirement in 1937 he was being vilified as the 'Guilty Man', whose failure to rearm had exposed his country to desperate peril. Although recent writers have shown the unfairness of some of the criticism, his reputation has only partly recovered.

His political career was short, only half the length of those of Gladstone or Churchill. By the time he became MP for West Worcestershire in 1908, he was over forty, and had been 'governing director' of E.P. & W. Baldwin, a large and successful group of iron and steel companies, for ten years. Financial Secretary to the Treasury in 1917, he entered Lloyd George's Coalition Cabinet as President of the Board of Trade in 1921. There he was the quiet, efficient man in a company of stars. Then came a political upheaval, from which nearly all the stars emerged on one side, with Baldwin on the other. Baldwin was the one minister to resign when Lloyd George decided to call an election in 1922. He had come to mistrust Lloyd George deeply, finding his sale of honours distasteful and his rash foreign policy dangerous, and led the attack on him at a Conservative Party meeting in the Carlton Club which brought about the break-up of the Coalition and the formation of a Conservative government under Bonar Law. Leading Conservatives in the Coalition stayed with Lloyd George, and Law made Baldwin Chancellor of the Exchequer. Within six months, cancer of the throat finished Law's career. This left King George V with a difficult choice for the next Prime Minister. Should he invite Curzon, a major and senior political figure but a peer, and overbearing, or Baldwin, the only possible candidate from the House of Commons but inexperienced and little known in the country? With the Labour Party emerging, the King felt that the choice of Curzon would be dangerous: so Baldwin it was. During the next fourteen years this unspectacular man became the leading statesman of his time.

He nearly fell at the first fence. In December 1923 he sprang an unexpected election on the country with Protection as his theme, and lost it. This was a bad misjudgment of the national mood, and only the lack of a proper alternative kept him as leader of his party. Thereafter he made it his chief aim to give the Conservatives a broad base. The erstwhile Coalition ministers Austen Chamberlain, Churchill and Birkenhead came over, disgusted with their Liberal partners, who had lent their votes to Labour to enable Ramsay MacDonald to form a minority government. Labour now emerged as the party of the Left, and there was a return to two-party politics, Conservative v Labour, with the Liberals falling apart. The Conservatives were the stronger: many British working men were ready to vote for Baldwin, whom they regarded as fair and 'very decent indeed', while disenchanted Liberals also became Conservatives under his centrist leadership. When MacDonald called another election in 1924, Baldwin won it with a majority of 225, and thereafter, with one break between 1929 and 1931, the inter-war Conservative majorities never fell below 200. Even when, from 1931 until 1935, there was a National Government with MacDonald as its Prime Minister, it was an overwhelmingly Conservative one, with Baldwin the power behind the throne.

Baldwin's was a complex personality. Behind his strong jaw and broad forehead was a serious and sensitive man. His father, the iron-master who had built up the family business, held deeply ingrained Christian beliefs; and Stanley himself talked to the nation as a Christian in a way which would have been embarrassing in the second half of the century. His mother, from a family of Methodist ministers, was the aunt of Rudyard Kipling, to whom Baldwin remained close, and sister-in-law of Burne-Jones, through whom he met William Morris. At Cambridge he had been impressed by Seeley's *Expansion of England*, with its hopes for civilisation being spread round the world by Britain as God's instrument. He was a capitalist with ideals of service, and in this and in many other ways his values remained Victorian. He was no academic, suspicious of theoretical economists and socialists alike, and his pragmatic approach to political issues explains much of his success. He understood the importance of words, using Kipling to help him with speeches; and of image, cultivating the appearance of a countryman with tweed jacket and waistcoat. He would come up with homespun proverbs: 'Never stand between a dog and a lamppost' was revealing about his approach to leadership. Books and music were important to him, and for recreation he went for long country walks. Easily tired and sometimes depressed to the point of nervous prostration, he was closely supported by his wife Lucy, who had played cricket well and wore large, old-fashioned hats: they were good companions until she died shortly before he did. They knelt together each morning to commend their day to God.

The years of Baldwin's pre-eminence were dominated by post-war exhaustion, industrial unrest and threats to freedom from Communism and Fascism: 'We are all dancing on a pie-crust,' he warned. He set himself to educate the British electorate and to bind it into the framework of a democratic constitution and responsible capitalism. He brought to this task modesty, transparent honesty, and a comfortable and traditional style which bred public confidence in a period of rapid change. He was instinctively inclusive – 'he don't sling no mud,' said a political opponent. He never talked down to the new women voters. When the first Labour government was formed he encouraged two non-Labour peers to join it, and he was happy to serve under Ramsay MacDonald in the National Government of 1931 as Lord President of the Council. His enemies were Lloyd George, whom he blamed for lowering the standards of public life with financial and sexual scandal, damaging democracy by short-circuiting the Cabinet and the House of Commons, splitting the Liberals and threatening to do the same for the Conservatives; and the Press Lords, Rothermere and Beaverbrook, who pandered to the lowest tastes to increase the circulation of their papers, and whose political activities showed, in his words, 'power without responsibility, the prerogative of the harlot throughout the ages.'

Industrial relations were bad in the early 'twenties: 1921 was one of the worst years of depression since the Industrial Revolution. Coal and cotton exports dried up, and there was a worldwide glut of shipping. Unemployment rose to over two million. Lloyd George handed the railways and the mines back to private ownership, and the old pre-war confrontations between unions and employers started up again, against a background of Red Revolution in Russia, reaching a climax in the General Strike of 1926. Baldwin, one of only two industrial managers ever to have been Prime Minister, preached the need for high production in an industrialised and overpopulated country, but he contributed towards the scale of unemployment himself by accepting the Treasury's deflationary policy and allowing Churchill, his Chancellor from 1924 to 1929, to return to the Gold Standard. Nonetheless, he showed skill in handling the problems he had thus exacerbated. He aimed to spread capital lower down the social scale, with War Savings certificates and subsidies for those building small houses for sale: he it was who coined the phrase 'a property owning democracy'. He understood the use of collective bargaining, and was sympathetic towards trade unions. When Macquisten, one of his back-benchers, produced a bill to stop unions imposing a contribution to Labour Party funds on their members, he persuaded Conservatives not to support it. To avert a General Strike he took the political risk of offering a government subsidy to the miners. This, and his pleas for social responsibility, coming as they did from a man who had helped his own workers through a pre-war strike by paying them when his factories lay idle, limited the support for the Strike when it did come, and shortened it, although he proved unable to stop the mine-owners from locking their work-force out after the miners' allies had gone back to work. His speaking style is well caught in his peroration to the House of Commons after the end of the Strike: 'The English language is the richest in the world in monosyllables. Four words, one syllable each, are words which contain salvation for this country, and they are Faith, Love, Hope and Work.'

In his approach to the big imperial problem of his time, India, he was not able to carry the whole of his party with him, but succeeded in isolating the rebels. The Empire was central to Baldwin's political philosophy. Influenced by Seeley and Kipling, he believed it to be the most effective international force for freedom and democracy in a dangerous world, and when he retired he was described as the foremost imperial statesman of his time. Business had taken him to Canada, and his Empire was that of white Dominions, which he saw as markets for our industries and sources of food and land for Britain's overcrowded population. India was peripheral – the glamour of oriental riches and princely power never caught his imagination as it did Churchill's – but it was forced onto his attention by Gandhi, and the Congress Party's drive for independence. When the Viceroy, Irwin, offered eventual Dominion status to India, he had Baldwin's full support. The revolt against him within the Conservative Party was dangerous, led by Churchill (who had been his

Chancellor of the Exchequer from 1924 to 1929), and backed by the press barons. After three years of simmering discontent, Baldwin was told (in 1931) that most of his colleagues thought he should resign as party leader. He survived with a mixture of concession (more safeguards for Britain in the proposed Indian constitution) and attacks on the gutter press. Churchill was marginalised; Baldwin was once more incontestably in charge at the centre.

Churchill was to get his revenge later in *The Gathering Storm*, in which he cast Baldwin as the leader who, ignorant of foreign affairs, left Britain defenceless against Hitler. How fair was this reputation? Baldwin was well travelled in western Europe and spoke French fluently. He left foreign policy to be conducted through the Foreign Office, but that was his method of leadership: all his ministers were expected to look after their own departments. He was fearful of a new war in which 'every man, woman and child' would be vulnerable: for 'the bomber will always get through', and talked of Britain's frontier being on the Rhine. So the emergence of totalitarian states filled him with foreboding: 'The world is stark mad. I have no idea what is the matter with it, but it's all wrong.' To judge his response to the growing threat honestly, one needs to look at some dates. For many years after the Great War, disarmament was at the top of Europe's agenda, and as late as 1932 a new Disarmament Conference was opened. There was a spate of anti-war literature between 1928 and 1931: Blunden's *Undertones of War*, Sassoon's *Memoirs of an Infantry Officer* and Sheriff's play *Journey's End*. Even after Hitler had seized power in 1933, the Oxford Union passed the motion: 'This House will not fight for King and Country'; the Peace Ballot (1934) pro-duced an 80% majority (out of eleven million responders) in favour of disarmament; and the Labour Party, led by the pacifist Lansbury, won a sensational by-election victory at East Fulham (1933), which (perhaps not entirely correctly) Baldwin took as a vote against rear-manent. There was a further problem. Where was the money for arms to come from, with the British economy in recession after the world collapse of 1931? So Baldwin's reaction to changing circum-stances on the Continent was cautious: defence estimates in 1934 were below those of 1924. He planned for air parity with Germany, and appointed the energetic Cunliffe Lister to organise it, but calmed the voters at the 1935 election with a promise that there would be 'no great armaments' (and won it with a majority of 242). He made collective security through the League of Nations 'the sheet anchor of British policy'. But no one stood up to the Fascists. Hitler was allowed to reoccupy the Rhineland and Mussolini to conquer Abyssinia. Baldwin was embarrassed by a leak which revealed his Foreign Secretary Hoare's pact with Laval for an Anglo-French arrangement with Mussolini over Abyssinia, and made matters worse for himself with a speech on armaments in which he made a confession 'with appalling frankness' that was wrongly interpreted as meaning that he had delayed rearmament to win the general election of 1935. Baldwin was ahead of most in anticipating the future storm. But fear of another war, the accepted nostrum that the Great War had been caused by an arms race, and the need to educate public opinion, all inhibited his approach to rearmament. In the light of history, he moved too slowly, but at the time he seemed to have judged the pace shrewdly. It was Churchill who wrote to Baldwin in 1935: 'You have gathered to yourself a fund of personal goodwill and public confidence which is indispensable to our safety at the present time.'

He planned to retire after the coronation of Edward VIII, but instead found himself managing Edward's abdication. He was shocked by the King's putting private happiness before public duty, and fearful of the reactions of the Dominions, linked almost solely by the monarchy. His authority kept Edward and his supporters from rash appeals to the country and there was palpable relief when the King went quietly. He eventually resigned after George VI's coronation in May 1937, to public acclamation. The *Punch* cartoonist saw him off as 'The Worcestershire Lad': 'Well done, Stanley,' says John Bull, 'a good long day and a rare straight furrow.' But the change in the climate of opinion between 1937 and 1940 was perhaps the most remarkable and complete in the whole of British history, and after Chamberlain's death Baldwin became the prime target for those in search of guilty men. When the gates of his house were removed for scrap iron, a Conservative MP asked in the House of Commons: 'Is the honourable Member aware that it is necessary to leave Lord Baldwin his gates in order to protect him from the just indignation of the mob?' He lingered on until 1947, his eightieth birthday unnoticed outside his family.

Baldwin was perhaps the most instinctively conservative leader the Tory Party has ever had. A quiet, unhurried pipe-smoker, he was approachable – 'drop in and have a word' – and reassuring, especially over the wireless, a new means of mass communication which suited his plain, reflective style. He was no administrator and rode his ministers on a loose rein. He took decisions slowly and painfully and his successes were those of a conciliator. His integrity was never questioned. Some marked him down as lazy: he always took long holidays and there were times when he switched off and government drifted. But he enjoyed a crisis, and his handling of them earned him Churchill's grudging admiration as 'the most formidable politician I have ever met.'

K. Middlemas & J. Barnes, *Baldwin: A Biography* (1969).
H. Hyde, *Baldwin: The Unexpected Prime Minister* (1973).

Ramsay MacDonald

J. RAMSAY MACDONALD (1866-1937), the first Labour Prime Minister (1924, 1929-31, and of a National Government 1931-5), had a tragic career. All his successes turned sour, all his hopes were blighted. Starting his political life as a member of the Independent Labour Party (ILP), he ended it with scarcely a Labour friend left. The creator of a united parliamentary party to represent the Labour movement in Parliament, he died when it was a mere rump, from which he had been expelled when he formed a National Government which was dominated by Conservatives. His two central objectives were to prove that Labour could govern and to foster world peace: but both his Labour Governments ended in failure, the second in near catastrophe, while he was as powerless as any of his contemporaries to halt the advance of Hitler. Behind these failures, and casting a deep shadow of loneliness over him throughout, was the early death of his wife. Long before he resigned his mind had deteriorated and he had become an embarrassment to his colleagues and himself. His subsequent reputation has been darkened by his closing years. Yet he was the architect as well as the first leader of the Parliamentary Labour Party, and in the 1920s he was the political hero of the British working classes.

Ramsay MacDonald was illegitimate, brought up in the fishing village of Lossiemouth by his mother and his grandmother, both proud ladies earning their living as dressmakers. A handsome and intelligent boy with the gift of the gab, he followed many an ambitious Scot down the road to London and made his way as a freelance journalist and secretary to a Radical politician. In 1894, frustrated by the Liberals' dislike of selecting working-class candidates, he joined the ILP. As a campaigner, administrator and conciliator he rapidly became so outstanding that, when in 1900 the unions and the political socialist groups, the ILP and the SDF, decided at a seminal meeting in Farringdon Street to form 'a distinct Labour Group in Parliament who shall have their own whips and agree their own policy', MacDonald was chosen as its Secretary.

From that base he was to turn this Labour Representation Committee into the Labour Party. Meanwhile he had married a social worker, Margaret Gladstone, daughter of a well-to-do doctor, who fell for him despite his red tie. They got engaged on the steps of the British Museum. She brought him a sense of personal security as well as financial independence. They had a close, affectionate working life together in the middle of the Labour movement. Their cheerful, untidy home saw streams of visitors, and their six children filled any time (and space) that was left; but in 1911 Margaret died. Thereafter Ramsay was a lonely man, suspicious of rivals and sensitive to criticism.

He had, however, already become both the leading theorist and the main strategist of his party. Much of his writing was romantically vague and even syntactically obscure, but the main river of his thought was one into which the many disparate streams of the early Labour movement could flow. Abhorring class war at home, he preached the evolutionary path to a socialist state. Abroad he denounced the secret diplomacy of the aristocratic chancelleries, and looked forward to world peace spreading through fraternal goodwill. To these ends he worked first to increase Labour's strength in Parliament through arrangements with the Liberals, and later to displace the Liberals as the leading party of the Left. His strategy was completely successful. In 1903, making use of the many two-member parliamentary constituencies, he persuaded the Liberal Chief Whip of the advantage to both parties of sharing some of them, so that in the Liberal victory at the 1906 election 29 Labour members were returned, including MacDonald himself, for Leicester; and in 1910 this number rose to 40, with a number of Liberal MPs joining Labour. Though his own ILP became restless as he supported the Liberal National Insurance Bill (being contributory, it was against Labour principles), the unions accepted this Progressive Alliance as being the best way of defending their interests. In 1911 he became Chairman of the Party. By then he was accepted as its outstanding figure. On public platforms he was charismatic, with his fine-boned face, high poetic brow, thick flowing locks and moustache, commanding voice and lilting Scottish accent. He could straddle the different groups in the Movement, from the Clydesiders to the Fabians, better than any of its other leaders. His Scottish background made him classless in London, and his Celtic romanticism was conveniently imprecise. He had many important qualities of leadership: electric energy, sensitive antennae, appetite for detail. He was a tireless negotiator and a patient chairman.

To all these he added another dimension, which for a time seemed to have ruined him politically, but which then raised him to new heights in the eyes of the public. In 1914 he declared his opposition to Britain's entry into the Great War. He did not think his country should be dragged into the rivalries of Emperors, especially where the Tsar of Russia was involved, and when his party joined the patriotic fervour he resigned his chairmanship. This required great political courage. *John Bull* called him 'Traitor, Coward and Cur', and told the electors of Leicester that they should have asked for his birth certificate. The Moray Golf Club at Lossiemouth expelled him. Letters arrived to Herr Ramsay MacDonald. In 1918 he lost his seat by 20,510 votes to 6,347. But his courage was soon to bring its reward. Reaction to the euphoria of 1918 came inevitably, and MacDonald's denunciations of the Treaty of Versailles rang true from a man who had consistently attacked the machinations of old-style diplomacy. Labour welcomed him back. In 1921 his war record still prevented him from winning a by-election at Woolwich, but in the general election of 1922 he was returned for Aberavon. He was elected Chairman again, since the existing Chairman, Arthur Henderson, had lost his seat: but this time it was as 'Chairman and Leader' of a party with 142 MPs, many of them able and experienced, and with the finance behind it of a trade union body which had doubled in size since the start of the war. The next year there was another election. At MacDonald's own campaign there were scenes which reverberated round the country. Outside Port Talbot his car took two hours to travel a mile as the crowds surged round it. It was, one paper wrote, 'a demonstration which reflected ... the enthusiasm which MacDonald's personality and single-minded intensity of purpose have created during the stern testing time of the past eight years.' The Conservatives, campaigning on a Protection platform, lost ground. 191 Labour members were returned, which made them the second largest party. With Liberal support, the first Labour government took office.

MacDonald headed two Labour administrations, from January to November 1924 and from June 1929 to August 1931. The fears of the gentry were great with the spectre of Lenin looming. The expectations of the poor were correspondingly high. 'In the slums of manufacturing towns and the hovels of the countryside', wrote a contemporary, 'MacDonald has become a legendary being ... the focus of the mute hopes of a whole class.' Anticlimax followed. There were modest achievements at home. The Housing Acts (1924 and 1930), the Coal Mines Act (1930) and the Agricultural Marketing Act (1931) all introduced central government machinery, working alongside private capitalism. But this was small beer. MacDonald's own interest was focused abroad: indeed, in his first ministry he was his own Foreign Secretary. Here he earned widespread respect. His drive for disarmament was persistent. In 1924 he persuaded the French to withdraw their troops from the Ruhr and to accept the Dawes Plan, moderating the savage reparations imposed on Germany at Versailles. In 1929 reparations were further modified and allied troops were withdrawn from the Rhineland. A reduction in the navies of Britain, the USA and Japan was envisaged by the Treaty of London in 1931 and a World Disarmament Conference was planned for 1932. For India, his policy was the active encouragement of self-government within the Empire, and over the winter of 1930 he devoted most of his time to reconciling Hindu and Moslem differences at the Round Table Conference in London. Fortunately he did not live to see the failure of that policy and the massacres which accompanied the birth of Pakistan. But he did witness the emergence of Hitler. Though understanding all too painfully the nature of German Fascism, he hated the bombers which his National Government started to build, and ended despairingly searching for ways of combating the Nazis without abandoning the assumptions of a lifetime.

But 'the mute hopes of a whole class' were wretchedly disappointed. Why was Labour in power so feeble? They never commanded a majority in the House of Commons, of course, but there were other reasons. MacDonald had had a clear strategy for gaining power, but such plans as he had for using it were fatally flawed. 'Without haste but without rest' he hoped to bring land, coal, transport, power and life insurance into public ownership, but neither he nor his ministers had thought through the problems of running a socialist state. Not that this was to matter greatly, as they never had the chance of doing so: they were cruelly unfortunate to be in power when the world's economy collapsed. The central problem for government in Britain between the wars was unemployment. Labour leaders assumed that this was caused by capitalism and would fade away once a socialist state was in place. Meanwhile MacDonald and his Chancellor of the Exchequer, Snowden, had to choose between Keynes's solution, of large-scale public works financed by loans to bring people back to work, and the Treasury orthodoxy of a balanced budget. With the catastrophic German hyper-inflation still a very recent memory, they stuck to orthodoxy. But they were also wedded to free trade, to encourage world fraternity and to keep food prices down. Here was a disastrous combination which proved fatal to MacDonald's hopes. Less protected than their rivals, British industries suffered most severely in world recession. Unemployment grew; so did the cost to the Exchequer of unemployment benefit. To balance the budget, Snowden had to raise taxes or reduce benefits, or both. Deflation followed; demand dropped. In the whirlpool of this vicious circle the second Labour government was dragged help-lessly down. The crisis which finally submerged it in August 1931 was caused by the incompetence of British bankers, who, having lent long and borrowed short, were unable to cope with a run on the pound. But the run itself was caused by the belief that Labour ministers would not face the consequences of their agreed policy of a balanced budget, and implement the large cuts in benefit recom-mended by the May Committee, formed to report on the state of government finances. And so it proved. MacDonald tried, but could not carry his Cabinet with him. Nine ministers voted against the cuts, and he resigned. The bitterness, when he decided to respond to the pleas of King George V and head a National Government to impose them and restore international confidence, was deep and long lasting. The worst sufferers were those who had expected most from him and from Labour. This was betrayal.

Though Prime Minister, he became a prisoner in a government which was supported, after an election in 1931, by 473 Conservative, 35 Liberal and only 13 Labour MPs, and he was despised by his former colleagues, the more so because of his friendship with the society hostess Lady Londonderry. He had not planned a National Government – that Labour myth is abundantly disproved in his diaries. His decision to lead one, rather than resign and allow the Conservatives to take over, was taken under the pressure of events, which allowed no time for contemplation, and partly out of wrath against his Labour colleagues, especially his old rival Henderson, who had prevented him from carrying through his policy as a Labour leader. There was also his vanity, responding to appeals from the King and Conservative and Liberal leaders, and the lack of a wife to consult. It proved a disastrous decision. The crisis was temporarily averted, but within a month Britain had left the Gold Standard. MacDonald had to watch helplessly as Labour's Land Tax was repealed, the Unemployment Assistance Board applied a tough policy with pettifogging inhumanity, and his own promise not to tax Co-operative Societies was broken. Bad eyesight hastened the deterioration of his mental powers: at the Conference at Stresa he rambled so strangely that the translator was advised to make up the speech, while his senior Foreign Office official had to provide him with collar studs. He clung to office, resigning as Prime Minister in 1935 but staying on as Lord President of the Council, a ghost in the lobbies, without patronage or a future. Finally departing when Baldwin retired, he died on board ship six months later, in November 1937.

D. Marquand, *Ramsay MacDonald* (1977, revised 1997).
A. Morgan, *J. Ramsay MacDonald* (1994).

Neville Chamberlain

NEVILLE CHAMBERLAIN (1869-1940) was Prime Minister from 1937 until 1940. His reputation, high when he took office as the obvious heir apparent to Baldwin, was destroyed by his attempts to appease Hitler. It has never recovered. Yet there is much else which should be known about him.

He inherited a famous name. While he was still a child, his father, Joe, created a political base in Birmingham by his achievements as Mayor there which survived intact through the whirligigs of politics until 1945. Joe bestrode, and his son Austen was a leading figure on, the national stage. Neville, son by a second marriage, was destined to be the businessman of the family: he was sent to grow sisal in the Bahamas, one of his father's wilder schemes. It failed. The poor quality of the fibre and overproduction elsewhere doomed it, despite his strenuous efforts over seven years. But on his return to Birmingham he built up his own business, Hoskins & Son, manufacturing ships' berths (its patent for folding beds enabled ships taking emigrants out to bring back full cargoes in their holds). Meanwhile he showed his father's vigorously active interest in Birmingham's affairs, becoming Mayor. His initiatives included the Birmingham Municipal Savings Bank (dear to his heart), the Birmingham City Orchestra and a Provident Dispensary, created to relieve the pressure on the hospital's out-patient department. His reputation as an efficient administrator was such that when conscription was introduced in 1916 Lloyd George asked him to become the Director of National Service. For a second time he was given an impossible task. Starting from scratch, he had no power base. Only with the support of the Prime Minister, against vested interests protecting important sources of manpower from conscription, could he have achieved success, and that was lacking. A mutual dislike between Chamberlain and Lloyd George quickly developed, which was to last through the rest of their lives. In August 1917 he resigned.

He was nearly fifty when he entered Parliament in 1918 as MP for Ladywood, a Birmingham constituency. With his brother Austen

Chancellor of the Exchequer, doors were soon opened to him in a Conservative Party which was short of talent after the war. He moved through them confidently. He had throughout his life an awe-inspiring capacity for hard work, sitting on more committees than any other MP. When Lloyd George's coalition was forced out of office by the Conservatives in 1922, promotion came rapidly. In Bonar Law's and Baldwin's Cabinets Chamberlain held a range of offices, ending as Chancellor of the Exchequer, and when Baldwin won his decisive electoral victory of 1924 he asked to return to one of them, choosing the Health Ministry rather than the more prestigious Treasury in order to carry through the plans he had laid there.

This was his most creative period: he and Churchill were the two big men in Baldwin's Cabinet. His National Insurance Act (1928) made insurance compulsory and contributory, covering unemployment, sickness, old age and widows. State pensions, too, became compulsory and contributory. His reform of local government was drastic, concentrating almost all local government activities under the County and County Borough Councils. In addition to police and education which they already controlled, these were now to run local transport and roads, public health, housing, slum clearance, planning, gas and electricity. As a result, the number of authorities was reduced from 15,546 to 1,767. Chamberlain showed tough perseverance in overcoming deep-rooted vested interests, and *The Times* opined that the Local Government Act (1929) would be recognised as one of the outstanding legislative achievements of the twentieth century. But to stimulate the economy he also de-rated agriculture completely and industry partly, compensating the local authorities for the loss of rates with subsidies from central government to the extent of two fifths of their income. He therefore left English local government with the widest powers in the world, but dangerously dependent on central government for its finances.

Though a forceful administrative reformer, Chamberlain was a Conservative through and through. His style and tastes were old-fashioned. He preferred the steel nib to the new-fangled fountain pen, and thought that Epstein's *Christ* must have been sculpted as a joke. The Conservative Research Department, of which he became Chairman in 1930, dealt in practical solutions to immediate problems, and he had no time for emotional rhetoric or ill thought-out ideas. He despised most of the Labour Party leaders, and they demonised him. There were policy issues dividing them. In a drive for economy, Chamberlain had cut the state contribution to National Health Insurance: 'plucking the feathers out of the pillow of a sick man,' Lloyd George called it. He also took powers to stop local authorities using the rates for social reform rather than direct poor relief: Poplarism, this tactic was called, after the district in which Labour leader George Lansbury had started to use it. But there was personal incompatibility too. A warm man in his family circle, he was stiff and cold in public. 'You can't get to know Mr Chamberlain until you've been with him for five years,' said his chauffeur. To relax, he was happiest fly-fishing alone on a country river. He was hardly ever seen in the Smoking Room of the House of Commons. In debate he was combative, and Baldwin had to urge him to stop treating Labour like dirt when he spoke at them across the House of Commons.

When the National Government was formed in 1931 to rescue the country from the financial crash, Chamberlain became the driving force in it. 'It amuses me', he wrote to his sister Hilda, to whom he was especially close, 'to find a new policy for each of my colleagues in turn.' As Chancellor of the Exchequer he restored confidence by balancing his budgets, and managed to convert War Loan interest from 5% to 3.5%. He fulfilled his father's dream by reintroducing Protection in Britain (though he could not achieve Empire Free Trade). In 1932 a general tariff of 10% was imposed on nearly all imports, with a superstructure of additional tariffs to protect especially threatened industries. This apart, Chamberlain was a conservative Chancellor, who had a low opinion of Roosevelt's New Deal and Keynesian deficit financing. For this he was castigated in the post-war Keynesian era, and unemployment remained obstinately high, but many would now agree that sound money was crucial for our economy in 1931, and go along with Lord Halifax's opinion, given in 1937, that his time at the Treasury provided the essential condition for all the improvements that those five and a half years had seen. By the time an exhausted Baldwin retired after seeing George VI safely through the Coronation, Chamberlain had for some time been recognised as his successor, and Conservatives looked forward to vigorous leadership.

Chamberlain wanted to be remembered for his domestic achievements, as a reforming Prime Minister. But the three years of his government were dominated by Hitler. Dark clouds had been gathering over Europe since 1936, when Hitler marched into the Rhineland, Mussolini invaded Abyssinia and the Spanish Civil War broke out. The German-Italian agreement (the Axis) and the pact between Germany and Japan further blackened them. There was little to comfort Chamberlain when he surveyed the world scene. The French were prepared to defy Germany from behind the Maginot line, but no further. Isolation still dominated American sentiment. In the League of Nations he had no confidence. Nor did he ever favour an alliance with Communist Russia, whose armies were at any rate regarded by British military experts as worthless after Stalin had purged their generals in 1937. Labour Party members were wholeheartedly pacifist, and though they were weak in Parliament they had the trade unions with them. British rearmament, which he had supported even as Chancellor, was two years behind the Germans', and the Dominions warned that they were not willing to join a war in defence of middle European states. There was, indeed, a universal horror of starting another Great War less than twenty years after the end of the last one, with the added menace of attack from the air. In England the bomber was regarded almost as nuclear warfare came to be ten years later; when war did break out there was a general issue of gas masks to civilians.

Most historians have judged Chamberlain with the hindsight knowledge of Hitler's determination to become master of Europe. But at the time, at least until the autumn of 1938, the policy of 'appeasement' had popular backing, and Churchill's clarion calls against Germany sounded strident and dangerous. 'Appeasement' was a respectable word in 1937, conveying a sense of honourable diplomatic hard work to settle genuine German grievances. Chamberlain pursued it with characteristic energy and single-mindedness. He dominated his Cabinet, confidently opinionated and leading from the front, and increasingly he got the diplomatic strings into his own hands. He lost his young but highly regarded Foreign Secretary, Anthony Eden, who had been accustomed to running his own show under the easy-going Baldwin. Eden disagreed with Chamberlain's policy of detaching Mussolini from Hitler, and had more hopes of the League of Nations than the Prime Minister did. Using his own senior civil servant, Sir Horace Wilson, as adviser and intermediary, Chamberlain accepted Hitler's occupation of Austria in March 1938 as reasonable: it was a German-speaking country. When Hitler started to threaten to settle the grievances of the German majority in the Czechoslovakian Sudetenland by war he set out to achieve a peaceful compromise: there *were* grievances, though they were being stirred up on Hitler's instructions. As Hitler moved his troops, Chamberlain flew to Berchtesgarten to talk with him face to face. Flying round the world is now routine for national leaders, but this was a double first: the first such flight for a British Prime Minister, and the first time that Chamberlain had ever flown. He was an old gentleman of nearly seventy, and his efforts caught the public's admiration and support. It took two more meetings to achieve the Munich settlement, which ceded the Sudetenland to Germany and thus deprived Czechoslovakia of the mountains from which it might (but probably briefly) have defended itself. The first reaction to the agreement in Britain was one of enthusiastic relief.

Had the premise on which the policy of appeasement been founded proved sound, there might, as Chamberlain rashly hoped in public, have been 'peace in our time'. But it was not. Hitler wanted his war while his rearmament programme was ahead of everyone else's and in March 1939 he marched into Prague and seized the rest of Czechoslovakia. Chamberlain had to change tack. He abandoned the policy of limited liability on the Continent. He set about creating an army to help France in the event of a German attack, and he and the French jointly guaranteed Poland, where the Polish corridor to the port of Danzig was Hitler's next target. Efforts were also made to create an Eastern group of allies round Russia, but Chamberlain's heart was not in this. With public opinion swinging fast against Hitler, he clung with failing hopes to the possibility of a peaceful deal over Danzig. But when Hitler, now astonishingly allied with Russia, invaded Poland, he honoured his commitment once the French had agreed to do so as well. The war which broke out in September was started on territory where Britain could have no military influence. Appeasement lay in ruins, and his own reputation with it.

That he remained Prime Minister for the first nine months of the war seems strange now. But his Cabinet and most of his party had been with him all the way to Munich and beyond, and Churchill now served under him willingly. For a while the war remained remote, but once Hitler had successfully invaded Norway it was clear that Chamberlain could never become a national war leader. In Parliament he was politically divisive, and in the country his image was of the umbrella, not the sword. When Hitler invaded the Low

Countries there was a substantial rebellion against him in the House of Commons. With Labour agreeing to join a National Government, but not under him, he resigned. Churchill, who had been loyal to him throughout, asked him to serve in the new Cabinet, realising his importance in keeping the Conservatives in line. This he did, his last service to the country. His tough constitution broke with his spirit: cancer attacked him and he died before the year was out.

For a whole generation, Chamberlain was the 'Guilty Man' who left Britain unprepared to meet Hitler, and appeasement became a term of opprobrium. The history of the period was dominated by Churchill, who wrote his own version of it, tendentious but powerful. Later writers have laid stress on the climate of opinion in which Chamberlain worked, and which changed so quickly and dramatically in 1939. They have pointed to the energy with which Chamberlain pursued rearmament after 1936, when Attlee accused him of producing a 'War Budget'; and especially to his switching production priority from bombers to fighters, without which the Battle of Britain would have been lost. In September 1940 the strength of Fighter Command was almost ten times that of September 1938. But there is little evidence that he regarded appeasement as playing for time. Taking full responsibility as a dominating Prime Minister, he misjudged Hitler, and that mattered more than anything else he did.

D. Dutton, *Neville Chamberlain* (2001).

Winston Churchill

SIR WINSTON CHURCHILL, KG (1874-1965) (Prime Minister 1940-5 and 1952-5), was made in the mould of heroes. Only Gladstone rivals him as a human being in the annals of 10 Downing Street, and, as the inspiring leader of the country in its most critical year since 1066, the importance of his influence on British history is unmatched. In 1940 he 'bestrode the narrow world like a colossus'. Alanbrooke, the soldier who worked most closely with him through the war, and who endured the most infuriating side of his nature, wrote in his diary in 1941, 'He is quite the most wonderful man I have ever met.'

He brought to Downing Street a unique and sometimes startling range of experience. He was born in Blenheim Palace, but relied on his Nanny for emotional support as a child since his father, Lord Randolph Churchill, and his mother, the American beauty Jennie Jerome, were too busy to give him attention. At Harrow he was already an original, winning from the bottom form a prize open to the whole school by reciting 1,200 lines of Macaulay by heart. But he failed the Army entrance exam twice. As a young soldier he fought on the North West Frontier and in Cuba (where he first learnt to smoke large cigars), and took part in the last cavalry charge at Omdurman; as a war correspondent he was captured by the Boers and escaped from an armed train. He became an MP (Conservative) aged twenty-five and a minister (Liberal) aged thirty-one. He entered the Cabinet as President of the Board of Trade in 1908 and joined Lloyd George in promoting social reform. He earned a trigger-happy reputation as Home Secretary by turning up in person at the Sidney Street siege of a gang of Latvian robbers in Stepney, which clung to him during the riots of Welsh miners at Tonypandy. And as First Lord of the Admiralty he prepared the Navy for the First World War, becoming one of Asquith's inner War Cabinet, from which he slipped away for a few days to try to rally the Belgian defence of Antwerp. His career as a minister came to a halt in 1915 after the failure of the Dardanelles expedition, conceived and run by him as the way to win the war away from the trenches of the Western Front. To those trenches he now went, to become colonel of the 6th Scots Fusiliers. Months later he was back at Westminster. Lloyd George, Coalition Prime Minister, made him successively Minister of Munitions, Secretary for War and Air, where he handled post-war demobilisation imaginatively, and Colonial Secretary at the time when the Middle East was being reshaped, under British influence, after the dissolution of the old Turkish Empire. Identified with the Coalition, he lost his seat in 1922 when Britain returned to party politics, but reappeared as Baldwin's Chancellor of the Exchequer (Conservative!) for five years (1924-9). It tells us much about his effectiveness in the House of Commons that Baldwin gave this senior post in his Cabinet to a man who had changed his party twice.

Many Conservatives disapproved. As a young man he was intolerably bumptious. On one occasion, while he was still a Tory, the whole of his own front bench had walked out when he rose to speak, and his rapid rise as a Liberal made him so unpopular among them that they had made it a condition of joining a Coalition Ministry in 1915 that he should be removed from the Admiralty. To Labour he was *persona non grata*, the minister who had sent troops against the miners at Tonypandy and tried to intervene against the Communists in the Russian Civil War. Their view was confirmed when he proved the most bellicose opponent of the General Strike in 1926. A remarkable man, but dangerously lacking judgement and a sense of proportion, was the general view. In the 1930s Churchill did much to lend colour to this picture. His romantic ideal of British imperial responsibilities led him to oppose with all the force of his oratory the plans to give India self-government and to break with Baldwin, and his romantic attitude to monarchy made him the quixotic champion of Edward VIII during the abdication crisis. So as the Cassandra urging rearmament against Hitler's Germany he was an outsider, suspect for his often-revealed fascination with war. Even when Chamberlain resigned in the critical days of May 1940, most of the Cabinet, and the King himself, would have preferred the establishment figure, Lord Halifax, as their next Prime Minister.

But by then it had become clear that Churchill must lead the country. When Hitler brushed aside the Munich settlement, Chamberlain's 'peace in our time', and invaded Czechoslovakia, a profound revulsion ran through the British public. Recalled to the Admiralty on the first day of the war ('Winston is back' was the signal round the fleet), his personality shone brightly from a grey front bench of erstwhile appeasers. He was a truly democratic Prime Minister, whose position depended on his popularity, chosen only because those at the centre, who still mistrusted him, realised that he had a charisma that none of them could match. Although depression, his 'black dog', occasionally bit him, his normal zest for life infected others. He rode hard, played polo, loved to swim, porpoise-like. He tried and failed to get a pilot's licence, crashing twice in a month. He learnt to paint, with bright-coloured oils. He became a bricklayer. He ate and drank well, with exhilarating talk over long lunches and dinners and much champagne (though he was a sipper, not a gulper). He was supported by a settled marriage with Clementine Hozier, a strong wife who put up with his whims, his rackety friends and his headstrong decisions (he bought Chartwell, a country estate in Kent, without consulting her). Their letters, his to 'my Cat', hers to 'my Pug', reveal deep and steadfast affection, and her advice to him was shrewd and forthright, though not always accepted. Their greatest concern was finance. Churchill was extravagant. 'He is always prepared to put up with the best of everything,' commented his friend, Lord Birkenhead. He was also a gambler. His largest gamble, on Wall Street on the eve of the Great Crash of 1929, brought them close to bankruptcy: indeed it was only after the war that they became financially secure through the help of a syndicate of rich men. With the habits but not the income of the landed aristocracy from which he sprang, he had to earn his living with his pen. His literary output was larger than that of any other Prime Minister, even the novelist Disraeli. From war reporting he graduated to major biographies of his father and of his ancestor Marlborough, to a *History of the English-Speaking Peoples*, and to two large-scale histories of his own time, *The World Crisis (1914-1919)* and *The Second World War*. These all shared the quality of being for the most part excitingly readable.

He was not, therefore, a man of the people – far from it. But British people then were happy to be led by a man flamboyantly different from themselves. With his bulldog expression under his old-fashioned or eccentric hats, and his big cigar, he became an exhilarating figurehead for them as he toured bombed sites with his fingers raised in a V sign. They were rallied by his speeches, some to them directly over the wireless (as he always called it), some to the House of Commons, which stirred them to face terrible danger with a buoyant spirit. 'Let us therefore brace ourselves to our duty, and so bear ourselves that if the British Commonwealth and Empire lasts for a thousand years, men will still say, "This was their finest hour."' He gave priority to the preparation of his speeches even when disasters crowded in daily, and their high-flown perorations gave new resolution to all who heard them, with their stark contrasts between good and evil, and their call to Britons to save not only themselves but the world from Nazi barbarism. They have been famous ever since.

This was how the people saw Churchill and why they followed him. But he was also the most powerful executive Prime Minister in British history. Churchill had always believed in destiny. Now, when he was sixty-five and long thought of as a has-been, destiny in the shape of Hitler had given him his opportunity. He led a coalition government to mobilise the whole nation for war, with Labour playing an important part, Attlee eventually becoming Deputy Prime Minister and Bevin carrying the trade unions with him. There was already a War Cabinet, but Churchill took a firmer day-to-day grip on the prosecution of the war by creating a Ministry of Defence and a Defence Committee, to which the Chiefs of Staff reported: he was Minister of Defence, and he met them almost every day while he was in the country, and normally had one with him when he went abroad. There was unity of direction for the three Services, and Churchill was in control. He picked and dismissed generals, and took the strategic decisions: the contrast with Lloyd George, who often argued in vain with Haig and Robertson, was much in his mind. But he remained a constitutional leader, reporting to the King and to the House of Commons, and depending on his (never seriously threatened) parliamentary majority.

His handling of this efficient machinery often put its members under almost intolerable pressure. His routine, working from bed in the morning, a siesta after a good lunch, and then maintaining a full output until the small hours of the next day, interrupted only by a well lubricated dinner, kept them up late with him, however exhausted they might be. From his fertile mind poured streams of ideas, a secretary always at hand to take his dictation. 'Winston had ten ideas every day', wrote Alanbrooke, 'only one of which was good, and he did not know which it was.' His interest in weapons, starting in the First War with the tank and the aeroplane, led to wild suggestions like using icebergs as floating airstrips off Norway, and inspired ones like the Mulberry Harbour. Many of them bore his trademark red label, 'Action This Day', with which he energised his government. He sat on the shoulders of his generals, demanding outgoing leadership and quick action, but his preference for the unorthodox worked, as with Montgomery; to his admirals he showed more deference. His moods varied and his language could be harsh. In June 1940, his devoted wife felt the need to write to him about his 'rough sarcastic and overbearing manner' to his subordinates. He was a bad chairman, leaving decisions untaken at the end of Cabinet meetings which he had filled with his wide-ranging surveys of world events. He also frequently operated outside the formal machinery, listening to the advice of special favourites, Bracken the wayward politician, Lindemann the scientific 'Prof', Beaverbrook the press baron, for which Attlee was eventually driven to rebuke him. But the sunshine after the storms, his still impish sense of fun and his resolute optimism kept the loyalty and commanded the admiration of those close to him.

He took brave early decisions. A fortnight after he had become Prime Minister, with the French beaten, the British Army surrounded, and he himself still unsure of Conservative backing, he resisted the attempt by Halifax to explore a compromise peace. He sent tanks from England to reinforce Wavell's army in Egypt even as the Battle of Britain was being fought, and gave the order to destroy the French fleet once it had become clear that it might fall into German hands. His strategic grasp was sound, and on the big issues he eventually listened to his Chiefs of Staff, even though he often took much persuasion to abandon some of his diversionary ideas, especially the invasion of Norway after which he long hankered. He resisted Stalin's insistent demands, and some American pressure, for a Second Front in France until the Allies were ready for it, and instead steered the Americans to North Africa, Operation Torch (1942), and thence to Sicily and Italy (1943).

Hitler provoked the Grand Alliance of the USA, the USSR and the British Empire which brought him down, but Churchill nurtured it. For the USA his affection was deep. His mother was American, and he had almost completed his *History of the English-Speaking Peoples* when the war started. He never cleared himself from the suspicions of Americans about the old imperialist lurking in him, but he devoted enormous care to trying to do so, with 200 letters exchanged between him and President Roosevelt, and nine wartime journeys across the Atlantic. 'Give us the tools and we will finish the job,' he had said, but he knew that Britain could not finish it by herself. He quoted Clough: 'In front the sun climbs slow, how slowly! But westward look, the land is bright!', and his reaction to the news of Pearl Harbor (December 1941) was: 'So we had won after all.' He was delighted that, despite the Japanese attack, the USA put the winning of the war against Hitler first. He recognised, though it hurt him to do so, the USA's emerging preponderance: that shared atomic research should take place in Los Alamos, and the command of the Second Front (Overlord) should go to an American general. Less readily he had to accept American insistence on Anvil, the invasion of the south of France in 1944, which pulled troops away from Alexander's advance towards the Po valley. His prejudices against Bolshevik Russia had been as strong as his attachment to America, but when Hitler invaded it (June 1941) his *volte face* was immediate. He respected Stalin, despite his 'surly, snarling and grasping' response to help. He went to Moscow in 1942, to Teheran in 1943 and to Yalta in the Crimea in 1945, to bind the alliance together. He did all he could to meet Stalin's demands short of opening a premature Second Front:sending convoys round Norway to Murmansk with heavy loss; returning, to their likely death, the White Russian and Ukrainian prisoners who had been fighting for the Germans; and authorising the saturation bombing of German towns, with its terrible climax at Dresden.

Churchill remained publicly buoyant through the bad early years of the Alliance (1941/2). Submarines threatened supplies across the Atlantic; the Japanese sank two of the battleships of which he was so proud, *Repulse* and *Prince of Wales*, overran Singapore and advanced through Burma towards India; and the Germans reached the approaches to Moscow and St Petersburg and had only Stalingrad between them and the oil riches of the Caucasus. Later, though the tide in Africa had turned with Montgomery's victory at El Alamein in October 1941, the strains on him began to tell. In 1943 he was out of Britain for 172 days, travelling uncomfortably and dangerously (a plane flying from Gibraltar on the same day as his was shot down, the film star Leslie Howard being killed). In Washington in 1942 he had a mild heart attack, and there followed three bouts of pneumonia, the one in 1943 laying him out for a month. By 1945 he was so tired after one Cabinet meeting in the underground bunker that marines had to carry him upstairs. He was also depressed at finding the UK the least powerful of the allies. He was unable to persuade Roosevelt of the threat to the liberties of Eastern European states posed by Russian Communism, and was dismayed at the end of the war when Truman ordered the immediate withdrawal of American troops from the areas they were occupying beyond the boundaries of influence agreed at the Yalta Conference.

But he led Britain to victory. D-Day was by far the largest amphibious operation ever attempted in the history of warfare, and it took the King to dissuade the old warrior from being there himself. He made his own special contribution to it, however, with his brainchild, the Mulberry Harbour, floated in parts across the Channel and assembled off the Normandy coast. Though there was much hard fighting to do, German surrender this time was unconditional. On VE Day, 8 May 1945, he addressed huge cheering crowds in Whitehall, and he went to Potsdam to settle the future of Europe. So it was a shock when the British voters decided that their wartime leader should not become their peacetime leader. Churchill wanted to prolong the Coalition until the Japanese had been defeated, but Labour did not. In the 1945 general election, the first for ten years, Churchill became robustly partisan once more, and conjured up a grim picture of a Socialist state which 'would have to fall back on some sort of Gestapo'. 'Let us think no more of Hitlee or Attler,' he had once growled after Attlee had stung him with a criticism. The electorate was not ready to accept this confusion and returned only 210 Conservatives to a House of 640 members. It was a decision not to go back to pre-war ways of running the country, and most expected that Churchill would shortly accept that his own chapter of leadership should be closed, and that Eden would take over.

But Churchill was not prepared to leave the world stage, and needed a power base from which to operate effectively on it: ten more years were to pass before Eden received his inheritance. Again, it was the orator who claimed his place on it, with two great speeches in 1946 which together set the agenda for the next generation of global politics. Both were ahead of their time. In the first, at Fulton, Missouri, he predicted the Cold War against Russia. He described the 'iron curtain' which had descended across Europe, 'from Stettin in the Baltic to Trieste in the Adriatic'. 'If the population of the English-speaking Commonwealth be added to that of the United States … there will be no quivering, precarious balance of power to offer its temptation to ambition or adventure. On the contrary, there will be an overwhelming assurance of security.' It was a suggestion which some Americans described as 'poisonous', and the *Wall Street Journal* stated: 'The United States wants no alliance, or anything resembling an alliance, with any other nation.' The second, at Zurich, to Europeans about Europe, showed a vision astonishing in the wartime leader against 'the Hun'. 'The first step in the recreation of the European family must be a partnership between France and Germany.' This was badly received in France at first. But it marked the start of his campaign for European unity, which led to the Council of Europe Assembly in Strasbourg in 1949. There he proclaimed his hopes for a new Europe to an open-air crowd of 20,000.

To his role as Leader of the Opposition at home, meanwhile, he gave only fitful attention, although, as he regained some of his energy, he led the attack by many able and forward-looking Conservative members on the austerity and bureaucracy of the Labour government, and enjoyed the slogan, 'Set the people free.' But when he regained power in 1952 his policies proved out of tune with his words. He accepted virtually all Labour's nationalisations and appointed a notable conciliator, Walter Monkton, to give the trade unions what they wanted. Nor did he try to reverse Labour's indifference to the Coal and Steel Community with which the French and the Germans were starting to put flesh onto his European dreams; and he was positively opposed to a European Defence force. For him there were three circles in the free world, the USA, the British Commonwealth, and Europe. Britain needed to be in all three of them. There was an inhibiting ambiguity here which was shared by succeeding Prime Ministers for the rest of the century. His style of governing was all too reminiscent of his late wartime decline, though he did attempt a short-lived innovation with 'joined-up government' by appointing Overlords. He gathered old friends around him, including Field Marshal Lord Alexander, who was out of his depth as Minister of Defence. He preferred playing bezique to doing his paperwork. Too deaf to follow Cabinet debates for long, he took decisions without consulting his colleagues. In June 1953 he was partly paralysed by a major stroke. His success in regaining his speech and his movement in time to address the Conservative Party conference four months later was only less astonishing than its concealment from the public – inconceivable today.

Nothing less than the fate of the universe kept him clinging to office for a further twenty-one months. His view of the future for civilisation had gradually darkened as he grasped the implications of nuclear weapons. At first he thought that 'safety will be the sturdy child of terror', but with Russia developing the hydrogen bomb, and with the risk of others getting it, he came to believe that the world was in danger of destruction. He devoted his closing years as Prime Minister almost exclusively to getting a summit meeting of the great powers to save it. In this he was too far ahead of the other leaders for practical progress. While Churchill feared Armageddon, Eisenhower, now President, looked on the bomb as just the latest improvement in military weapons. The Russians, playing nuclear catch-up, were suspicious. When they finally aborted his plan, he resigned.

Much of his second term of office must therefore be regarded as an unsuccessful, sad and, for Eden especially, a frustrating aftermath. But his funeral, ten years after he finally left Downing Street, was the proper epilogue to his career, a huge public celebration of a famous historical life.

R.S. Churchill and M. Gilbert, *Winston S. Churchill* (8 volumes, 1966-88).
R. Jenkins, *Churchill* (2000).
V. Bonham-Carter, *Winston Churchill: An Intimate Portrait* (1965).
D. Reynolds, *In Command of History: Churchill Fighting and Writing the Second World War* (2004).

Clement Attlee

CLEMENT ATTLEE, 1ST EARL ATTLEE (1883-1967), was Prime Minister from 1945 until 1951, leader of a famous Labour government. He summed up his career himself in a limerick written for his brother Tom:

> Few thought he was even a starter
> There were many who thought themselves smarter
> But he ended PM
> CH and OM
> An Earl and a Knight of the Garter.

Seventh child of a successful City solicitor whose hero was Gladstone, he was brought up in a middle-class Victorian tradition of public service, and went to school at Haileybury, and to University College, Oxford. He was a late developer, small and shy, and came to politics through working in the Boys' Club in Stepney which had been founded by Haileybury. There he joined the Independent Labour Party, and started a fourteen year residence in the East End of London, absorbing the problems of working-class families, sweated labour, slum landlords and the hated Poor Law. He helped to run a campaign for Poor Law reform, and was briefly Secretary at Toynbee Hall, where he was regarded as 'a bit of a bolshie'. But when the war started, and brother Tom became a conscientious objector, Clem pulled a string to join the South Lancashire Regiment. He served at Gallipoli, and was in command of the rearguard at the evacuation from Suvla Beach. He went on to Mesopotamia, where he was wounded by 'friendly fire', and ended on the Western Front. When he stood for Parliament, it was as Major Attlee. In 1919 he was adopted as candidate for Limehouse despite his Oxford accent, and co-opted as Mayor of Stepney. Efficient, energetic and without swank, his unflamboyant style enabled him to work with people from a wide range of backgrounds. He won the seat in 1922, defeating the Liberal incumbent.

His rise to the leadership of the Labour Party owed much to the safety of his majority. He had no base outside Parliament. Ramsay

MacDonald had no special regard for him, giving him a junior post in his first government (1924), and nothing at all at the start of his second one (1929), though he eventually made him Postmaster General. Attlee, for his part, came to see MacDonald as an ineffectual windbag. As a loyal Labour man, he refused to support the National Government which MacDonald formed in 1931. At the election which followed only 46 Labour MPs were returned, but, Limehouse being a strongly Labour seat, Attlee, by 551 votes, was one of them. With only one former Cabinet Minister, George Lansbury, among them, Attlee was chosen as his Deputy Leader. At that stage he was seen as a stop-gap, and even when Lansbury, a committed pacifist, resigned over the party's vote to support sanctions against Italy after the invasion of Abyssinia, and Attlee became leader, no one expected him to be there after the next general election. But, when Labour's heavyweights got back into Parliament in 1935, Attlee defeated Greenwood and Morrison in the ballot, thanks to the support of MPs, mostly trade unionists, who had learnt to respect him in the previous Parliament. Dalton, one of the heavies who had backed Morrison, was disgusted: 'and a little mouse shall lead them.' A little mouse he remained to many of them, even when he became Churchill's Deputy Prime Minister in the wartime Coalition Government. In 1942, in a national poll on who should succeed Churchill if he died, 34% supported Cripps, erstwhile leader of the Socialist League; only 2% chose Attlee. Bevan aimed much of his powerful Welsh anti-government rhetoric at him personally during the war, especially at his failure to push for more socialist measures at home, including the immediate implementation of the Beveridge Report. There was a strong move to replace him when the 1945 election loomed. Even after Labour's remarkable win, Morrison wanted a fresh election for leadership of the party before a government was formed. His physical insignificance was a handicap, his voice thin and dry. He had no expertise in economics or planning, and no industrial experience. After Churchill, he cut a poor figure as a public leader.

He survived partly because of the flaws of others. Herbert Morrison had his power base in the LCC rather than Parliament, Ernest Bevin was a union leader and only latterly an MP, Dalton too spiky an intellectual who was widely distrusted, Cripps tainted by his Communist sympathies. Bevin disliked Morrison, and brought union votes to Attlee in the wider party. But he himself won trust within the Parliamentary Labour Party, which was his own power base. His beliefs, springing from his life in Stepney, were simple and widely shared. 'The Labour Party is the only practical instrument ... for the attainment of a new order of society,' and to that new society he was unswervingly committed: full employment, wider affluence, decent housing, full and equal education, medical care for all. This could only be achieved by state control of the economy. Nationalisation was the means to the end, which was social justice. This approach commanded broader support than more theoretical socialism, and Attlee's central contribution to the widely disparate Labour Party was to hold it together. He was also recognised by those who worked with him as a capable man of business who got things done.

Experience in Churchill's wartime government was important to his success as Prime Minister. From its start in 1940 he was responsible for the management of home affairs, and he was the only man who sat on all the key Cabinet committees throughout. He filled Churchill's place during his increasingly frequent absences abroad, and from 1942 was formally Deputy Prime Minister. His knowledge of world affairs, started when he was on the Simon Commission for India in 1927, was broadened, especially after he became Secretary for the Dominions, and he and Eden saw a lot of each other as they shared the problems of working with Churchill. He was pivotal in the relationship between the Labour Party and the government, leading it into the coalition in 1940, after refusing to serve under Chamberlain, and keeping it mostly loyal throughout the bad years of the war. He managed to implement significant social reforms against the grain of the Prime Minister. He patched up differences between Tory and Labour ministers, Bracken and Dalton (he regarded Beaverbrook as the only wicked man among Churchill's cronies), and between Labour leaders, Bevin as Minister of Labour and Citrine, Secretary of the TUC, over the conscription of skilled workers. Bevin's admiration for him, dating from wartime experience, became crucial.

Government was his natural milieu, and his contribution to the achievements of what, with the Liberal government of 1906, was the most creative ministry of the twentieth century, has come to be far more widely recognised than it was at the time. He had led his party intact into the wartime Coalition Government, kept it intact all through the war, and led it out again, still united, to an election victory which astonished everyone by its scale. Labour had an overall majority of nearly 150 in 1945, a well digested programme and able leaders with long experience in government. But they had to carry out their reforms against a background of huge economic strain. Britain had lost a quarter of its entire capital during the war. Truman cancelled the wartime programme of Lend Lease a month after Labour came to power. Five million Britons were still in the armed forces. The subsequent bottlenecks in manpower and also in raw materials presented critical problems: bread, always available across the counter throughout the war, was rationed for the first time in 1946, and that winter the shortage of coal was such that domestic use of electricity was banned for five hours each day, and 1,800,000 workers were laid off. Meanwhile, Britain was still a worldwide military power, and ruling an Empire.

Despite such apparently overwhelming difficulties, and leading a nation exhausted by six years of war, Attlee could truthfully claim that 'the legislative programme on which the 1945 Labour government embarked was more extensive than that launched by any peacetime government.' The Bank of England, coal, civil aviation and overseas cable and wireless were all nationalised in 1946. Electricity and all inland transport followed in 1947, gas in 1948 and iron and steel in 1949. Four measures, National Insurance, National Assistance, Industrial Injuries and National Health Acts, provided security and an acceptable standard of living for every British citizen, the culmination of years of planning and the bedrock of British Social Democracy for the future, accepted by all parties. The Butler Education Act was left in place, but the school-leaving age was raised to fifteen. Abroad, Indian independence was achieved through the India Act in 1947. As much as the size of the Labour majority and the ability of many of his ministers, Attlee's management skills as Prime Minister made all this possible. He organised Cabinet Committees to make sure that the minister in charge of the legislation was fully briefed. He set the priorities, got all proposals fully discussed in Cabinet, took clear decisions and insisted that thereafter the Cabinet should present a united front. Behind his more flamboyant colleagues, he ensured that things got done. He preferred to leave the minister to run his own show: 'If you have a good dog, don't bark yourself.' But he took charge himself when things got difficult. So when Shinwell, Fuel and Power Minister, failed to take precautions against the coal shortage in time, Attlee created and chaired a Fuel Committee to speed up production and keep the public properly informed. After a fierce Cabinet discussion over whether health control should be nationally or locally based, Attlee's decision to back Bevan's National Health Service against the opposition of Herbert Morrison tipped the balance

These decisively creative years of the Labour government, 1945-7, were very unsettled ones globally, as world patterns shifted after the end of the war. Attlee left the conduct of foreign affairs largely to Bevin, his closest political ally, with whom he shared a belief in the importance of the Commonwealth and a suspicion of a federal Europe. His personal strategic policy, that Britain should withdraw altogether from the Middle East, was blocked by the Chiefs of Staff, who threatened joint resignation. But in two issues he took command. He it was who determined that Britain should have her own atomic bomb. In 1946 the McMahon Act prohibited the sharing by the USA of any atomic secret, even with Britain. Attlee, whose ideals for future peace had been centred on a strong United Nations, now realised that power lay with nations with nuclear capabilities, and launched and funded in secret a programme to enable Britain to become one of them. He it was, too, who took charge of the dramatic final phase of the long march to Indian independence. On the Simon Commission in 1928 he had learnt on the spot about the communal tensions between Hindus and Muslims and the attitudes of the Princes. As Prime Minister, he chaired the India and Burma Committee, minimising the potentially damaging interventions of Labour MPs who wanted to hand over only to a socialist regime there. Realising the need for speed to avoid British troops being drawn into mass rioting which they could not control, he pushed through fresh elections in 1945 and chose Mountbatten to succeed Wavell as Viceroy. He grasped the need for partition, accepted Mountbatten's recommendation to bring forward its implementation by a year, and ensured that the whole process was constitutionally achieved under the terms of the India Act of 1935.

After 1947 Attlee's shortcomings were increasingly exposed. During the run on the pound which led to its formal devaluation he dithered: he was no economist. Leading socialists felt that he failed to seize the opportunities that the Labour majority presented. Worker participation in industry remained minimal and there was no overall planning ministry. Attlee even backed capital punishment. His judgment, so shrewd in selecting Bevan to launch the Health

Service, failed him when he picked Morrison, ambitious but all at sea off his own ground in the LCC and the Home Office, to succeed the sick Bevin as Foreign Secretary. 'Great mistake,' he admitted afterwards. 'He'd spent his life organising – foreign policy is about negotiating.' The Labour majority was reduced to five at the election of 1950. The Korean War put fresh pressure on government finances, and the strain between left and right in the party finally became a split: while Attlee was in hospital Bevan and Harold Wilson resigned over the introduction of prescription charges in the NHS. The nationalisation by the Iranian leader Musaddiq of the Anglo-Iranian oilfields was a humiliation. With Bevin dead and Cripps dying, Labour morale became low and a further election became necessary in 1951. The Conservatives won it narrowly, with a majority of 17. In opposition Attlee did not shine, but he remained leader for four more years to ensure that he was not succeeded by Morrison, but by the younger Gaitskell.

Attlee's own standing at the end of Labour's period of power was higher than that of his party. Those who worked closely with him came to admire his remarkable memory: he astonished them when he addressed a conference in fluent Italian, a language which he had picked up in his youth. He was seen as ruthless, firing more ministerial colleagues than almost any other Prime Minister. His terse comments had become famous: 'No, not you, him,' to Gaitskell, who had offered to end his dispute with Bevan by resigning. The wider public enjoyed his homely style, in contrast to Churchill's grandeur. He sucked at his pipe, did the crossword, was driven to his election meetings by his wife Vi in their small car. The purpose of his public life was close to the heart of the national mood before, during and after the war, and was expressed in his riposte to Churchill's accusation that Labour was levelling down, 'It depends on where you started from. If he had been an agricultural worker or a housewife living on the Means Test he might have seen it differently. For the majority it was a great levelling up.' This indeed was the achievement of the man whom many consider the most capable Prime Minister of this century.

K. Harris, *Attlee* (1982).
F. Beckett, *Clem Attlee* (1997).

Sir Anthony Eden

ROBERT ANTHONY EDEN, 1ST EARL OF AVON (1897-1977), an outstandingly successful Foreign Secretary, was an unhappy Prime Minister (1955-7). He had a golden start. Two of his father's forebears were Cabinet Ministers; his mother, a Grey, was great-granddaughter of a Prime Minister, and cousin to a Foreign Secretary. Brought up in a large Durham country house, Windlestone, he went straight from Eton into the 60th Rifles, survived 29 months on the Western Front, and finished with an MC, as a very young Brigade Major. At Christ Church, Oxford, he gained a first, specialising in Arabic and Persian. Elected MP for Warwick and Leamington in 1923, he held the seat for the whole of his time in the House of Commons. He had a powerful patron, Baldwin. Strikingly handsome and courteous, he was widely admired and marked for future greatness. But all was not quite as it seemed. Sir William Eden had a famously explosive temper, which his son inherited. It was about all he did inherit, for his mother was a spendthrift who got through the family silver (Anthony saw his christening spoon in a pawnbroker's window), and his brother had to sell Windlestone. Two other brothers had been killed in the First World War, and his closest son was lost over Burma in the last weeks of the Second. His early marriage became loveless and ended in divorce. Highly strung, unclubbable and shy, Eden was fundamentally a lonely man until in 1952 he married again, Clarissa Churchill, Winston's niece.

His life was centred on his work, and this was focused almost exclusively on foreign affairs until he became Prime Minister. Baldwin made him Foreign Secretary in 1935. There followed what Churchill dubbed 'the gathering storm': Mussolini invaded Abyssinia, Hitler reoccupied the Rhine and moved into Austria, the Spanish Civil War broke out. Yet from all this he emerged with an enhanced reputation, resigning in protest against Prime Minister Chamberlain's plan to meet Mussolini while he still had troops fighting for Franco in Spain. This won him the applause of the

British public as a fresh, brave man in the middle of a grey and timid world; and the admiration of Churchill, who became his next patron when he returned to office at the start of the war and persuaded Chamberlain to make him Dominions Secretary. When Churchill formed his own government, he made Eden Secretary for War, and then once again Foreign Secretary. In 1942 he told the King that he regarded Eden as his natural successor if he should die. Thenceforward Eden was seen as the Conservative Prime Minister in waiting.

It was a long wait. During it, Eden achieved much in the Foreign Office, where perseverance, thorough mastery of detail and patient good manners (he never lost his temper while negotiating) brought him many diplomatic successes. In wartime he inevitably played second fiddle to Churchill, but used his influence on behalf of de Gaulle, and, as a former supporter of the League of Nations, took the British lead in setting up the United Nations Organisation. His hopes for a strong post-war Europe, centred on France and a reunited and restored Germany, were dashed by Stalin. But it was on his initiative as much as Churchill's that Greece was kept on the right side of what was to become the Iron Curtain. His main successes, however, were during Churchill's last government. 1954 was a great year for him. He negotiated the withdrawal of British forces from the Suez Canal, with a US guarantee of freedom of passage through it and the right for British forces to return in an emergency. He brought West Germany into NATO, with an agreement that she should be allowed limited rearmament, getting France on side by promising the presence of British forces on the Continent virtually in perpetuity. He ended the struggle for the control of Iranian oil by restoring the Shah and setting up an international oil company in which Britain had a nearly 50% share. But the success of which he was most proud was the settlement of French Indo-China. The French were being driven out by the Communist-inspired Viet Minh. The Americans threatened to come to their rescue with air and ground forces, and did not exclude the use of nuclear weapons. China, fresh from intervention in Korea, waited in the wings. Eden got all those concerned together at Geneva, and emerged with separate armistices for Laos and Cambodia, and an agreement to divide Vietnam into a Communist north and a non-Communist south. All in all, his was a record to match that of any other British Foreign Secretary.

There were high hopes for Eden when he at last succeeded Churchill as Prime Minister in April 1955. Though he had no experience of domestic politics, he had spoken warmly of a property-owning democracy and of industrial partnership. He called a general election, led from the front, with posters of himself and his young second wife, Churchill's niece, bearing the caption 'Working for Peace', and won it with a majority of nearly 60. But his shortcomings in this new role soon became apparent. From the start he felt the pressure, and showed it. In 1953 he had undergone three major operations: the first had gone so badly wrong that two more were needed to patch him up. He was left with recurring high fevers and dependent on drugs. His naturally febrile temperament suffered: 'He used to get terribly het up,' recalled a senior Foreign Office official. His ministers found him difficult. Reacting against Churchill's long, meandering Cabinet meetings, he did most of his business with them individually, much of it on the telephone at all hours, and his temper could be explosive. They found him unwilling to delegate and fussy over details, not least in domestic and economic problems of which he had little grasp. He knew few Conservative MPs, and did not like the right-wingers: 'I'm afraid I have never been a good party man,' he confessed. He failed to keep the press informed, which mattered the more because he was sensitive to criticism. He came across as indecisive: the *Daily Telegraph* enjoyed the contrast between his habit of emphasising a point by smacking one fist into the palm of his other hand and the lack of any smack of firm government.

There was little change in policy and only a modest reshuffle of the Cabinet. Butler had to produce two budgets in one year, first reducing taxes and then, after a shift in the balance of trade, increasing them again. When trade unions rejected proposals for wage restraint, Eden did not press them. Like Churchill he showed no enthusiasm for the birth of the European Community, and sent only a civil servant with a watching brief to the discussions leading to the Treaty of Messina. Only in Cyprus was the smack of firm government felt. Determined to keep the island a British colony, and equally to maintain his recently formed alliance with Turkey, he deported the Greek archbishop Makarios to the Seychelles. He also took a spectacular initiative in inviting the two Russian leaders Bulganin and Khrushchev to visit Britain. There was embarrassment when the body of a British frogman was discovered near the hull of a Russian warship in Portsmouth harbour.

But Eden was more seriously embarrassed when the young King Hussein of Jordan suddenly dismissed the British commander of his Arab Legion, Glubb Pasha. Four months later, in July 1956, Gamal Abdul Nasser, Arab leader of Egypt, nationalised the Suez Canal. Eden was immediately clear that he must take up this challenge. He was already seen as weak by his own back-benchers and much of the press for withdrawing from Suez. Now, with the dismissal of Glubb so recent, he feared the Arab nationalist threat to the rulers of British Middle Eastern allies in the Baghdad Pact, especially in Iraq, Iran and Jordan. He believed, correctly, that Russia was planning to undermine British influence in the area and deny Western powers their oil supplies. His mind went back to the appeasement of the 'thirties: he saw Nasser as another Mussolini, who must be overthrown before he set the whole region ablaze. He found a ready ally in the French, struggling with their own Arab rebels in Algeria. He also expected to have a friend in the US, but the American attitude was to be crucially ambivalent. For Secretary Dulles fear of Communism was often overriding, but President Eisenhower was closer to the anti-imperial tradition of American foreign policy. Fatally, despite forthright warnings, Eden never fully understood this.

Anglo-French preparations to re-enter the Canal zone by force went ahead in parallel with efforts to win international support. The Russians vetoed a Security Council resolution. Dulles produced two schemes, a conference of maritime nations and a Suez Canal Users Association, but made it clear that the US would not shoot their way through the Canal. So Nasser stayed put. The French hatched a plan for Israeli armies to attack Egypt through Gaza, giving France and Britain an excuse to move in to protect the Canal and order both sides to withdraw from it. With this secret collusion Eden went along on condition that Israel did not attack Jordan. But the timing of the operation went awry: the Israeli attack was launched a week before the allied forces reached Port Said. As they steamed slowly from Malta, they found the US 6th Fleet threateningly alongside them. Eisenhower blocked British access to IMF credits, and encouraged the UN to impose oil sanctions on the UK and France. There was a run on the pound and Britain lost 15% of her gold and dollar reserves. The dependence of Britain on American support was now revealed, and Eden ordered a ceasefire the day after the main force had landed.

Throughout the Suez crisis, Eden kept control of policy in his own hands, using an 'Egyptian Committee' instead of the Cabinet, and concealing from all except those closest to him the collusion with the French and the Israelis, although he did obtain broad Cabinet agreement for military action. He did not brief his generals about his aims and there were no plans for what would happen after the troops had occupied the Canal zone. Eden had aimed to topple Nasser and create an international alliance to protect the Canal and strengthen anti-Communist influence in the Middle East. He ended with Nasser an Arab hero, the Baghdad Pact destabilised, America and half the Commonwealth alienated and British prestige destroyed. Exhausted and with fever recurring, he accepted his doctors' advice and went off to Jamaica. By the time he came back, our troops had been withdrawn and his authority was diminished. His doctors warned him that his fevers would continue, and a month after his return he resigned, never to return to the House of Commons. Since taking the political stage as the *beau ideal* of the 1930s, he had worked for twenty years under intense pressure. Suez was his nemesis: but many felt, with hindsight, that his tragedy was ever to have become Prime Minister.

R. Rhodes James, *Anthony Eden* (1986).
D. Dutton, *Anthony Eden: A Life and Reputation* (1997).

Harold Macmillan

HAROLD MACMILLAN, 1ST EARL OF STOCKTON (1894-1986), was Prime Minister from 1957 until 1963. He was a late political developer. Though he liked to recall that he was a Scottish crofter's grandson, he had a successful family publishing business and a powerful American mother behind him. He went to Eton and Balliol, fought a 'good war' in the Grenadier Guards, where he was twice wounded in the trenches, married a daughter of the Duke of Devonshire and became Member for Stockton in 1924. But the Cavendishes looked down on this gauche, bookish man, and his fellow MPs regarded him as a bore. Worse, he became a cuckold when his wife, Lady Dorothy, to whom he remained devoted, and who was eventually to prove an impeccable and effective political partner, began a relationship with another politician, Bob Boothby, which, though a well-kept secret from the public, wounded him deeply. When Eden, three years younger, became Foreign Secretary, Macmillan was still a back-bencher. He had had to make his own way; only Churchill, increasingly an outsider himself, gave him fitful patronage. Concerned to find an alternative solution to socialism for the unemployment which he saw at close quarters in Stockton, he wrote *The Middle Way*, which urged greater government intervention, using some of Keynes's ideas. The war altered the balance in the Conservative Party, but it was not until 1942 that Macmillan was given real responsibility, when Churchill invited him (as his second choice) to become Minister Resident in North Africa, where the Allied armies had landed. As they advanced, so did his career, until he was dubbed Viceroy of the Mediterranean, negotiating the Italian armistice and being in the front line of policymaking over the liberation of Greece and Yugoslavia. He made important friends, including Eisenhower, the commander of the Allied forces, and his horizons were dramatically broadened.

His second breakthrough was as Minister of Housing from 1951. Lord Woolton had promised that a Conservative government would build 300,000 houses a year. Labour said it could not be done. In difficult economic conditions, with import restrictions and rising interest rates, Macmillan did it. He used the political importance of meeting the target to get subsidies from the Exchequer for local authorities and increase the allocation of steel and timber to private builders. Some argued that his pressure distorted the government's economic policy, but he had proved himself a powerful administrator and a skilful political operator. Churchill made him Minister of Defence in 1954 and Eden promoted him to Foreign Minister, and then to Chancellor of the Exchequer. He was thus a central player in the Suez drama. He emerged from it as Prime Minister.

Macmillan later admitted that Suez was not his finest hour. Harold Wilson described his part succinctly: 'first in and first out.' He shared with Eden a belief in British greatness, a fear of Russian Communist influence and a dread of appeasement, so he urged him to deal with Nasser before British influence in the Middle East was fatally compromised. However, when Eisenhower withheld American support and there was a run on the pound, it was Macmillan who told the Cabinet that they could not go on. Afterwards some felt that he had deliberately undermined Eden. How true was this? He certainly failed to pass on Treasury warnings about the threat to British gold reserves, and did not take the precaution, as the French had done, of drawing the permitted tranche of funds from the IMF in advance. But though his bedside literature at the time included a life of Machiavelli, the general verdict is of cock-up rather than conspiracy. Macmillan was a patriot for whom scheming to damage his country would have been anathema; he was as surprised as Eden at American policy. Moreover, Eden's natural successor was not him but Butler. There is more truth in Enoch Powell's memory of the way in which Macmillan 'succeeded in false-footing Rab' in the days which followed Eden's resignation. 'Horrible,' he called it. Macmillan followed Butler's lacklustre speech backing Suez by confidently launching an upbeat defence of what the government had been trying to do. Conservative leaders were still chosen by informal consultation within the party, and when Lord Salisbury asked his senior colleagues, 'Well, which is it, Wab or Hawold?', three at most supported Butler. Macmillan was summoned to the Palace next day, 10 January 1957. In the aftermath of Suez, he thought he might be out of office after six weeks. He lasted for more than six years.

There was an immediate change at the heart of government. Eden had betrayed high tension with his explosive temper, and interfered constantly in all departments. Macmillan cultivated a studied calm behind his drooping eyelids. He always found time to read spacious novels, George Eliot, Stendhal, Tolstoy and his favourite, Trollope. He was at ease in his job, delegating confidently. The bore had become an amusing, later even a spellbinding, conversationalist. He spent much time in the Smoking Room at Westminster talking to MPs – 'dear boy', with the arm round the shoulder – and in clubs: on his first night in office he took the Chief Whip, Ted Heath, to supper and champagne at the Turf. He managed his Cabinets with natural authority, consulting all round the table but never taking a vote, and 'guffaws of laughter' could often be heard through the door. In opposition a witty speaker, he now became an orator with a broad vision, putting events into historical perspective. Like Churchill, he understood the importance of image in democratic leadership: 'the old actor manager' Powell was to call him. His appearance was transformed, pince-nez spectacles removed, moustache trimmed, teeth straightened, baggy trousers replaced by Savile Row suits. He learnt how to use television, doing informal interviews at airports and inviting the cameras into Downing Street when Eisenhower was there. He relished his part on the world stage, dressing up in a large white Russian hat on his visit to Moscow, and entertaining Kennedy and de Gaulle at Birch Grove, his Sussex home.

Between 1957 and 1959, Macmillan rescued the Conservative Party and restored the morale of the country. His policy was based on regaining power and prestige abroad through a rapprochement with the United States, and on developing prosperity at home by expanding the economy. He re-established a 'special relationship' with Eisenhower, later to become even closer with Kennedy. At Bermuda, in March 1957, there was agreement to work together in the Middle East, and for America to supply Britain with Thor missiles. Nuclear co-operation was resumed, the act banning the sharing of research information was repealed, and Britain produced her own hydrogen bomb. His influence in Washington should not be exaggerated: Kennedy consulted him after, not before, he decided to risk nuclear war by blockading Cuba. But their friendship was warm, their telephone conversations regular and their visits frequent. At home, post-war austerity was finally thrown off, and Macmillan, while famously telling an audience, 'You've never had it so good,' did so in the context of a warning, and started to become concerned about inflation. Nevertheless, setting out on a Commonwealth tour, he dismissed the resignation of his three Treasury ministers who attacked him for overheating the economy as 'a little local difficulty', and at the 1959 general election, less than three years after Suez, the Conservatives were returned, their majority over Labour increased from 67 to 107. This was Macmillan's personal triumph. The cartoonist Vicky had mockingly dubbed him 'Supermac': it became a term of affectionate admiration with the public.

Was it a triumph of style rather than substance? His record is more impressive overseas than at home, where the British economy, burdened by debt from two wars and worldwide defence commitments, was not strong enough to protect sterling as a reserve currency. There were structural flaws in British industry and powerful trade unions made reform difficult. Macmillan could understand the problems, but was instinctively pragmatic. He made little impact on the economy. He wanted above all to avoid the wretched unemployment he had known between the wars, and tried to put the ideas of *The Middle Way* into practice, government working actively through employers and the unions. He created the National Economic Development Council (Neddy) and launched a national incomes policy. His policies were taken further by subsequent governments, Labour and Conservative. They were not successful. Nothing fundamental changed, and the country drifted into a period of mounting inflation and unemployment. It was left to Thatcher to wrench the steering wheel.

With economic decline came a loss of status in the world. In 1957 the Russians put a satellite into orbit, and American nuclear hegemony was at an end. In 1958 the European 'Six' signed the Treaty of Rome and de Gaulle came to power in France. Macmillan was determined that Britain should punch above her weight. His threefold policy was to withdraw from Empire, to retain an independent deterrent, and to get into the European Common Market. The withdrawal from British African colonies proceeded apace, and Iain Macleod, the Colonial Secretary, handled it so that the Commonwealth was strengthened and Communist infiltration kept to a minimum, despite the active probing of Krushchev. Macmillan was less successful in Rhodesia, where he failed to keep the new Federation together, and earned the reputation of a slippery customer or worse among white settlers. Although he spoke to the South African Parliament in 1961 of 'the wind of change blowing through this continent', he failed, too, to persuade South Africa to moderate apartheid or to keep it in the Commonwealth. But he did manage to fight off Conservative right-wing rebels, dangerous since the Suez Group was formed, and to shed nearly all the remaining African colonies without either leaving chaos, as the Belgians did in the Congo, or having to fight a debilitating war, as the French did in Indo-China and Algeria.

His world view was dominated by the threat of Russian Communism, and of nuclear war. Hiroshima was only eleven years in the past when Macmillan became Prime Minister, and the Russians were just becoming a nuclear power. In 1962 the Cuban confrontation brought Armageddon nearer than at any time before or since. Macmillan's Grand Design, Churchillian in concept, was to bring the British Commonwealth, the United States and Europe together to contain the Russian menace. His hope, too, was to achieve world peace through summit meetings, treaties banning the testing of nuclear weapons, and ultimately nuclear disarmament. One low moment was when the Paris summit he had painfully set up between Eisenhower and Krushchev in 1960 proved a fiasco after an American spy plane was shot down over Siberia. Another was when, in 1962, de Gaulle rejected his application to join the European Economic Community. These were both blows to his Grand Design. After Suez he had put the American alliance first; its fruits now included Polaris, the submarine-launching pad which kept Britain a nuclear power. But he never saw this as being incompatible with membership of a European Community. De Gaulle did – he was having to become a nuclear power on his own – and the French Grand Design was different. De Gaulle's '*Non!*' resounded through Downing Street and Whitehall, and his tall presence stood between Britain and Europe for more than ten years.

As the significance of rejection sank in, the image of Supermac became tarnished. He had already lost some of his reputation for never flapping when, in May 1962, he suddenly dismissed seven of his ministers in 'the night of the long knives'. In the burgeoning decade of 'sixties satire, he became a natural target, the old Edwardian clubman. Spy scandals chased each other across the headlines: Vassall, Fell, Philby and Blunt. Then came Profumo, the promising young Secretary of State for Air, who lied to the House of Commons about his association with an up-market prostitute, Christine Keeler, who had also slept with a Russian defence attaché. Macmillan had refused to believe the rumours about him: 'I do not live among young people much myself.' The old actor was becoming trapped in his self-portrait. His last success as Prime Minister was at the heart of his policy, a nuclear test ban treaty for all except underground tests. Qualified as that sounds now, it was difficult to broker, and proved the start of a process towards full test banning and arms reduction. The end of his ministry came amidst drama. With the Conservative Party assembled in Conference at Blackpool in October 1963, waiting for his address, he had to have an emergency prostate operation, and, fearing cancer, resigned. From his sickbed he pulled the strings which led to Alec Douglas-Home being chosen as his successor. He then staged a full recovery, and was to live for more than twenty years, enjoying, especially as Chancellor of Oxford University, a prolonged Indian Summer of wisdom and wit.

A. Horne, *Macmillan* (2 vols, 1988 and 1989).
J. Turner, *Macmillan* (1994).

Sir Alec Douglas-Home

LORD HOME OF THE HIRSEL (1903-95), formerly Viscount Dunglass, the 14th Earl of Home, and from 1963 until 1964 Sir Alec Douglas-Home, was the most unexpected Prime Minister of the twentieth century and, except for Bonar Law, the most transient, holding office for just one year from October 1963. Until the year of his appointment no one thought of him as a possible successor to Harold Macmillan, because he was a peer. The last peer to be Prime Minister had been Lord Salisbury (in 1903), and long before 1963 it had become a constitutional convention that the government must be led from the House of Commons. So Lord Home (a keen follower of racing form himself) was out of the running, not even an outsider. Moreover, he came from an unlikely stable: an aristocrat from the Scottish borders who was brought up to inherit a landed estate. At Eton and Oxford cricket played a large part in his life. He enjoyed fishing and shooting and became a knowledgeable naturalist: he recalled spending the first hours of the war in 1939 with his brother looking for Chalk Blue butterflies on the South Downs.

But he was also a political animal, who was later described by Macmillan as 'steel painted as wood'. He became MP for Lanark, against his father's wish, in 1931. His early career, full of promise after he had become Neville Chamberlain's Parliamentary Private Secretary, led him down a cul-de-sac. Much photographed at Chamberlain's shoulder during the Munich crisis, he seemed damned by his association with appeasement. He was then struck down by tuberculosis of the spine, cured only after an operation which kept him flat on his back for more than two years. It came as a surprise when James Stuart, Secretary for Scotland and a friend of Churchill's, asked for him as his Minister of State in 1951. 'Home, sweet Home, it shall be,' growled Churchill. For the next four years his work kept him mainly north of the border, and he was not widely known at Westminster. His move centre stage was made in 1955, when Eden, looking for a younger man with the right style for Dominion leaders, invited him to become Commonwealth Secretary in his new government. The work he did there brought him a new and crucial patron, Harold Macmillan, who invited him to become Foreign Secretary in 1960.

Home's strengths were admired by those who worked with him. He was a good administrator, who took decisions and could delegate. As a negotiator he knew where he was trying to get to, was patient and listened. He had a warm smile and an open personality. Labour leader Tony Benn, no admirer of Macmillan's, reflected later of his emergence, 'That's why they picked him, they wanted a straight man after a fixer.' He was a true Conservative. As Commonwealth Secretary he worked to prepare colonies for independence through education, but did not want them to have it until they were ready to respect minorities. At the centre of his foreign policy was his determination to stand up to Russia. In reply to Soviet attacks on the British Empire, he asked where the new imperialism was if not in the Baltic states, where Russia had colonised 22 million people, and he risked a diplomatic explosion by expelling 105 members of the Soviet embassy as spies. He wondered publicly whether the United Nations Organisation, which was sometimes used as a platform for Communism, had had its day. He was in favour of joining the EEC mainly to strengthen European traditions of freedom and democracy against the threat from the other side of the Iron Curtain, and he believed that it was the first duty of a British Foreign Secretary to keep the NATO alliance intact.

In July 1963 the Peerage Bill, allowing peers to renounce their titles, became law. So, when Macmillan fell suddenly ill on the eve of the Conservative Party Conference in October 1963, he saw in Home a potential Tory Prime Minister. Determined to keep out Rab Butler, his old rival and natural successor, he first favoured Lord Hailsham. But in the highly charged atmosphere of the Conference at Blackpool Hailsham shook the leadership by stirring up mass fervour among his supporters, and appearing with his baby daughter and her bottle. Macmillan turned to Home. Reports from his soundings revealed overwhelming backing for him in the Cabinet, majority support among Tory MPs, and nothing conclusive from the constituencies. The Queen accepted Macmillan's recommendation and Home, soon to be Sir Alec Douglas-Home and an MP, became Prime Minister.

'The machinery of aristocratic cabal, producing a result based on family and hereditary connections,' was Harold Wilson's verdict, widely echoed in a Britain which had entered the age of television satire. With his strengths little known by the electorate, the former 14th Earl did not cut a powerful figure in public. His speaking voice was light, he was no crowd swayer, and on television he had a head like a skull. An earlier unguarded remark about doing his sums with matchsticks was quickly exploited by the mercurial Wilson, himself a former economics don. This was surely not the man to lead the Conservative Party into the 1964 election, from the deep unpopularity into which it had descended after a period of scandal. Wilson was a brilliant opposition leader. Two important ministers, Macleod and Powell, refused to join a Home Cabinet, and Butler, who did, proved an ambiguous supporter. The Liberals were gaining ground, especially in Scotland. Above all there was a feeling that it was time for a change after 'the thirteen years of Conservative misrule'. Yet Sir Alec came astonishingly near to winning the election. The year was dominated by its approach, and there was only one major policy initiative, the abolition of Resale Price Maintenance, which stopped manufacturers fixing prices, a liberal trade measure which helped to change the shopping habits of the nation and was predictably unpopular with small shopkeepers. But Sir Alec ran his government firmly; his methods were described in his autobiography: 'short and precise paper work ... a Cabinet agenda which is cleared of all but the absolute essentials ... and a programme of legislation for Parliament which is not overloaded.' As chairman of a Cabinet he was better than any other Prime Minister except Attlee at getting through its business. His calm common sense restored the confidence of his party and he won the 'deference vote', still a factor in the early 'sixties. His foreign policy was popular: keeping our own nuclear deterrent – the Campaign for Nuclear Disarmament had caught the headlines but not the votes. Sir Alec delayed the election while the mood swung back to the Tories. Had he done so for a week longer it would have been held after the Chinese exploded their first nuclear bomb, and he might even have won it. As it was, Labour's overall majority was four.

It was, nonetheless, the end of a Conservative era. Sir Alec made his contribution towards the start of the next one by sensing this, setting up a more open method of selecting his successor, resigning as leader nine months after the election, and giving an example of loyalty by serving as Foreign Secretary under Heath when the Tories got back in 1970. Though his social background made him seem dated, and he came to be seen as a postscript Premier, his efficiency in government and his obvious sincerity enhanced the reputation of politics, and he embodied the better values of a Conservative.

D.R. Thorpe, *Alec Douglas-Home* (1996).

Harold Wilson

JAMES HAROLD WILSON, BARON WILSON OF RIEVAULX (1916-95) was Prime Minister from 1964 until 1970 and from 1974 until 1976. He won four out of the five general elections he fought, and retired voluntarily, the only serving Prime Minister in the twentieth century to do so without the pressure of ill-health. It was the record of a skilful leader.

He did not fit naturally into any of the main streams of the Labour Party. He was a Lancastrian, who spoke like one to the end, but he was not a trade union man. He gained a first-class degree at Oxford and went on to become a lecturer and a Research Fellow (and to be married in academic dress); but, having once been a keen Boy Scout, he did not become a Marxist intellectual of the Left, nor did he move in the circle of the Public School intellectuals who went on to play a leading role on the Right of the Labour Party. Wilson liked his unfashionable college, Jesus, describing the undergraduates there to his parents as 'a very decent set, no snobbery'. Gaitskell's friends looked down on him as a philistine, whose interests were narrowly political. During the war he worked on the Beveridge Report on which the social security policies of the Attlee government were to be based, and in the Ministry of Fuel and Power on plans for the post-war coal industry. When he was elected in 1945 he brought to Parliament valuable experience but no political friends.

He entered the Cabinet in 1947 as President of the Board of Trade, at thirty-one the youngest member of any Cabinet since 1806, and grew a (short-lived) moustache to add gravitas to his chubby looks. He abolished clothes rationing, developed trade with Russia, and started his lasting interest in the film industry by creating the National Film Corporation to provide funds for British producers. But he soon acquired a reputation for neat-footed ambition. He was seen as a man of the Left when he resigned with Aneurin Bevan over the imposition of charges for National Health prescriptions, but moved back to the centre when he refused to support Bevan in opposing German rearmament. It took good fortune to propel him to the top of the Party. His challenge to Gaitskell for the leadership in 1960 was decisively defeated, and he even lost the election for Deputy Leader in 1963 to George Brown. Then, completely unexpectedly, Gaitskell, who was only fifty-seven, became ill with a mysterious virus and died. The Left united behind Wilson as his successor. The Right had a potential majority in the Parliamentary Party, and it was widely assumed that George Brown, their candidate, would win. But his pro-European views alienated some, and his personal weaknesses alarmed many: 'Are we to be led by a neurotic drunkard?' asked Gaitskell's friend, Crosland. James Callaghan emerged as an alternative, and split the Right vote. Wilson successfully wooed the TGWU, the largest union, and gained provincial backing against the sophisticated Londoners. Callaghan dropped out after the first ballot, and Wilson beat Brown on the second by 144 votes to 103.

The choice proved wise. Wilson was a brilliant debater, and against Macmillan and Douglas-Home he shone as the modern man of his times. 1963 was the year of 'the Lady Chatterley Trial and the Beatles' first LP', with *Private Eye* and *That Was The Week That Was* spreading irreverence towards the establishment. In this climate Wilson's attacks on fuddy-duddy Tories rallied the forces of change behind the Labour Party. His first party political broadcast as leader attracted the largest audience for any television programme to date, and he wowed them with his confidence, his classlessness, the fun in his satire, his energy. Even his low-brow tastes appealed to them. Here was the plain man, bringing politics out from the country houses and the corridors of power. When the Tories chose the Fourteenth Earl of Home to succeed Macmillan, Wilson did not conceal his glee, and in due course he won the 1964 election. The only surprise was that his overall majority was only four.

Wilson, Labour and most of Britain saw this as the start of a new era. With the decadent Tories out of power after thirteen years, this was to be a fresh Britain, 'to be forged in the white heat of the [scientific] revolution'; an educated Britain with opportunities for all; a mobile, classless Britain; a Britain led by a government with a National Plan for growth. Through these early months of his first ministry, Wilson was dynamic. His leadership was presidential. Into Downing Street he brought his own advisers, headed by Marcia Williams, the *chef de cuisine* of his 'kitchen cabinet'. All ministerial speeches had to be cleared through No. 10. He appointed the first formal peace-time inner cabinet, and often allowed the full Cabinet to talk itself out while he doodled. By nature suspicious and acutely political, he liked to balance factions. He set up a Department of Economic Affairs to balance the Treasury and organise expansion, and chose his chief rival, George Brown, to run it. Though Barbara Castle and Richard Crossman from the Left got Cabinet places, and Tony Benn was put in charge of the new Ministry of Technology, most positions went to moderates or former Gaitskellites, and Callaghan became Chancellor. He also brought in outsiders, Frank Cousins from the TGWU and the author C.P. Snow. There were constant reshuffles, which Roy Jenkins described as 'Harold's annual gymkhanas'. Like Blair in the next Labour surge, he led his government from the front; but being, unlike Blair, an economist, Wilson took the crucial economic decisions himself.

The first of these proved fatal for his National Plan. The plan was for a 25% growth for the economy in six years, with improved technology, better management and higher production leading to more exports and a cut in overseas spending. But on the night he took office Wilson was told that the country faced a budget deficit of £800 million and one of the sterling crises which had been a recurring post-war feature for British governments. The simplest economic solution was devaluation, but Wilson set his face against it. Two Labour governments had devalued the pound, and he was determined that his should not be the third. Moreover he believed that if his plans were given time devaluation would be unnecessary. He was wrong. The world's financiers regarded sterling as over-valued. Deflationary budgets and attempted wage control led to a seamen's strike which caused another run on the pound in 1966. A worse one in 1967, after a dock strike and a sudden rise in oil prices following the Israeli-Arab Six Day War, drove him finally to agree to a change in its value from $2.80 to $2.40, but this came too late to save his plan.

By then, nonetheless, Wilson had won a majority of 97 in the 1966 general election. It was the peak of his career. Thenceforward he wrestled, often frenetically though with resilience, with forces beyond his control. In Rhodesia Ian Smith was already set on the path towards a unilateral declaration of independence (UDI), and Wilson found himself powerless to stop him, despite two sets of negotiations on British warships, *Tiger* and *Fearless*. He tried to join the Common Market, to succeed where Macmillan had failed, but the immovable object of de Gaulle was still in place. Realising that trade union attitudes stood in the way of industrial reform, he gave his full backing to Barbara Castle's paper *In Place of Strife*, which proposed legislation to regulate union behaviour. This was brave, but it split the Cabinet, and in the face of opposition led by the powerful James Callaghan he retreated, to Castle's fury. Again, his alternative, a solemn and binding agreement by the unions, was ineffectual, soon labelled 'Mr Solomon Binding'. Pay freezes came and went, and Downing Street negotiations over beer and sandwiches late into the night became a regular feature of his life. Wilson was a gregarious man who enjoyed political manoeuvering, but the pressure began to tell, and it was made worse by a disastrous deterioration in his relations with the press after the 'D' Notice affair, when he attacked a well-known journalist, Chapman Pincher, for breaking the agreement under which defence information had to be cleared before publication. Thereafter he became paranoid about the media, and they swung from adulation to contempt.

The story was not all bad. Wilson had earned credit for refusing to send British forces to Vietnam despite being under pressure from President Johnson; and he had strongly handled what were to prove the opening stages of the troubles in Northern Ireland, by sending troops in to keep order. Devaluation had won him a respite from economic threat, and the resignation of George Brown, by then a sometimes inebriated Foreign Secretary, strengthened his position. His Home Secretary, Roy Jenkins, had carried broadly popular liberal reforms of the laws on capital punishment and abortion. So defeat by Ted Heath's Conservatives in the 1970 election took him by surprise. But there was no threat to his leadership: his fractious party never looked like agreeing on a replacement. The more divided it became – and over Europe its divisions were increasingly bitter – the more indispensable he was. In February 1974 he won another election, when the country refused to back Heath's stand against the miners. He did not gain an overall majority, and had only a very slender one when he went back to the voters in October. But, with the Conservatives having thirty-three seats fewer than Labour, it was enough.

'The Second Coming of Mr Wilson,' was how the *Daily Mirror* described it: a new Mr Wilson, who seemed much more than ten years older than his first incarnation, a homely, reliable figure with his pipe and his Gannex mackintosh. He was to prove a less fit man than he had been ten years earlier, and his paranoia was becoming alarming: he thought that someone had hidden a listening device behind Gladstone's portrait in the Cabinet room. He presented himself to the country in football parlance as a 'sweeper', operating behind a forward line of gifted and often experienced ministers, Callaghan, Jenkins, Crosland, Healey, Castle and Benn, and his programme was modest. Indeed, his priority now was to keep his party in power, and himself too, until the retirement which he was already planning. There was one important innovation, the No. 10 Policy Unit, a group from outside the Civil Service to give him strategic advice, and the first in a long line. But he shelved most problems. In Northern Ireland he accepted the failure of Heath's attempted power-sharing in Northern Ireland (the Sunningdale Agreement), and reverted to direct rule. His 'social contract' with the TUC added up to an agreement that as long as he gave them most of what they wanted they would not cause trouble. He settled with the miners largely on their terms, and rescued Chrysler, a significant player in the car industry, with £160 million of government money. The unions helped him to tackle inflation, which had reached 25% in 1974, by agreeing to a wage compromise, pay bargaining within certain limits, which was not going to last. The creative achievement of this ministry, and Wilson's own personal triumph, was the 1975 referendum by which Britain confirmed that it would stay in the European Common Market. He was not an instinctive European, this north countryman who preferred meat and two veg with HP sauce to French cooking and went to the Scilly Isles for his holidays, but he believed that Britain had to be inside the Common Market for economic reasons. For once he took a clear public stance in pushing through the referendum and recommending a 'Yes' vote. He risked isolation from his own party, whose NEC was strongly against it, and gambled on the fears of the Parliamentary Party that 'If he's out, we're all out.' His aims were to keep his party in one piece, and Britain in Europe, and he succeeded in both. His judgment of the country's mood was sound: there was a 67% 'Yes' vote.

In March 1976 he took everyone by surprise by resigning: his plans had been a well-kept secret. Almost immediately his reputation plunged. The press, after a puzzled and suspicious pause, exploded with glee when he published his Resignation Honours List, dubbed the Lavender List after the paper on which Marcia Williams, now Lady Falkender, had written it. It included several shady capitalists:

one was later jailed for fraud and another committed suicide. Then there were rumours, subsequently proved accurate, that MI5 had had their eye on Wilson, who had visited Russia often, as a minister and while advising a timber trading company. Next came the Crossman diaries, with their detailed descriptions of the in-fighting in his Cabinets and among his advisers. Through all this, retired in the Scilly Islands, he remained the friendly, cheerful man whom his civil servants had always liked, and to whom his quiet wife Mary, who wrote poetry and had hated life in Downing Street, remained loyal right through his sad decline into Alzheimer's Disease. The record has become more balanced since. Two Race Relations Acts, the Fulton Report on equal access to the Civil Service, the launch of the Comprehensive Schools and of the Open University (his own special baby) all promoted the equality of opportunity which he had set out to achieve. But the red sky in the mornings back in 1964 portended stormy days, and Wilson was not able to check the decline in Britain's economy at home or in her power overseas.

B. Pimlott, *Harold Wilson* (1992).
P. Ziegler, *The Political Life of Lord Wilson of Rievaulx* (1993).

Edward Heath

SIR EDWARD HEATH, KG (1916-2005), Prime Minister from 1970 to 1974, was the first Conservative leader to come from a modest home: his father was a carpenter who developed a small building firm. He went to Balliol College, Oxford on a grant from Kent and his parents' savings, won an Organ Scholarship and became President of the Union. He ended the war as an acting lieutenant colonel, passed out top in the Civil Service Examination, won Bexley for the Conservatives in 1950, and by 1955 had become their Chief Whip. From boyhood he was focused, purposeful and self-sufficient, spared the washing-up at home so that he could get on with his studies, with musical interests which kept him alone at the piano or in the organ loft. He was brought into contact with others by his enterprise and efficiency as an organiser: he ran a memorable Union Ball when he was President, and formed and conducted a choir at Balliol.

Throughout his life he worked best with small groups, winning their admiration and often affection. His Cabinet, mostly dubbed Heathmen, were staunchly loyal to him. When he took up sailing he led his crews to many successes, winning the Sydney-Hobart race in 1969. In 1971, while Prime Minister, he captained the victorious British team in the Admiral's Cup, and conducted Elgar's *Cockaigne* overture in the Festival Hall. But he did not easily command in a wider circle. He did not bother with those who did not interest him, who found his long silences intimidating, and he was normally a poor speaker, with artificial perorations tagged on to a dense mass of dry detail. His jokes, accompanied by much heaving of his shoulders, were ironic and not always shared. Later he was able to inspire audiences, especially younger ones, with his vision of a Europe at the centre of world civilisation, but his stiff manner in the House of Commons, on the floor and in the Smoking Room alike, and his inability to find the words to carry the country with him in a crisis, were fatal handicaps to him as Prime Minister. *Private Eye* dubbed him 'The Grocer'.

Politically ambitious from his youth, Heath was by instinct and ability an administrator, who wanted power in order to improve people's quality of life by running the country more efficiently and creating a society in which merit replaced class as the route to the top. He gained stature as Chief Whip, preventing rebellion during the Suez crisis, and in 1965 the Tories chose him, in preference to Reggie Maudling and Enoch Powell, to lead them against Harold Wilson's glitzy Labour government, for his efficiency and modern outlook. But they were not all ready for him. Defeat in the election which followed came too soon for them to blame him, but when he regularly failed to match Wilson's debating pyrotechnics they prepared to abandon him after the 1970 election. But Heath was stubborn, and came across as honest in wanting to replace Wilson's 'cheap and trivial style of government' with steady leadership which would take decisions carefully and stick to them. He formed a close-knit group of policymakers to plan for government, led from the front, did well on the streets and won a working majority (Conservatives 330, Labour 287) against all the odds and the polls. It was a personal triumph, and his party now rallied behind him.

The government through which he set out to transform Britain's economy and modernise its society is largely a story of failure. His one vital success was to take his country into the European Economic Community. Heath's commitment to Europe was whole-hearted and unswerving throughout his life. He was the only Prime Minister to put both feet decisively on the French rather than the American side of the Atlantic divide. In 1970 circumstances were on his side, with de Gaulle at last out of the way. Having been chief negotiator for the previous attempt under Macmillan he brought experience to the table, and understood that the heart of the solution lay in Paris, not Brussels. Compromise eased the difficulties over New Zealand lamb, sterling balances and the size of the British contribution to the European budget. This last, at 8.6% rising to 19% over 5 years, was widely accepted in Britain at the time, and it was only the poor performance of the British economy in the 'seventies that led to Margaret Thatcher's fierce demands for its reduction in the 'eighties. But there were many Tories more wedded to the Empire than to Europe, and it took the support of Labour pro-Europeans to get the enabling legislation through Parliament, and confirm Heath's lasting achievement. Of his three follow-ups towards European co-operation, the Maplin air and deepwater sea port vanished without trace, the Channel Tunnel had to wait for a decade, and only Concorde survived his defeat.

The 'sixties had been a period of economic decline for Britain, but Heath believed that it was possible to recover prosperity, with full employment, by running the traditional mixed economy more efficiently. Most of the moves he made to transform the way the country was governed were transient or unpopular, sometimes both. He wanted to give Cabinet Ministers more time for policymaking; the strategic 'think tank', effective under Lord Rothschild (Heath's imaginative choice) in looking at long-term issues and alerting ministers to looming problems, lasted until Thatcher. But the large super-ministries through which he proposed to co-ordinate government activities proved hard to manage and were split up again. The reorganisation of local government into two tiers was much needed, but deeply disliked by many traditional conservatives who felt disorientated (alas, poor Rutland!). Keith Joseph's reform of the National Health Service was a bureaucratic disaster.

After a policymaking weekend at Selsdon while in opposition, Heath preached that the economy would work better if government interfered less. Inflation was the central economic problem, and he was cruelly unlucky, not only in the death of his gifted Chancellor, Iain Macleod, but especially in coming to power when the structure of international finance created at Bretton Woods was collapsing. Inflation was generally assumed in this pre-monetarist period to be caused by wage rises outstripping productivity. Heath introduced the Industrial Relations Act, which made agreements between employers and workers legally binding, created an industrial court to enforce them and made unions financially responsible for illegal industrial practices. His purpose was to end statutory wage control, with its beer-and-sandwiches preliminaries at 10 Downing Street, and return to free collective bargaining between employers and unions. There was much here that unions might have accepted, but they were not consulted as the bill was being framed, and set out to kill it. It embittered industrial relations, was widely evaded and repealed as soon as Heath fell.

Long before that, Heath had abandoned his policy of non-intervention. Unemployment was anathema to all Tory leaders since the war, and when it reached a million in 1972 he rescued industrial lame ducks in Glasgow shipbuilding and Midlands motorcycles, subsidised coal and steel, passed a new Industry Act as a catch-all measure to revive firms with taxation relief and regional grants, and produced a budget to stimulate growth. These were new methods of pursuing the same aim in different circumstances, and he made this U-turn without losing any members of his Cabinet, but the hopes that boom would lead not to bust but to a new era of expansion within the European Community were destroyed by a sudden and astonishing rise in commodity prices as the Arabs realised their economic muscle. Oil prices rose from $2.40 to $11.65 a barrel in 1973, copper by 115%. With no North Sea oil yet flowing, the UK trade balance became disastrous and there was a flight from sterling.

The thunderous atmosphere of *Götterdämmerung* hung over Heath's fall in February 1974. He had been working under exceptional pressure. The problems in Ulster, that 'bloody awful country' in the opinion of his Home Secretary Maudling, had been escalating since Wilson sent British troops to the province. The IRA had reverted to militarism in 1970, and the support for them surged when the Army attempted to deal with them through internment, reaching a climax after Bloody Sunday, 30 June 1972, when 13 were killed as troops fired on Catholic marchers in Derry. There was a brief interlude of calm when Heath prorogued the Stormont Parliament and introduced Direct Rule from Westminster, and even of hope, when his well-chosen Minister Whitelaw drew up the outlines of a new Northern Ireland constitution with power-sharing between Protestants and Catholics, and Heath negotiated the Sunningdale Agreement with the Irish government, with a Council of Ireland and cross-border security measures. But the rank and file of the Unionists never backed this, and the climate of violence remained.

It spread into England when Angry Brigade anarchists tried to blow up the Home Secretary, and became widespread when Mick McGahey and Arthur Scargill led the miners into militant confrontation. They had used flying pickets in their strike in the winter of 1971/2, the first national miners' strike for fifty years, and when Lord Wilberforce recommended a pay increase for them far in excess of the already mounting inflation, Heath had had to give way. Sensing their power, they now set out to destroy the government. Heath took them on, well prepared for battle this time with fuel reserves high; he believed that public opinion would give him the right answer as he held a general election on 'Who governs Britain?' His campaign was serious and moderate, but the power cuts and the three-day week which followed the strike added darkness and drama to the scene. The public were alarmed by inflation at 20% and inclined to blame Europe for their woes. The orators were against him. Harold Wilson painted him as pigheaded, divisive and dictatorial. Enoch Powell, traditional romantic Tory facing this modern technocrat, rallied disaffected reactionaries and announced on the eve of poll that he was voting Labour. The result was close (Labour 301, Conservative 297), but Heath had lost the support of the 12 Ulster Unionists after the Sunningdale agreement, and when the 14 Liberals rejected coalition he had to resign.

He confidently expected to be back, for his authority was formidable and his Cabinet colleagues loyal; he saw himself leading a government of national unity to rescue the country from economic disaster and social turmoil. But his party had other ideas. He had lost three elections and appeared a public liability as well as being brusque with back-benchers, so in 1975 he was challenged by Margaret Thatcher, and lost. He found this very hard to take, and increasingly allowed his bitterness to escape. Personal considerations aside (though the media never left them there), her Conservatism was far from his, dogmatic rather than pragmatic, more divisive than his, especially after she had espoused monetarism as the cure for inflation and driven unemployment up to three and a half million as part of the medicine. But the self-sufficiency which was so fundamental to his make-up kept him apart from the 'wets' when they writhed under her rule. He had the vision to recognise the emerging importance of China, but his advocacy of negotiated settlements for the Falklands War and Saddam's invasion of Kuwait left him isolated; he remained, eventually to become Father of the House of Commons, a lonely figure, the last of the post-war generation of One-Nation Tories.

J. Campbell, *Edward Heath* (1993).

James Callaghan

LEONARD JAMES CALLAGHAN, LORD CALLAGHAN OF
CARDIFF (1912-2005), Prime Minister from 1976 until 1979, was
brought up in Portsmouth by his mother, a naval widow who had to
struggle to make ends meet after his father's early death. He was a
Labour man from the day that the 1924 Labour government provided his mother with her first small pension. He went to work as an
income tax clerk, joined his union, became its Assistant General
Secretary and earned a reputation for debating and organising skills,
there and in the Fabian Society. In 1938 he married Audrey Moulton,
daughter of a businessman, a teacher and a fellow Fabian, who
proved a devoted wife and mother. He joined the Navy in the war,
was recommended to South Cardiff as a Labour candidate, and
won the seat comfortably in 1945.

Callaghan quickly made his mark in the House of Commons, even
among the host of new Labour MPs. He was a large man and a forceful debater, and his experience in union life made up for his lack of
a university education. He had started as a militant. At Labour's
Annual Conference in 1944 he helped to carry a motion against the
Executive requiring the party to adopt a programme of full nationalisation: Herbert Morrison went up to him and said, 'Do you realise
that you have just lost us the next general election?' But Callaghan's
instinct was to work through power, not rebellion, and by the end of
Attlee's governments he had been Parliamentary Secretary in
Transport (when 'cat's-eyes' were introduced) and at the Admiralty.
He was, and remained all his life, the complete traditional down-to-
earth Labour man. The Parliamentary Party elected him to the
Shadow Cabinet every year, and the Labour Party to its National
Executive Council every year except one: he became its Treasurer.
He was popular in the constituencies, a good union man, and effec-
tive in the House of Commons. Putting party unity above what he
called 'theological arguments about the precise meaning of social-
ism', he backed Gaitskell against his old friends on the Left.
Gaitskell made him Shadow Secretary for the Colonies and then

Shadow Chancellor. When Gaitskell died in 1963, some Gaitskellites encouraged him to stand for the leadership. He came third, behind Harold Wilson and George Brown, but Wilson saw Callaghan as a powerful and potentially dangerous rival, a great pike swimming below the water. When Labour came to power in 1964 he made him Chancellor of the Exchequer.

Callaghan held the three major Cabinet offices, the only Prime Minister to have done so. He was Chancellor from 1964 until 1967, Home Secretary from 1967 until 1970 and Foreign Secretary from 1974 until he succeeded Wilson in 1976. His record in them was uneven. He often had a wretched time as Chancellor, for he had had to learn his economics at specially arranged seminars, and lacked confidence. His years at the Treasury were punctuated by three sterling crises, starting on his first day there when a huge balance of payments deficit was revealed, and finishing with the devaluation which Wilson and he had constantly reassured the world was not going to happen. In his efforts to avoid it, Callaghan raised existing taxes and introduced new ones, the Selective Employment Tax and a tax on betting. He annoyed other countries by introducing import surcharges and export subsidies, and angered fellow ministers, especially George Brown who eventually resigned, by postponing public spending projects: and all to no avail. After a tactical shambles, when he delayed raising the bank rate while waiting for President Johnson's reply to his appeal for a loan and had to beg for a much larger one to bail him out after the resulting selling of sterling, he lost his nerve in private: officials were shaken to hear this solid man exclaiming, 'We can't go on.' He handled the actual devaluation in 1967 from $2.80 to $2.40 skilfully, but with his policy in ruins he was determined to resign.

Wilson, still regarding him as a threat on the back benches, moved him to the Home Office. Callaghan, following the liberal Roy Jenkins, was a reactionary Home Secretary. Wilson was to comment, 'Jim isn't as much a Minister of Justice as a Minister of Police,' and an off-the-cuff remark, 'I cannot bear the young men with hair hanging over their shoulders,' showed him to be a man of the respectable 'fifties rather than the swinging 'sixties. The Commonwealth Immigration Act let down Asians wanting to leave Kenya and Uganda by giving the right of British citizenship only to those with fathers or grandfathers born in Britain. When riots in Ulster got out of police control in 1969 he sent in the Army. But that is not the whole story. He had a sure touch with the public. On the Falls Road in Belfast, 'he has a great smile and a great wave and a great way of approaching people', said a Catholic. He showed shrewd judgment when he refused to ban a demonstration against the Vietnam War: police and remaining demonstrators eventually moved off together singing Auld Lang Syne. As Home Secretary his reputation for straight common sense was restored, and with it his confidence. However he stored up future trouble for himself by leading the opposition in Cabinet to Barbara Castle's proposals in *In Place of Strife,* to control trade union procedures by laws enforced by industrial courts. They offended his deepest instincts and beliefs.

As Foreign Secretary in the 1974 Wilson government, Callaghan made the Atlantic alliance and the Commonwealth his priorities: he was never a wholehearted European. He got on well with President Ford (with whom, after retiring, he was to enjoy several cruises), and also with Henry Kissinger. He persuaded Kissinger to shift his African policy from backing anti-Communist regimes of whatever type to moving closer to the new rulers of African countries, the 'will-bes' rather than the 'has-beens'. Less happily, he allowed Kissinger to dictate British policy in Cyprus, which led to the creation of a Turkish enclave and the long-lasting partition of the island. The robust patriot in Callaghan showed when he sent frigates to help our fishermen in the 'Cod War' with Iceland. He enjoyed his time in the Foreign Office and travelled widely, including a seven-nation safari round Africa. Kissinger found him a shrewd and experienced judge of world affairs.

When Wilson retired in 1976, his successor was elected by Labour MPs. Right-wing members predominated, and with Roy Jenkins withdrawing after the first ballot Callaghan was sure of success over Michael Foot, the standard bearer of the Left. Although he was sixty-four, he was at the peak of his powers, fit and experienced. Shirley Williams saw him as having 'toughened over time from the outside in'. In his wrath he could be formidable, but he was also 'Sunny Jim', 'Big Jim', friendly and avuncular behind his large moon spectacles. He delegated confidently. 'One of the great pleasures of being Prime Minister', he wrote, 'is that you can pick and choose to some extent. You have ... room for manoeuvre.' Bernard Donoughue, the head of his Policy Unit, commented on his capacity to ask the simple question at the heart of the issue, and on his natural authority in his Cabinet – which Wilson had lacked. He believed that, starting at a different time in British history, Callaghan would have been rated a great Prime Minister. But events decreed otherwise. Britain's fundamental economic weakness was unchanged. There was a balance of payments deficit, made worse by union-backed pay demands unrelated to production increase, and by the international use of sterling as a reserve currency. Inflation had been well into double figures since 1971. The world expected sterling to be devalued again, but Callaghan believed that it was possible to restore confidence in it. The unions had already agreed to a Social Contract keeping wage claims to 6%. North Sea Oil was starting to flow, with the promise of new riches when Britain became an oil-exporting country after 1980. Now he had to win time by obtaining a loan from the International Monetary Fund, for which the IMF asked for £5 billion cuts in public spending. Haunted by the catastrophic Labour split in 1931, he was determined to hold his party together through this economic crisis. His Cabinet included three divergent groups. Tony Benn and his allies wanted import controls and no cuts at all; Tony Crosland thought that the modest cuts already proposed would be adequate; only the Chancellor, Denis Healey, with one other, was ready for deeper cuts. Callaghan showed exceptional leadership qualities in reaching consensus and commanding the collective loyalty of the Cabinet after nine long, tough meetings. With their hard-won agreement, Callaghan and Healey brought negotiations to a successful conclusion in December, with £2 billion of cuts over two years and a loan of £3.9 billion. The party stayed intact.

His stature grew at home and abroad, and there followed a period of calm. Travelling widely and chairing a World Economic Summit meeting at Downing Street, he was more of an international statesman than Heath or Thatcher. He eased the strained relationship between German Chancellor Schmidt and President Carter; and Carter consulted him all through the Camp David negotiations which led to the accord between Israel and Egypt. He quietly got on with clearing the way for a replacement for Polaris, and agreed that Americans might station Cruise missiles in England. But he was cautious: 'steady as she goes' was one of his favourite nautical expressions. His reaction to the new idea of monetary union for Europe was suspicion, and he kept the Army in Ulster without searching for new initiatives there. At home he encouraged initiatives, but did not press when he encountered opposition. He launched a 'Great

Debate' on education but the Green Paper which followed it was bland, and nothing happened. He was interested in industrial democracy, but when the Bullock Report suggested putting workers onto company boards and there was an outcry from employers and some unions, he dropped the idea. Initiatives to reduce restrictive practices in the City and amongst lawyers and doctors ran into the sand. His one major move for change on the statute book was Devolution for Scotland and Wales, for which neither he nor the Welsh had much enthusiasm.

The government's parliamentary position was precarious. By 1977 Labour held only 314 out of the 634 seats. It was defeated 30 times in the Commons and Callaghan achieved a margin of security only by negotiating a pact with the Liberals. But Callaghan's personal ratings were far higher than the Tory leader Margaret Thatcher's, and in 1978 he playfully kept the country in suspense about an autumn election. His decision to postpone it until 1979 was famously disastrous, for there followed the 'Winter of Discontent'. In Parliament the government's position became even more exposed after the Lib-Lab Pact ended and the Scottish Nationalists were embittered by the failure to obtain the required 60% 'Yes' vote in the referendum on devolution. In the country pay restraint ended when the TUC rejected a new agreement with the government. There followed an explosion of wage demands of up to 40%, and strikes which sometimes started even before the unions had submitted their claims. Rubbish piled up on the streets, gravediggers and ambulance drivers stopped work and there was violence on picket lines – all relayed on television. Callaghan returned suntanned in the middle of it all from a summit meeting in Guadeloupe. 'Crisis, what crisis?' he responded to reporters. But on 28 March a vote of censure was carried in the Commons after the defeat of an amendment to the bill on the Nationalisation of Ship Repairing, and he was forced into the election he had so unwisely delayed. The Conservatives won it with an overall majority of 56, and the Thatcher era began.

Callaghan saw his defeat as a sea change in British politics, and he was right. The Labour Party and the unions were his church, in which he had grown up, and he had failed to educate them to the realities of modern Britain. Both were shifting to the left. The growing unpopularity of the unions became an incubus, first to him and then to the unions themselves. Thatcher conquered them; and the party, a coalition kept intact by Wilson and Callaghan, fell apart. Eighteen long years passed before there was another Labour Prime Minister, with a very different agenda.

K. Morgan, *Callaghan: A Life* (1997).

Margaret Thatcher

MARGARET HILDA THATCHER, BARONESS THATCHER OF KES-
TEVEN, (1925-), the first and so far the only female Prime Minister,
was also the longest serving in the twentieth century (1979-90). So
much is incontrovertible; and, though controversy has dogged her
then and since, few will deny that she had a stronger personal impact
on the course of British history than any other peacetime Premier.

She was a conviction politician. 'I am in politics because of the
conflict between good and evil,' she told an interviewer, 'and I
believe that in the end good will triumph.' Many of her convictions
she learnt from her father, Alderman Roberts, a self-educated
shopkeeper who became Mayor of his Lincolnshire home town,
Grantham. Her evangelical beliefs sprang from his Methodism (she
shook her Cabinet by reading the Old Testament from cover to
cover). She saw the national economy as a shopkeeper's writ large.
She shared his energy, his public spirit, his belief in the family and
in the need for self-improvement through education. She was all he
could have hoped for in a daughter, winning a place at Oxford to
read Chemistry, becoming President of the Conservative Club, and
being called to the Bar, as a tax lawyer. But she was not to remain a
Lincolnshire girl for long. In 1951 Margaret Roberts married Denis
Thatcher. He gave her much more than his name: financial resources
and devoted, shrewd, unobtrusive support throughout her career, all
the while remaining an unpolitical figure (after their dinner parties
in Downing Street he retired with the ladies, leaving her to talk with
the men). In 1959 she won the seat of Finchley, representing it
throughout her time in the House of Commons. From then on she
was seen as a southerner from the Home Counties.

As Heath's Education Secretary she soon earned a tough reputation by abolishing free school milk: 'Thatcher the Milk Snatcher'
cut a decidedly unfeminine figure. But her toughness was largely
devoted to getting a full share of resources for her Department, and
she was a big spender on behalf of nursery and primary schools. She
was loyal to Heath through a dramatic reversal of economic policy,

the storms of miners' strikes, the three-day week and an election called and lost, and became his Shadow Environment Secretary. It was his proposal for a coalition government to solve the country's problems which led her to stand as a candidate against him for the party leadership in 1975, for coalitions were anathema to her. She started as an outsider. Indeed she only stood because her more senior political guru, Keith Joseph, decided not to: 'somebody who represents our point of view *has* to stand,' she told him. But her campaign was energetically organised by a popular back-bencher, Airey Neave, while more senior men like Howe, Prior and Whitelaw held back from the first ballot. So all the Tories who could no longer endure Heath backed her, and she won in such a way that the momentum proved overwhelming. The Tory establishment was swept aside by a back-bench 'peasants revolt', and the party found itself with a leader about whom it knew remarkably little. Four years later she was Prime Minister, and it was not long before the whole country found out more.

Margaret Thatcher had a first-class mind of a particular type: the mind of a lawyer and a scientist. She dealt in facts and had an exceptional memory for them. She enjoyed argument, mastering briefs and solving problems. She asked penetrating questions. But she had no time for inconclusive theorising, pretentious or abstract language, or the subtler shades of grey. This clear-cut, limited outlook she carried into her personal relations. 'I make up my mind about people in the first ten seconds,' she told her Permanent Secretary at the DES, 'and I very seldom change it.' Throughout her political career she made enemies. Most of them came from privileged backgrounds and were part of the 'Establishment'; many looked for compromise and consensus, both dirty words to her. Tory grandees, Church of England bishops, Civil Service mandarins (especially in the Department of Education), the Foreign Office, the ancient universities, the BBC, the trade unions, the Commonwealth, the Brussels bureaucracy: it was a formidable list.

Her style, as well as her mind, was challenging. In Cabinet and the House of Commons, and at European and Commonwealth meetings, her approach was almost invariably confrontational. She gave her opinion forcefully, and respected that approach in others. As a small lady coming onto a male-dominated stage (there were only 25 women in the House of Commons in 1959), she intended to be taken seriously. She inherited an interest in clothes from her mother and dressed smartly, with a matching range of handbags ready to brandish. She made up skilfully and never had a hair out of place, developing as Prime Minister a backcombed and sprayed hair style which gave her height and dignity. She took breathing lessons to lower the pitch of her voice. There was a feminine side to her: she was as distraught as any mother when her son went missing in the Sahara, she prepared her dinner parties meticulously, and there are many stories of small kindnesses to her staff. Those who lived close to her appreciated her efficient organisation; others found her bossy.

Margaret Thatcher's ten and a half years as Prime Minister involved a series of battles – against inflation, the Argentine, the miners, the trade unions, the IRA, the GLC, and the demands and ambitions of Brussels. She fought them, as she saw it, on behalf of the mass of individuals and families who made up the British people, and she fought them with courage as well as conviction. The central problem of the British economy through the 1970s had been inflation. Under the tutelage of Sir Keith Joseph, she had come to believe that the cure for this was to control the money supply, and she now set about doing so for the long-term benefit of her country, regardless of the short -term consequences. Her government's actual increase in money supply was much the same as Labour's had been latterly, but a 12% increase in the value of the pound and the doubling of VAT forced prices up. There followed the biggest decline in industrial output since 1931, and three million unemployed. There were major riots in Brixton and Toxteth, and Thatcher herself became a hated figure, her approval rating dropping to 23% in 1981. She did not flinch, and in a broadcast told the nation: 'After a major operation you feel worse before you convalesce. But you do not refuse it when you know that without it you will not survive.' The eventual success of the treatment won her the confidence of the nation.

The next election came too soon for that, however, and she was saved only by the Falklands War. The mistakes of her government which encouraged General Galtieri to invade the Falklands in April 1982 were forgotten in the courage she showed in recovering them. She was admired by the military leaders for the decisive way she took the risk, on their advice, of sending an armada to far distant enemy waters, and giving them an order to break the rules of war by sinking the *General Belgrano*. Her friendship with President Reagan won crucial American support, even through her refusal to consider a compromise peace. When *HMS Sheffield* was sunk she wept but was unshaken. Constitutionally correct, she carried the Cabinet and the House of Commons with her through all the major decisions, but she had the fortitude, the single-mindedness and the public bravura of a wartime leader, and the victory was recognised as hers, with a march-past at which she and not the Queen took the stand. 'Rejoice,' she had told the nation when South Georgia was recaptured – and it did. She won the election of 1983 by a majority of 144.

She therefore faced without hesitation the next challenge, from Arthur Scargill and the miners. This was the show-down with the unions which she needed to consolidate her transformation of the economy, and she had prepared for it, building up fuel stocks, getting smaller unions onside with timely concessions, facing down an earlier steel strike to demonstrate her resolution, and building up a trained police force. It was a long, bitter battle with ugly scenes at picket lines, but this time there was no compromise; instead, the first total defeat of a major strike since 1926. With the closed shop banned, secondary picketing forbidden and unions liable financially for breaches of the law, their political power was destroyed. Thatcher eventually managed to ban union membership altogether in the Government Communication Headquarters.

The problems of Ireland she approached as a Unionist. The IRA had murdered Airey Neave with a car bomb in the precincts of Westminster: later they came near to killing her too, with the bomb which they planted in the Grand Hotel in Brighton during the Conservative Party Conference in 1984, which helped to confirm her heroic status. She toughed it out with their hunger-striking prisoners, allowing Bobby Sands to starve himself to death. She set herself against changes in the status quo: 'that's out, that's out, that's out', she wrote across the suggestions of the New Ireland Forum. Because she was a 'can-do' politician, she did agree with Dublin to the Anglo-Irish Agreement of 1985, with regular inter-governmental conferences, cross-border security operations and a joint secretariat, but she gave the assurance that there would be no change in the status of Northern Ireland without majority consent.

Commonwealth nations she treated with ill-concealed impatience, especially when they pressed, on moral grounds, for sanctions against South Africa, which would damage its economy. 'Blacks and their families out of work. Moral? Poof! Moral?' Russia was at first her central enemy abroad. She was horrified by President Reagan's plans for total nuclear disarmament, which would leave Europe exposed to the Russian army. But she welcomed the arrival of Gorbachev: 'I like Mr Gorbachev. He and I can do business together.' Her central ally was the USA, and her relationship with Reagan was as 'Special' as any in the twentieth century. They shared a philosophy, both believers in self-help and the struggle between good and evil, both growing up outside the establishment. They enjoyed each other's company, too: the sparky, bright-eyed lady and the tall, dark, confident former filmstar. He let her have the latest Trident at cost price, and provided vital support in the Falklands War. She derided his Star Wars scheme for anti-nuclear protection and was outraged by the American invasion of the formerly British Grenada, but was ready to provide UK bases for the bombing of Libya.

By 1987 the economic medicine had worked, and share prices had risen five-fold since 1983. Privatisation was unpicking much of the socialist state – telecommunications, oil, gas, air and road transport and shipbuilding – and the number of shareholders had increased to nine million. Meanwhile the sale of council-houses to their tenants had made a million more of the electorate property owners. With the opposition hopelessly divided between a Labour Party led from the left, and an Alliance of Liberals and the new SDP whose leaders publicly disagreed on defence, the Tory majority at the election was 102. Three times victorious, Thatcher was coming to see herself as an institution, and her confidence, boosted by having proved doubters wrong so often, was verging on the vainglorious. In this mood she fought her last two battles, against local authorities and Brussels. These were to bring about her downfall.

Margaret Thatcher wanted to manage, and she was a centraliser, frustrated by organisations which came between her and the proper running of the country. The Education Reform Act of 1988 took power away from local authorities in two directions, giving schools their own governing bodies and creating a single national curriculum. In 1989 hospitals, too, were allowed to become self-governing trusts financed from Whitehall. With powers to cap high-spending authorities, the government waged war on notorious socialist regimes in Liverpool and Lambeth, and all authorities were compelled to put most of their services out to tender to private organisations. The climax of her attack was the abolition of the Greater London Council and of other metropolitan giants. But local authorities still accounted for 30% of all public spending, and she was irked by the system through which they raised their money – the rates. Rates were paid by a property-owning minority who did not have the voting power to discourage local over-expenditure, and for their regular increase central government tended to get the blame. So Thatcher determined to make the change from a property to a personal tax, and launched the Community Charge, soon to be dubbed the Poll Tax: fair in that everyone paid for services they received, but manifestly unjust on the poor since it was a flat rate charge, the same for everyone. In the euphoria of the third election victory, the Cabinet agreed to push it through forthwith, and to start in Scotland, where a rates review was due. But there was widespread outrage, and the Scots gave a lead which England and Wales followed: half of them withheld all or part of their payment. By 1990 Conservative MPs with small majorities were becoming fearful.

Over Europe, Margaret Thatcher had early fought a famous battle and won it. She believed that Britain should be inside the European Community, but on the right terms and in the right sort of Community. Britain was paying more than its fair share, and she used her power of veto over any increase in the Community's expenditure to bargain for a drastic reduction in the UK's contribution. In 1980, rejecting with contempt the offer of a £350 million rebate, she finally settled for an annual reduction of £760 million for three years and in 1984 got this converted into a permanent rebate of 66% of the difference between what Britain paid in and got out of the Community. She remained impervious to crises, immutable in her demands. 'She doesn't really believe that there's any such thing as useful negotiation,' commented an ambassador, Sir Nicholas Henderson. President Mitterand saw 'cette femme Thatcher! Elle a les yeux de Caligule' – adding, however, 'mais elle a la bouche de Marilyn Monro.' So far, so good. But in 1988 the battle ground changed when the re-elected European Community President, Jacques Delors, sketched his vision of a Federal Europe, with its own embryo government within six years and 80% of all social and economic laws coming from Brussels. Margaret Thatcher was appalled. Galtieri, Scargill, Delors: demons all! She delivered a landmark speech at Bruges. She spoke of a wider Europe, of 'Warsaw, Prague and Budapest as great European cities', and of the value of a European single market: but 'we have not rolled back the frontiers of the state in Britain only to see ... a European superstate exercising a new dominance from Brussels.' From this broad position she narrowed her hostile focus onto the single currency for the European Community and the Exchange Rate Mechanism (ERM) leading to it. That was to bring about her downfall.

Thatcher was a populist Prime Minister. 'I'm in the business to try to make Britain great again,' she told a reporter, and she had the popular press, headed by *The Sun*, and the Tory Party workers behind her. *Sun* readers liked the Iron Lady, who had seen off the 'Argies' abroad and the rioters at home, and most felt the benefits of lower inflation and taxation. But she had many enemies in the Establishment. Only two members of her first Cabinet had voted to make her their party leader in 1974, and after the 1983 election she cleared out most of the 'wets'. But her methods as well as her policies made some of those who replaced them unhappy. As time went on, Cabinets met less often, and she spoke in them more than she listened. Cabinet committees gave place to ad hoc groups. She was ready to undermine her ministers if she did not like what they were doing: Jim Prior found her PPS, Ian Gow, lobbying Conservative MPs to vote against his Irish Bill for gradual devolution. Two important ministers, Michael Heseltine and Leon Brittan, resigned in 1986 over the sale of the Westland helicopter firm to an American rather than a European company, both feeling that she had been duplicitous.

After the 1987 election, the Greek tragedy unfolded. She lost through illness her Home Secretary Willie Whitelaw, a friend, moderating influence and channel of communication. As hubris set in, she relied increasingly on a close circle of personal advisers, Charles Powell from the Foreign Office, Bernard Ingham, her Press Secretary, and Alan Walters, her erstwhile pet economist now recalled to her side. In 1989 her attitude towards Europe led to a show-down: her Foreign Secretary, Geoffrey Howe, and her Chancellor, Nigel Lawson, told her that they would resign if she did not agree at the Madrid Summit of 1989 that Britain should set a timetable for joining the ERM on certain conditions. Cornered, she did so, but she did not forgive them (and later events proved them wrong and her right). Lawson resigned over the outspoken criticism of his policy by Alan Walters. Howe had been the Chancellor who had carried through her economic revolution, a key player in all her Cabinets. Now she moved him from the Foreign Office, making him an unconsulted Deputy Prime Minister. On her return from the next Summit, she took off in the Commons. Delors wanted a European

Government with its Parliament, its Commission and its Council of Ministers set over all national governments. 'No ... No ... No,' she cried. Her tone made Howe despair. He resigned, and a fortnight later delivered a resignation speech which ended, quietly but deliberately, with a suggestion that others might 'consider their own response to the conflict of loyalties with which I have myself wrestled for perhaps too long.' Nemesis duly arrived in the leonine form of Michael Heseltine as a challenger for the leadership of the party. She needed a 15% lead over him to avoid a second ballot, and she missed it by four votes. This opened the floodgates. One after another, her ministers advised her not to fight on, and, listening perhaps to her husband most, she resigned.

Faith in the City (1985), the report of a Commission set up by the Archbishop of Canterbury, Robert Runcie, deplored the philosophy of Thatcherite Conservatism which emphasised the individual at the expense of society. Her policies led to a widening of the gap between the rich and the poor, and the scars of the operation with which she started her decade of power were slow to heal. They, the divisions in it over her approach to Europe, and the decadence which often develops during a long period of power, eventually left her party unelectable for a period not yet over. But for her country she had done what she set out to do. She decisively reversed its economic decline, and pulled it out of a period in which it seemed to be becoming ungovernable. This Conservative Prime Minister remained, moreover, a radical reformer to the end.

H. Young, *One of Us: A Biography of Margaret Thatcher* (1991).
J. Campbell, *Margaret Thatcher: Grocer's Daughter* (2000).

John Major

JOHN MAJOR (1943-), was Prime Minister from 1990 until 1997. His background was the most extraordinary for a Conservative leader since Disraeli's. His elderly father, once a juggler and acrobat, had to sell his garden ornament business, so from the age of twelve young John was brought up in Brixton, in a two-room flat with a gas stove at the top of the stairs outside it. He left school at sixteen with six 'O' Levels. He was unemployed while he helped to look after his parents and only got regular work, as a bank clerk, three years later. In the Standard Bank he made his way steadily up until he was asked to run its new marketing department at the age of thirty-three: an average dealer, but a capable organiser with a friendly personality. His political career started from an equally modest base, in the Brixton branch of the Young Conservatives. His winning of a seat on the Lambeth Council in 1968 was wholly unexpected, the Conservatives being swept in on the tide of Enoch Powell's anti-immigration campaign.

1970 was a formative year for him. He gained a settled and affectionate home when he married Norma, a teacher and a dressmaker, and he became Chairman of both the Brixton Conservatives and the Lambeth Housing Committee. With growing confidence he put in for parliamentary seats and, after many rejections and to his considerable surprise, was adopted for the safe, upper-crust seat of Huntingdonshire in 1976, being duly returned as its MP in 1979. He started up the ministerial ladder in 1981, became a Whip in 1983, successively Parliamentary Under-Secretary and Minister of State in the Department of Social Security between 1985 and 1987, Chief Secretary to the Treasury in 1987, Foreign Secretary for ninety-four days and then Chancellor of the Exchequer in 1989, and Prime Minister in 1990. He had climbed Disraeli's 'greasy pole' with the panache of an acrobat's son rather than the long struggle of that Hebrew conjuror.

The Major Enigma was the title of one of the earliest books about him: the enigma being that there was, in fact, absolutely no panache, and nothing of the acrobat, in John Major. He owed his rise to a lot of hard work, a clear mind, mastery of detail, negotiating skill, and an open friendliness which made those who met him feel the better for it. He went to the Treasury at Chancellor Lawson's urgent request, when Margaret Thatcher would have liked him as Chief Whip. Events then propelled him to the top. Thatcher's relations with her senior ministers were becoming dangerously strained. After Howe and Lawson had combined to force her to accept Britain's entry into the ERM, she planned her revenge. Seeing Major as a loyal man who was liked by his colleagues, she chose him to succeed Geoffrey Howe when she pushed him out of the Foreign Office in a Cabinet reshuffle, and then made him Chancellor when Lawson resigned four months later. When, the next year, her leadership was challenged by Michael Heseltine, she did not win by a large enough majority to avoid a second ballot, and, advised by her ministers that she might be defeated in it, she retired from the fray to allow others from her Cabinet to stand unimpeded against him. The same qualities which had commended Major to her now commended him to Conservative MPs. Against the establishment figure Douglas Hurd, he was seen as a man of the people; against the leonine, disruptive and passionately European Heseltine, he was felt to be a conciliator who would restore party unity. So the man who had thought his background might prevent him from ever winning nomination for a Conservative seat found himself, only eleven years after entering Parliament, Conservative Prime Minister.

Within the Cabinet, there was a deep sense of relief. Margaret Thatcher had always liked to give her views at the start of any debate there, and these became increasingly dogmatic assertions. More and more, too, she had come to consult her own advisers rather than ministers. Experience and instinct alike led John Major to restore the Cabinet to its central position, and to seek consensus through discussion. He used its meetings to define problems and to share responsibility for their solution. Chris Patten described the Thatcher ministers coming out of their first Cabinet Meeting under Major's chairmanship as resembling the prisoners in *Fidelio* emerging blinking into the sunlight. But antidote became anticlimax. His balanced summing-ups soon led to grumbles about his indecision; as the memory of her became more distant, they started to look back with regret to the stamp of Thatcher's authority. Even his natural modesty seemed inappropriate in a leader. What to make of a Prime Minister who is found clearing up the beer cans in a hotel room himself after the celebrations over his negotiating success at Maastricht? What was true for the Cabinet was true also for the country at large. People found Major a grey man, and compared him unfavourably with Thatcher's vivid colours. He was uncomfortable with theories and ideals. 'I am not a moral philosopher,' he said, 'Nor an economist. Nor an intellectual. I am a practical politician.' This made it hard for him to unfurl bright banners around which to rally the nation: while in government, the very strengths which had eased him to the top inhibited him from coming down on one side or the other when compromise was unsatisfactory or impossible. It was to be his misfortune that this was to happen when the split over Europe widened right at the heart of the Conservative Party.

The early days of his premiership were the most successful. During the Iraq war he cut a good figure as a leader. He got rid of the hated Poll Tax. He introduced a Citizen's Charter to deliver better public services to all, through inspectors, performance targets, league tables and a Charter line for complaints: the young man from Brixton setting out to improve the day-to-day lives of his fellows. His European policy had the makings of an acceptable compromise: to be at the heart of the Community, but to oppose moves towards federalism. He was at his best in negotiating favourable terms for the UK in the run-up to the Maastricht Treaty: opt-out clauses from the single currency and the Social Chapter, both anathema to the Euro-sceptic wing of his party; keeping the dreaded 'f' word, federalism, out of it; and establishing the principle of subsidiarity – national governments to be left with everything which they could do better than Brussels, including foreign, defence and security policy. The House of Commons gave the treaty a majority of 244 at the bill's second reading. By then he had fought a general election in 1992 and won it against the predictions of the polls. This was seen as a personal victory, and his decision to campaign from soap boxes around the constituencies caught the public imagination. He made much of his underprivileged background. 'I know what it's like ... when you have to search for the next job. I haven't forgotten – and I never will.'

But within a year of this triumph his popular rating in a Gallup Poll was lower, at 21%, than that of any previous Prime Minister. Many of his troubles were foreseeable, some of his difficulties unavoidable. The recession which he inherited proved long and deep, exacerbated by the problems of the German economy as Chancellor Kohl tried to revive East Germany after reunification. A collapse in the value of houses hit the middle classes in the South East far more heavily than earlier recessions. But Major badly mis- handled the inevitable closure of coal pits, allowing Michael Heseltine to announce, without consulting the Cabinet, that 31 of them, more than half the remains of the mining industry, would be shut down; and then having to beat a rapid retreat.

There had already been another spectacular retreat, on 16 Sep- tember 1992, when the pound was forced out of the ERM by spec- ulation against sterling. This was dramatic, with the Bank of England selling £15 billion of its reserves trying to defend it, and interest rates going up to 15%; and humiliating, since having sterling in the ERM to prevent inflation was a cornerstone of John Major's economic policy. Black Wednesday became recognised as the point from which the Conservatives spun into irreversible decline. The government's reputation for economic competence took a fatal knock, the immediate improvement in the British economy as it lost the incubus of an overvalued pound merely proving how wrong Major's policy had been.

At her farewell party, Margaret Thatcher had ominously described herself as 'a good backseat driver'. Tories who had been uneasy about her departure and the manner of it now followed her call to arms against the drift into a federal Europe. The 'Maastricht Rebels', further encouraged by the Danish rejection of the treaty in their referendum, fought its progress through the Commons, clause by clause, for a year. Eventually Major banished eight of them by removing the party whip – only to restore it again in order to keep a majority eroded by lost by-elections. 'We give the impression of being in office but not in power,' commented his dismissed Chancellor, Norman Lamont. In the Balkans Major was cutting a much less impressive figure than he had in Iraq. A London Conference to stop the Serb ethnic cleansing in Bosnia, hailed at first as another diplomatic success for him, merely served to show the weakness of Europe without American involvement, as the Serbs made a mockery of the 'Safe Areas' designated for fleeing Muslims under United Nations protection, and slaughtered them there. At home, his 'Back to Basics' initiative, to restore 'traditional values, common sense and a concern for the citizen', proved uninspiring, and was soon being narrowly interpreted as a crusade for sexual morality. This made the scandals which littered the path of his government all the more uncomfortable for him. He set up two judicial enquiries, leading to the Scott Report on the licensing of arms sales to Iraq before the Gulf War and the Nolan Report on standards in public life, both of which came back to hit him like boomerangs, when they broadened their remit into widespread criticism. The press made lurid displays of the steamy sex allegations about David Mellor and the lies of Jonathan Aitken, two of his ministers, and the cash accepted for asking parliamentary questions by Conservative MPs; these and much else pulled together under the heading of 'Sleaze'. 'What fools we were to back John Major', proclaimed *The Sun*.

After 1994 *The Sun* found someone else to back, the new leader of the Labour Party, Tony Blair. To Major, Blair appeared superficial, brash, full of rhetorical cliches and ad-man speak. But to the public and the media his youthful idealism had exciting appeal, spoken in the language of his generation. Moreover, he was reshaping his party, reducing the influence of the trade unions, the National Executive Committee and the Party Conference, and abandoning its commitment to nationalisation. Here was New Labour, ready to work with private enterprise, announcing that it would not raise income tax. There were the old Tories, divided and corrupt, led by someone who now seemed more a man of the past than a man of the people. Major made a brave effort to achieve a new start. In 1995 he resigned the leadership of the Conservative Party and stood again for it, demanding: 'Back me or sack me.' He defeated his right-wing challenger John Redwood, and brought the charismatic Michael Heseltine back as Deputy Prime Minister. But the margin of his success (218 to 89, with 20 abstentions) was too small to convince the world that he could lead a united party, and his personal frustration with 'the bastards', as he was heard to call the Euro-sceptics over a live microphone, was painfully obvious. When the general election was held in May 1997, the national mood against Brussels had been darkened by BSE, the 'mad cow disease' which led to the imposition by the European Union of a ban on the export of British beef; and over two hundred Conservative candidates announced their opposition to a single European currency. Major's European compromise was damaged beyond repair.

The country returned New Labour with a majority of 179, the Conservative defeat being the worst they had suffered since 1906.

Their failure to recover since throws light on the limited extent to which John Major, who had immediately resigned, should be held personally responsible for this. Much was due to the length of time they had been in office, with blame for mistakes accumulating and the number of disappointed ex-ministers and back-benchers increasing. The bitter schism over Britain's relationship with Europe bedevilled the party as a similar divide over Tariff Reform had done before 1906. It is doubtful whether anyone could have led the Conservatives remotely near to success in 1997. Major had won victory against the odds in 1992. He had inaugurated measures which were in tune with popular hopes: the shifting of more government into the private sector, more open government, better auditing of public expenditure, the National Lottery. His skill as a negotiator won favourable terms for Britain at Maastricht. It was also shown to advantage in Northern Ireland, where with political courage he achieved a ceasefire and movement towards self-government in which Protestants and Catholics could share, only to see it halted by the refusal of the IRA to decommission its weapons. But John Major had no instinct for presentation, and his reforms could appear banal as well as worthy, as when improvements in public toilets and a 'Cones Hotline' for motorway drivers were included in his Citizen's Charter. Under constant pressure from a hostile media he was vulnerable, and increasingly unable to set his own agenda. Six years in power had shown that, capable, agreeable and often brave as he was, he lacked the authority and the charisma needed at the top of a democracy.

A. Seldon, *Major: A Political Biography* (1997).

Envoi

AT THE TIME of writing, Tony Blair (1953-) is still Prime Minister, having won his third victory at the polls. But, although an overall assessment of his premiership is not possible, he has been too striking a leader to omit him altogether from this book. This is therefore an attempt to set out his approach to his task and the office which he holds, and to summarise his achievements to date and his future prospects.

On 1 May 1997 he found himself on the brink of a new era in British politics: the head of the first Labour government for eighteen years, with an even larger majority (179) than Attlee had in 1945 (144). He led a party whose structure and attitudes he and his close friend Gordon Brown had transformed, bringing to fruition work which had started under the leadership of Neil Kinnock and John Smith. The historical power of the trade unions in it was reduced when union votes at its annual conference were reduced to 50% of the total, and union-nominated members on its national executive to a minority. 'One member, one vote' replaced the block-voting system for choosing parliamentary candidates and the party leader. Crucially, Blair and Brown persuaded party members to accept a new Clause IV in the Labour Party Constitution, which ended Labour's commitment to common ownership of 'means of production, distribution and exchange'. Their New Labour movement aimed for full employment, not through the Keynesian use of government expenditure but by stimulating demand with low taxes, free markets and sound money: accepting the Thatcherite approach to the economy. Thus did they make the Labour Party electable, and steal from the Conservatives their command of the central ground of politics.

Tony Blair was one of fortune's favourites. There was no vacancy either in the highly regarded Inner Temple Chambers or on the short list of candidates for the safe Labour seat of Sedgefield to which he applied, but in both he was a successful 'Johnny-come-lately' – his name being added to the short list at Sedgefield by one vote. John Smith's fatal heart attack in 1994 led to a totally

unexpected vacancy for the leadership of the Labour Party and happened just when his political charisma was being felt at Westminster.
As Leader of the Opposition and a brilliant debater, he faced a tired
and decadent Conservative government whose reputation had
suffered irreparable damage on Black Wednesday, and whose bitter
division over Europe was being paraded across the pages of the
press. John Major cut a flat and defensive figure alongside him: to
win the 1997 election he had only to push at an open door. He was
the first Labour Prime Minister to inherit a stable and promising
economy.

The victory was a personal one for him and he entered Downing
Street on a high-rolling wave of popularity. His youth (he was not
quite forty-four), his fresh good looks and big smile, his easy confidence and ebullient optimism presented to the public the mood of
a new start, a clean break from the sleaze of some post-Thatcher
Tories. He was serious-minded. At Oxford he had come under the
influence of an Australian Christian Socialist, Peter Thomson, and
through him of John Macmurray, a philosopher who based his thinking on the importance of community, and was confirmed into the
Church of England. At the Bar he met and married Cherie Booth, a
gifted lawyer and a Roman Catholic: interest in religion played a part
in drawing them together. But he was also high-spirited, lead singer
in an Oxford band, and a natural populist. 'I am a modern man, from
the rock 'n' roll generation. The Beatles, colour TV, that's my generation.' He won the endorsement of *The Sun* by wooing Rupert
Murdoch with his vision of a classless, meritocratic Britain. When
Princess Diana was killed four months after the election, he hailed
her as 'the People's Princess', and led the mourning of the nation.
His shirtsleeves style appealed to the broad public; so, at that time,
did his openly expressed affection for his wife, and the birth of their
son Leo (Walpole, the first, and Blair, the latest Prime Minister, both
had a child born while they were in Downing Street). His political
instincts were timely, too. The British people, after a lengthy dose of
Thatcher, were ready for a community-minded approach in their
government: ready for Tony Blair.

Their expectations were to be gradually disappointed; and one
must wonder why, from a position of exceptional strength, New
Labour so far has had such an unspectacular record of reform
compared with those of similar governments, the Liberals in 1905
and Labour in 1945. The answer lies partly in the complexity of the

reforms needed. But it is partly to do with Blair's background and the nature of his talents. He was not as well equipped to take advantage of his opportunities as he had been to win them. He has no power base in the traditional Labour Party. His father had had political ambitions as a Conservative until he was crippled by a stroke, and had sent Tony to Fettes, the leading Scottish independent school. There young Blair was a rebel but a cautious one. He is essentially *politique* rather than *dévot*, as pragmatic in his politics as he is ecumenical in his religion. Asked why he joined the Labour Party, he replied, 'Well, I could never be a Tory.' His political education was with Gordon Brown. Their relationship is fundamental in Blair's story. For nine years after 1983, when they both entered Parliament, they shared a tiny windowless office, and became close friends. New Labour was their joint creation. Brown was the senior, with proper roots in the Scottish Labour Party, the star of the 1983 intake who was made shadow Chancellor by John Smith. As late as 1991 Brown said, 'I think Blair could well one day be leader after me.' But Blair, the extrovert, became recognised as a natural vote-winner, while Brown dourly preached fiscal restraint. By 1994 the mood among their fellow MPs had shifted so far that, when John Smith died, Brown agreed, over a famous meal in the Granita restaurant in Islington, to stand aside to let Blair lead the party in the ensuing election. It hurt him; and the long shadow of their lost friendship has lain across Blair's governments. Blair, no economist himself, accepted that Brown should run the economy from his own empire in the Treasury, but their rival camps have fought battles in the media ever since, with rumours of a deal done over the succession. This relationship between two dominant men has been unique in the story of British governments, saved from breakdown only by their mutual recognition that each needs the other. It has proved inhibiting.

Inhibiting, too, has been the priority Blair has given to establishing New Labour as the long-term party of government, which has made him move carefully. With the devaluations of the Labour governments of MacDonald, Attlee and Wilson haunting them, Blair and Brown were determined to prove that the pound would be safe under New Labour. They committed themselves to Conservative spending plans for two years, kept their promise not to raise income tax, and handed over the control of interest rates to the Bank of England, with instructions to keep inflation low. They thus gave themselves a base from which to expand government expenditure in the social services later. But when this opportunity did come Blair's lack of experience in office caused problems in using it effectively. He had worked not with men who had run businesses or departments but with lawyers and politicians. In Downing Street he relied on a team of his old friends and allies rather than on his senior civil servants: Alastair Campbell, Jonathan Powell and Angie Hunter in his office were closer to him than the Cabinet Secretary. His leadership was centralised and personal, 'sofa government', and there was much talk of 'cronyism' when he gave old friends and allies important ministerial posts: Peter Mandelson, Derry Irvine, Charlie Falconer. Under Smith he had sat near the door during Shadow Cabinet meetings and often slipped out early. Now his Cabinets were for the passage of business rather than centres of policy discussion, and he had no time for Cabinet committees: the contrast with Attlee is significant. The themes of New Labour emerged as proclamations of intent, in particular for consumer choice in health and education, but early initiatives often ran into the sand, and involved more quangos and civil servants, more paperwork – and targets (e.g. for reduced hospital waiting lists) which often distorted proper priorities. One success was the introduction of numeracy and literacy hours into primary schools, honouring Blair's promise of 'education, education and education' as his top three priorities. But Frank Field's ambitious scheme for higher pensions for all was soon blocked by the Treasury. It took two years for Gordon Brown to launch his Welfare to Work measures to encourage the unemployed back to work, and to introduce the minimum wage – at a lower level than had been promised. As late as the election of 2001 Blair had not thought through the details of his reforms, so only towards the end of his second administration were foundation hospitals started and specialist schools developed, while the introduction of 'top-up' fees for students to help to solve the crisis in university finances still lies ahead. Throughout he has been hampered by opposition from Brown in the Treasury, to the devolution of financial power and the increased use of private resources in the social services.

By contrast, the constitutional reforms heralded by New Labour were introduced speedily, and Scottish and Welsh devolution safely delivered. London has an elected Mayor (not the one Blair wanted). But changes in the House of Lords were botched. Eight years on, the hereditary principle is almost dead there, but there is still no agreement between the supporters of an elected and of an appointed second chamber: Blair has shown little interest in achieving one. He did focus his attention on Ireland, and there he achieved the Good Friday agreement, which restored its own devolved government to Northern Ireland, with Unionists sharing power with Nationalists and working with the Irish government on cross-border issues. This was a remarkable achievement of sustained negotiation, and only a leader with Blair's charm and skills could have conjured it from such divided roots. But it did not last; and it left Blair with confidence in his powers of diplomacy which proved to be over-confidence when the Iraq crisis developed.

The shift from Old to New Labour was as great in foreign policy and defence as in their approach to the economy. Support for unilateral disarmament had been one of the factors which made Old Labour unelectable. Blair has swung to the opposite extreme, and has been ready to use force to make the world a better place. He was strong in his support of intervention in Iraq in 1998, with Anglo-American air strikes to enforce co-operation with UN weapons inspections on Saddam Hussein. When the refugee crisis in the Balkan province of Kosovo worsened, with native Muslims fleeing from Serb troops who were brutally enforcing Milosevic's ethnic cleansing policy, Blair became convinced that NATO would have to send in troops on the ground. He was eventually successful in persuading an unwilling President Clinton to commit US soldiers; and in keeping the British public and Labour left-wingers onside. It was his own policy, and he left himself no exit strategy. Had it failed he would probably have had to resign. But Milosevic became convinced of the reality of the threat, and, when his Russian ally abandoned him, ordered his troops out of Kosovo. Blair became a statesman of world standing, while at home he won the admiration of the generals, the troops, *The Sun* and the people.

At Chicago, while working on Clinton, he had set out his five criteria for intervention. Is the cause just? Has diplomacy proved futile? Are we confident of winning? Is there a will for long-term commitment? Are national interests involved? To these he has remained consistent. They led him into the war in Iraq in 2003 which has cost him his popularity. His Manichean view of the world scene, good versus evil, light versus darkness, was deepened by 9/11. He went to America nine days after it, and then threw himself with sustained energy into the war on terror. He won Pakistan's President over against the Taliban, but his tour of the Middle East was fruit-less, earning him a televised snub from President Assad of Syria; nor did he carry France or Germany with him. When the Bush adminis-tration decided to follow up its success in Afghanistan by regime change in Iraq, Blair signed up to the war there in September 2003, six months before it started. He pushed hard for his second criter-ion, that the US should work through the UN to persuade Saddam to get rid of his weapons of mass destruction (WMD); and Bush did try to get a fresh UN resolution authorising the war, against the advice of most of those close to him, so Blair can claim to have had some influence on him. But Blair had already agreed that if this route failed he would send British troops to join the Americans: he was as ready as Bush to rid the world of Saddam, an evil and poten-tially dangerous man.

He was less successful than he had been in 1998 in keeping the people, his party and the press on his side. By presenting Saddam's WMD as the *casus belli*, he laid himself open to accusations of deceiving Parliament and the public. Saddam had used chemical and biological weapons before, and might well have acquired nuclear warheads in the future – Blair had knowledge, which he could not share, of their distribution from Pakistan. But to justify the war in Britain he built up slenderly based intelligence evidence that Saddam had WMD ready to hand. It proved false, and this has cost him dear. He has used up his capital of trust at home, and in future his efforts to make the world a better place will have to be con-ducted peacefully, or on a much smaller scale.

In his domestic policies Blair is so pragmatic that it is hard to dis-cover any principles beyond the retaining of power. But abroad he is a Gladstonian idealist and looks to a lowering of barriers to spread peace and prosperity. He believes that it is in British interests to be at the centre of Europe, but that Europe must run a free-market economy both internally and externally, to make it more competitive against strong economies and to help poorer parts of the world, especially Africa, by ending agricultural subsidies. He has played a lively part in European politics, and pushed successfully for the enlargement of the Community. He hoped that this would lead to a more liberal approach in it towards economic management, which in turn would make it more acceptable to a sceptical British public. But his support for the Americans in Iraq has revived French suspicions, never completely dormant, of the perfidious Anglo-Saxons.

Nationalism in Britain and France alike is a powerful force, and the French are still protectionists at heart. Their rejection of the Constitution designed to make the larger Community work has cast a dark cloud over the future of the Europe Blair would like to see. His diplomatic skills will be challenged through and beyond his presidency of the European Commission.

Blair faces an uncertain future. It is too early, in the summer of 2005, to assess the impact of the London terrorist bombers on his reputation. His immediate response to them struck the right note, but those who thought that the invasion of Iraq was a dangerous diversion from the war against al-Qaeda will be powerfully reinforced. With a reduced majority he depends more than he did on the support of the Old Labour wing of his party. There are doubts about the sustaining of government expenditure on its present scale without increased taxation when there is a downturn in the economy. Success brings its own problems. Longevity adds costs to the NHS and to the financing of pensions; prosperity clutters roads with cars, and pavemens with the drunk and the drugged; choice raises expectations; interest in politics declines when there are few great issues dividing the country. Reaction to the terrorist threat may put at risk traditional civil liberties, and the tolerant multicultural society which has been emerging in Britain. The gap between rhetoric and performance, the use of 'spin', and his handling of the entrance to the Iraq war, let alone the war itself and its aftermath, have all damaged Blair's reputation. Youth fades, the hairline recedes. But despite the impact of events and policies on the popularity of any long-term government – the empty Dome, the stench of burning cattle during the foot-and-mouth outbreak, the hunting ban, traffic jams and train crashes, and illegal immigrants roaming the country – New Labour remains the dominant party at the centre of the political spectrum. Its economic model, based on that of Conservative chancellors, still works – just; its investment in health, education and transport has recently been massive, even if the improvements resulting from it have been uneven (some would say non-existent in transport); and under Blair's governments the British people have become more prosperous, and more fully employed, than in any previous period of national history. Three successive victories in general elections can be explained by this, as much as by the destructive divisions within the Conservative Party.

It is too soon to hazard a verdict on Blair's New Labour governments. Will they be seen as strengthening the welfare structure of
the country and achieving a redistribution of wealth without limiting the openings for the entrepreneur, or, measured against both
expectations and opportunities, will they be written down as the
most disappointing governments of modern times?

Further Reading

AFTER MOST essays an accessible biography or two have been suggested. The following additional list, far from comprehensive, includes books which we have found most valuable or which can take the reader further towards understanding the political world and the society and culture which shaped it.

There is now a source of unique value in the *New Dictionary of National Biography* (2004).

Among books specifically about Prime Ministers, P. Hennessy, *The Prime Minister: The Office and its Holders since 1945* (2000) is a masterly work by a leading expert on the workings of British Government. R. Eccleshall and G. Walker (eds), *Biographical Dictionary of British Prime Ministers* (1998), reflects recent research and specialist work.

There are several notable new Oxford histories. For background: Julian Hoppit, *A Land of Liberty? England 1689-1727* (2000); for the Whig Ascendancy: Paul Langford, *A Polite and Commercial People: England 1727-1783* (1999); for the Victorians: K. Theodore Hoppen, *The Mid-Victorian Generation, 1846-1886* (1998).

Among textbooks which have stood the test of time are: J.B. Owen, *The Eighteenth Century, 1714-1815* (1974); Asa Briggs, *The Age of Improvement, 1783-1867* (revised edition, 1979); Dorothy Marshall, *Eighteenth Century England* (1962); R.C.K. Ensor, *England 1870-1914* (1936); H.J. Perkin, *The Origins of Modern English Society, 1780-1880* (1969); A.J.P. Taylor, *English History, 1914-1985* (1965).

See also: W.A. Speck, *Stability and Strife: England 1714-1760* (1977); R. Christie, *Wars and Revolutions: Britain 1760-1815* (1982); J.C.D. Clark, *English Society, 1688-1832* (1985); E.J. Evans, *The Forging of the Modern State: Early Industrial Britain, 1783-1870* (2nd edition, 1996); K. Robbins, *The Eclipse of a Great Power: Modern Britain, 1870-1992* (2nd edition, 1994); N. Gash, *Aristocracy and People: Britain 1815-1865* (1979); N. Feuchtwanger, *Democracy and Empire: Britain 1865-1914* (1985); R. Rhodes James, *The British Revolution: British Politics 1880-1939* (1978); M. Pugh, *The Making of British Politics 1867-1939* (1982).

For contemporary views of the state: S. Checkland, *British Public Policy, 1776-1939* (1983).

For the Constitution: G.H. le May, *The Victorian Constitution: Conventions, Usages and Contingencies* (1979); J. Cannon, *Parliamentary Reform, 1640-1832* (1973); P. Hennessy, *Whitehall* (1980); *The Cabinet* (1986).

For political ideas and practice: (still influential) L. Namier, *The Structure of Politics at the Accession of George III* (2nd edition, 1957); J. Black, *The Politics of Reform, 1688-1800* (1993); J. Cannon, *Aristocratic Century: The Peerage of Eighteenth Century England* (1984); C. Jones and D.L. Jones, *Peers, Politics and Powers: The House of Lords, 1603-1911* (1986); P.D.G. Thomas, *The House of Commons in the Eighteenth Century* (1971); J. Cannon, *Parliamentary Reform, 1641-1832* (1973); A.S. Ffoord, *His Majesty's Opposition, 1714-1839* (1964); D.G. Wright, *Popular Radicalism: The Working Class Experience, 1780-1880* (1988); P. Adelman, *Victorian Radicalism: The Middle Class Experience, 1830-1914* (1982); E.P. Thompson, *The Making of the English Working Class* (1963); D. Cannadine, *The Decline and Fall of the British Aristocracy* (1992).

For influences on politics: G. Kitson Clark, *The Making of Victorian England* (1962); Linda Colley, *Britons: Forging the Nation, 1707-1837* (1992); J. Black, *The English Press in the Eighteenth Century* (1987); A.J.P. Taylor, *Beaverbrook* (1972).

Among royal biographies: R. Hatton, *George I: Elector and King* (1978); J. Brooke, *King George III* (1972); Elizabeth Longford, *Victoria R.I.* (1973); P. Magnus, *King Edward VII* (1964); K. Rose, *George V* (1983); S. Bradford, *King George VI* (1989); B. Pimlott, *The Queen: A Biography of Elizabeth the Second* (1996).

Among those of exceptional importance who did not become Prime Minister: L.G. Mitchell, *Charles James Fox* (1992); on Joe Chamberlain, Curzon and Butler: D. Thorpe, *The Uncrowned Prime Ministers* (1980); of double interest: J. Enoch Powell, *Joseph Chamberlain* (1977); brilliantly perceptive: Winston Churchill, *Great Contemporaries* (1937); D. Gilmour, *Curzon* (1994); A. Roberts, *The Holy Fox: A Biography of Lord Halifax* (1991); A. Howard, *Rab: The life of R.A. Butler* (1987); P. Williams, *Hugh Gaitskell: A Political Biography* (1979).

For political parties: Linda Colley, *In Defiance of Oligarchy: The Tory Party 1714-1760* (1982); R. Blake, *The Conservative Party from Peel to Thatcher* (1985); H. Pelling, *A Short History of the Labour Party* (1965); D. Southgate, *The Passing of the Whigs* (1962); R.B. MacCallum, *The Liberal Party from Earl Grey to Asquith* (1963).

For the Church: O. Chadwick, *The Victorian Church* (2 vols, 1966 and 1970).

For foreign policy: M.E. Chamberlain, *Pax Britannica: British Foreign Policy 1789-1914* (1988).

For Ireland: R.F. Foster, *Modern Ireland, 1600-1972* (1988).

For the Empire: B. Porter, *The Lion's Share: A Short History of British Imperialism* (3rd edition, 1996).

Index